TRIALOGUE AND TERROR

Trialogue *and* Terror

Judaism, Christianity, and Islam after 9/11

EDITED BY
Alan L. Berger

CASCADE *Books* · Eugene, Oregon

TRIALOGUE AND TERROR
Judaism, Christianity, and Islam after 9/11

Copyright © 2012 Alan L. Berger. All rights reserved. Except for brief quotations in critical publications or reviews, no part of this book may be reproduced in any manner without prior written permission from the publisher. Write: Permissions, Wipf and Stock Publishers, 199 W. 8th Ave., Suite 3, Eugene, OR 97401.

Cascade Books
An Imprint of Wipf and Stock Publishers
199 W. 8th Ave., Suite 3
Eugene, OR 97401
www.wipfandstock.com

ISBN 13: 978-1-60899-546-2

Cataloging-in-Publication data:

Trialogue and terror : Judaism, Christianity, and Islam after 9/11 / edited by Alan L. Berger.

xvi + 272 p. ; 23 cm.—Includes bibliographical references and index.

ISBN 13: 978-1-60899-546-2

1. Religions—Relations. 2. Abrahamic religions. I. Alan L. Berger (1939–). II. Title.

BL410 T75 2012

Scriptures marked (NRSV) are taken from the New Revised Standard Version Bible, copyright 1989, Division of Christian Education of the National Council of Churches of Christ in the United States of America. Used by permission. All rights reserved.

Scriptures marked (JPS) are taken from *JPS Hebrew-English Tanakh*, copyright 1999, Jewish Publication Society, 1999. Used by permission. All rights reserved.

Thanks are due to the University of Minnesota Press for permission to reprint in an abridged version Professor Anouar Majid's "Muslim Jews," from his book *We Are All Moors: Ending Centuries of Crusades against Muslims and Other Minorities* (University of Minnesota Press, 2009) and to the Brookings Institution Press for permission to reprint in an abridged version Ambassador Akbar S. Ahmed's "Lifting the Veil," from his book *Journey into Islam: The Crisis of Globalization* (Brookings Institution Press, 2007).

Manufactured in the USA

Contributors

Ambassador Akbar S. Ahmed is the Ibn Khaldun Chair of Islamic Studies at American University in Washington DC. He has taught at Princeton, Harvard, and Cambridge Universities, and is former High Commissioner of Pakistan to Great Britain. He is the author of over a dozen award-winning books, including *Discovering Islam* (revised edition, 2002). His books have been translated into many languages, including Chinese and Indonesian. His most recent book is *Journey into America* (2010). Along with Professor Judea Pearl, Ahmed was awarded the first Purpose Prize. He has also received the annual Rabbi Abraham Joshua Heschel/Martin Luther King Award for Interfaith Activism.

Alan L. Berger is the Raddock Family Eminent Scholar Chair of Holocaust Studies at Florida Atlantic University, where he also directs the Center for the Study of Values and Violence after Auschwitz. Among the dozen books he has authored, coauthored, and edited are *Jewish-Christian Dialogue* (2008; coauthor); *Second Generation Voices* (2001, co-editor; winner of the B'nai Zion National Media Award), and *Children of Job* (1997). He holds a Doctor of Letters, *Honoris Causa* from Luther College.

Mary C. Boys is the Skinner and McAlpin Professor of Practical Theology at Union Theological Seminary in New York City. Among the eight books she has written or edited is the award-winning *Has God Only One Blessing?* (2000). She has been a Henry Luce II Fellow in Theology, and is the recipient of the Sir Sigmund Sternberg Award from the International Conference of Christians and Jews.

Donald J. Dietrich, Professor of Theology at Boston College, has focused his research and publications on German Catholic experiences ranging from the Tübingen School of Theology to the Third Reich. Among his books are *Christian Responses to the Holocaust: Moral and Ethical Issues* (2003; editor) and *Human Rights and the Catholic Tradition* (2007). He is a member of the Committee on Church Relations and the Holocaust at the United States Holocaust Memorial Museum.

Rabbi Riccardo Di Segni was born in 1949 in Rome, where he received his medical degree and rabbinic ordination. He still practices medicine as a radiologist. In 2010 he was appointed Chief Rabbi of Rome. He has been involved in research and publishing in different aspects of Jewish traditional culture. Among his books are a guide to Jewish dietary laws, in Italian; a collection of anthropological essays (*Le unghie di Adamo*, 1981); a study in Hebrew on the traditional explanations of the dietary laws (*Noten Ta'am leshavach*, 1998); and a book on the Jewish legends of Jesus (*Il Vangelo del Ghetto*, 1985). He has been extensively involved in Jewish-Christian dialogue, attending meetings and conferences as well as widely publishing on the subject.

Eugene J. Fisher is Distinguished Professor of Catholic–Jewish Studies at Saint Leo University (Florida). He directed Catholic-Jewish relations for the U.S. Conference of Catholic Bishops from 1977 to 2007. He was also Consultor to the Holy See's Commission for Religious Relations with the Jews and a member of the International Catholic-Jewish Liaison Committee, representing the Holy See. He also represented the Holy See at international conferences in Stockholm (2000) and Budapest (2001). In 2003 he was the Rabbi Hugo Gryn Fellow at Cambridge University. He is the author or editor of over thirty books and three hundred articles, many of which have been translated into French, Spanish, Italian, Portuguese, and German. He holds honorary doctorates from Seton Hall University and St, Mary's Seminary and University.

Anouar Majid is Director of the Center for Global Humanities and Associate Provost for Global Initiatives at the University of New England. Majid's books on Islam in the age of globalization and Muslim-Western relations since 1492 have all been critically acclaimed. He has been described by Cornel West as one of a few "towering Islamic intellectuals." Majid's work has been profiled by Bill Moyers on the PBS program *Bill Moyers Journal* and by Al Jazeera's *Date in Exile*. He has written for the *Chronicle of Higher Education*, the *Washington Post*, and other publications. Majid is also a novelist, the author of *Si Yussef*, first published in 1992.

Khaleel Mohammed is Associate Professor in the Department of Religious Studies at San Diego State University, where he also is a core faculty member in the university's Center for Islamic and Arabic Studies and its

Master's Program in Homeland Security. He received his PhD in Islamic law from McGill University. He also received a Kraft-Hiatt postdoctoral fellowship at Brandeis University. He has published numerous journal articles and is a frequent participant at interfaith conferences

A. Rashied Omar is a Research Scholar of Islamic Studies and Peacebuilding at the Joan B. Kroc Institute for International Peace Studies at the University of Notre Dame. He received his PhD in Religious Studies from the University of Cape Town. His research and teaching are focused in the area of religion, violence, and peacebuilding, with a twin focus on the Islamic ethics of war and peace, and Interreligious dialogue. He is a contributor to the *Encyclopedia of Islam and the Muslim World* (2004) and is coeditor of the forthcoming *A Dictionary of Christian-Muslim Relations*. Dr. Omar is the coordinating Imam at the Claremont Main Road Mosque in South Africa.

David Patterson holds the Hillel Feinberg Chair in Holocaust Studies at the University of Texas at Dallas. A winner of the National Jewish Book Award and the Koret Book Award, Professor Patterson has published more than thirty books and over 140 articles and book chapters on philosophy, literature, Judaism, and the Holocaust. His writings have been widely anthologized. Among his books are *Genocide in Jewish Thought* (2012), *A Genealogy of Evil* (2011), *Emil L. Fackenheim* (2008), *Jewish-Christian Dialogue* (2008; coauthor), and *Open Wounds* (2006).

John T. Pawlikowski, OSM, is Professor of Social Ethics and Director of the Catholic-Jewish Studies Program at the Catholic Theological Union in Chicago. He is the author or editor of some fifteen books in the area of Christian-Jewish relations. He has been a member of the United States Holocaust Memorial Council by Presidential Appointment for four terms and currently chairs the Museum's Church Relations Committee as well as serving on its Academic Committee and its Committee on Conscience. He is part of a major theological study on Christ and the Jewish People, which will soon release its first book, to which Fr. Pawlikowski has contributed an important essay.

Rabbi Gilbert S. Rosenthal is director of the National Council of Synagogues, a partnership of the Reform, Conservative, and Reconstructionist movements in Judaism dealing with interfaith affairs nationally. He served as pulpit rabbi for thirty-three years and as Executive Vice President of the New York Board of Rabbis from 1990 to 2000. He has authored or edited eleven books, most recently, *What Can a Modern Jew Believe?* (Wipf & Stock, 2007), and *Let Us Reason Together* (2010; coeditor). His many articles and essays have appeared in journals in America and Israel. For eleven years he hosted the television program, *Point of View*. He co-produced the film, *Walking God's Paths*.

Rabbi A. James Rudin received his master's degree and rabbinical ordination from Hebrew Union College–Jewish Institute of Religion (HUC-JIR). He holds honorary doctorates from Saint Leo University, Saint Martin's University and HUC-JIR. In addition to serving as a pulpit rabbi, he was an Air Force chaplain stationed in Japan and Korea. He served as director of the Interreligious Affairs Department at the American Jewish Committee (AJC) and is now the AJC's Senior Interreligious Advisor. Rabbi Rudin has participated in eleven meetings with Pope John Paul II or Pope Benedict XVI. He is the author or editor of nine books and since 1991 has written weekly commentaries for Religion News Service/Newhouse Syndicate. His latest book is *Christians and Jews Faith to Faith* (2010).

Theresa Sanders is Associate Professor of Theology at Georgetown University, where she teaches courses such as "The Problem of God" and "Sacrifice and Suffering." Her most recent books include *Tenebrae* (2006) and *Approaching Eden* (2009).

Muhammad Shafiq is Professor and Executive Director at the Center for Interfaith Studies and Dialogue at Nazareth College in Rochester, New York. He is also Executive Director of that city's Islamic Center. Professor Shafiq has been an active worker and participant in several interfaith forums and dialogue groups in America and abroad for over three decades. He has written over fifty articles and several books, including *Interfaith Dialogue* (2007).

Deborah Weissman has lived in Israel since 1972 and received her PhD in Jewish education from the Hebrew University in Jerusalem. A prize-winning Jewish educator, she has become extensively involved in interreligious education and dialogue. Debbie currently is President of the International Council of Christians and Jews. She is the first Jewish woman to be elected to that post in the Council's more than sixty-year history.

In memory of Mr. Emanuel (Manny) Shemin (z"l)
and for Mrs. Rhoda Shemin

Contents

Preface | xiii
Acknowledgments | xv

Introduction | xvii
ALAN L. BERGER

1. The Interreligious Golden Age: Has it Ended? | 7
   A. JAMES RUDIN

2. Salvation Jewish Style | 23
   GILBERT S. ROSENTHAL

3. Life and Afterlife: Judaism's Contribution to the Jewish-Christian Muslim Trialogue | 37
   DAVID PATTERSON

4. Pride without Prejudice: Towards a Dialectical Education for Religious Identity | 51
   DEBORAH WEISSMAN

5. Jewish–Christian–Muslim Dialogue after 9/11 | 71
   RICCARDO DiSEGNI

6. 9/11: Dialogue and Trialogue | 87
   EUGENE J. FISHER

7. Defining Catholic Identity against the Jews: Pope Benedict XVI and the Question of Mission to the Jewish People | 102
   JOHN T. PAWLIKOWSKI

Contents

8. This I Believe | 121
   MARY C. BOYS

9. Globalization, Human Rights, and the Catholic Response | 134
   DONALD J. DIETRICH

10. Blow on the Coal of the Heart": September 11 and the Book of Job | 150
    THERESA SANDERS

11. Dialogical Interaction or Post-Honor Confrontation? | 166
    KHALEEL MOHAMMED

12. The Semitic Solution: Renewing the Natural Alliance between Jews and Muslims | 185
    ANOUAR MAJID

13. Islam and Peacebuilding | 201
    A. RASHIED OMAR

14. Transformation through Dialogue: A Muslim Scholar's Search for Identity | 211
    MUHAMMAD SHAFIQ

15. Lifting the Veil | 229
    AKBAR S. AHMED

Conclusion | 247
ALAN L. BERGER

Index | 257

Preface

This volume emerged from four Global Shemin Trialogues held at Florida Atlantic University from 2007 to 2010. The late Mr. Emanuel Shemin and his wife Rhoda established the Trialogue in the aftermath of 9/11 in order to create a forum that would facilitate interfaith dialogue and educate the public about the tenets of the three Abrahamic traditions. The Shemins' hope was to foster clarity and understanding in order to help build an informed foundation for a meaningful trialogue to occur. Moreover, their goal was to help form a clearer picture of the vital contemporary role played by religion in human life. This involved educating in order to overcome ignorance about the religious Other. The aim was to underscore the commonalities and seek a better understanding of the differences embedded in Judaism, Christianity, and Islam. Attaining this goal could potentially lead to the celebration of differences rather than fear of the other. Being cognizant of differences means neither acquiescence nor uncritical acceptance. It does, however, reveal the possibility for a richer appreciation and deeper understanding of both one's own tradition and that of the other.

The Shemin Trialogue bore no illusions about the fact that there are essential differences among the Abrahamic traditions. These differences are both historical and theological in nature. Moreover, the relationship between Judaism and Christianity, on the one hand, and Judaism and Islam, on the other, is uneven. This is not to mention the slowly emerging dialogue between Christianity and Islam. Furthermore, the three traditions are demographically unbalanced and ideologically diverse.[1] While Judaism birthed both Christianity and Islam, the three monotheistic faiths went their separate ways. This is the case even with the differing ways in which the three faith communities understand the role of Abraham; each

---

1. There are approximately 1.4 billion Muslims and 1.2 Christians worldwide. Judaism claims approximately 14 million adherents.

tradition views the patriarchal figure differently as seen in the theological claims they make about him.²

The essays in this volume reveal both commonalties and very real differences among the Abrahamic traditions in response to the altered post-9/11 religious landscape. On the one hand, condemnation of the murderers frequently morphed into condemnation of the entire religion of Islam. People were justifiably enraged by what was correctly perceived as an attack on America, on modernity itself, and on western culture. However, it needs to be kept in mind that not only Americans or Jews or Christians were the murderers' sole victims; citizens of other nations as well as Muslims were also killed. On the other hand, the attack drew Jews and Christians closer, at least in the American context because of the realization that followers of both traditions were united by their shared sense of victimhood. Some Muslims also condemned the attack, although regrettably, that response was for the most part—at least initially—not as vigorous or widespread as it should and could have been.

I thank the contributors to this volume, who, although born in different lands, are united by the fraught nature of the post- 9/11 interreligious world. They have demonstrated that a trialogue, which is still in its infancy, is possible even while the obstacles are formidable and many. The essays assembled here approach the issue from a variety of perspectives including education, globalization, personal meditation, and theological reflection. Clearly, there are differences in points of view. However, each of the contributors has personal experience in both interreligious trialogue and dialogue. They know firsthand the perils and the promise of such efforts. Moreover, the urgency of the task and the future outlines of an authentic interreligious exchange are the uniting themes running throughout this volume.

---

2. Jon D. Levenson, "The Idea of Abrahamic Religions: A Qualified Dissent," *Jewish Review of Books*, no. 1 (Spring, 2010) 40–44. Levenson crucially distinguishes between the figure of Abraham as bond and barrier for interfaith trialogue. He writes: "If an appeal to Abraham simply invokes his name in pursuit of inter-communal peace and harmony but disregards the teachings with which these three communities associate him, it can only be shallow and self-defeating" (p. 42).

The Quran (3:65–68) chides Jews and Christians for failing to recognize that Abraham was neither a Jew nor a Christian. Rather, Levenson notes, "Abraham was more ancient . . . one who was muslim, submitted to God and untainted by idolatry of any sort." Consequently, "what he prefigures . . . is not a confraternity of Abrahamic religions, but rather the one true Abrahamic religion, Islam, which the Jews and Christians, for all their disputatious prattle about the patriarch, have distorted" (p. 44).

This volume nonetheless utilizes the phrase "Abrahamic traditions" because of its widespread public acceptance.

Acknowledgments

I am pleased to acknowledge the support of two Boca Raton clergy, the Very Reverend Andrew Sherman, St. Gregory's Episcopal Church, and Rabbi David Steinhardt, B'nai Torah Congregation, for their assistance and insights in planning the Shemin Trialogues, although they bear no responsibity for any claims made in this volume. I also acknowledge the support of Mr. Dennis Hall, my graduate student, and especially my assistant, Ms. Bonnie Lander, for their help in preparing the manuscript. Bonnie Lander, as always, was both professional and patient throughout this process. Finally, I want to acknowledge the support of the Shemin Trialogue and the FAU Foundation in bringing this project to fruition. I am also indebted to Ms. Heather Carraher of Wipf and Stock for her guidance and wisdom.

Introduction

ALAN L. BERGER

The 9/11 attacks against the United States carried out by nineteen Muslim fanatics radically altered the religious landscape—not only in America but in many other parts of the world. A decade later, the reverberations of these attacks continue to have global implications which are manifest in a variety of areas, including politics and international relations. The essays in this volume focus on the role of religion in the mass murder and specifically the response of the Abrahamic traditions. This is not to say that people of other faith communities, or those professing no faith, have nothing to contribute. They do. The traumatic wounding of America impacts the entire human community. However, Judaism, Christianity, and Islam remain in the forefront of the contemporary discussion about how to achieve what Judaism terms *tikkun ha-ʿolam*, repair or restoration of the world. For obvious reasons, it is Islam and its response that has received the most attention in the post-9/11 world.

In the past decade, religion has been pilloried as the cause of wars and hatred. Jonathan Swift's caustic observation: "We have just enough religion to make us hate one another but not enough to love one another" seems as pertinent today as it was during his lifetime (1667–1745). A large number of books since 9/11 have reinforced Swift's position. Writers such as Richard Dawkins, Daniel Dennett, Sam Harris, Stephen Hawking, and Christopher Hitchens seek to prove the falsity or irrelevance of religious belief.[1] Collectively, their works are the intellectual grandchildren of Sig-

---

1. Richard Dawkins, *The God Delusion* (Boston: Houghton Mifflin, 2008); Daniel C. Dennett, *Breaking the Spell: Religion as a Natural Phenomenon* (New York: Penguin, 2007); Sam Harris, *The End of Faith: Religion, Terror, and the Future of Reason* (New York: Norton, 2005); Sam Harris, *Letter to a Christian Nation* (New York: Knopf, 2006); Stephen Hawking and Leonard Mlodinow, *The Grand Design* (New York: Bantam, 2010); Christopher Hitchens, *God Is Not Great: How Religion Poisons Everything* (New York: Twelve, 2007). Each of these works presents a reductionist and, therefore,

mund Freud's skewed understanding of religion as an *illusion*. Religion in the modern as well as the postmodern world is derided as having lost its credibility. Yet, one of the abiding truths that emerged from the carnage of 9/11 is that religion and religious beliefs, for both good and evil, are very much a factor in human existence.

Everywhere with the exception of Western Europe, religion appears resurgent. The sociologist Peter Berger attests that modernity "tends to undermine the taken-for-granted certainties by which people lived through most of history."[2] This is "an uncomfortable state of affairs," Berger maintains, "and for many an intolerable one, and religious movements that claim to give certainty have great appeal."[3] There is, of course, no greater certainty than that possessed by the fanatic. Berger astutely contends: "Very probably religion in the modern world more often fosters war, both between and within nations."[4] Religion is, however, a two-edged sword. On the one hand, religion can serve as a "sacred canopy" for adherents providing a "plausibility structure" against the absurdity of evil while giving meaning to their existence and a transcendent purpose to their death.[5] Yet, on the other hand, religion can also provide *justification* for terror and mass murder.

It is also possible that religion may hold a vital key to opening the door to peaceful coexistence. The challenge, however, is daunting. The Catholic thinker Hans Küng, addressing a 1989 UNESCO conference on world peace and dialogue among religions, pointedly observed: "There will be no peace among nations without peace among the religions, but there can be no dialogue between the religions without each religion engaging in a fundamental re-examination of its basic assumptions." Küng's powerful insight is both a stimulus and a warning. On the one hand, he is calling for the need for religious pluralism. Modernity means interaction among peoples and cultures previously isolated and insulated from each other. There is a need for mutual learning and for informed teaching. On the other hand, he sounds a caution against triumphalistic assertions.

---

flawed vision of religion and its role in human existence.

2. Peter L. Berger. "The Desecularization of the World: A Global Overview," in *The Desecularization of the World: Resurgent Religion and World Politics*, edited by Peter L. Berger (Grand Rapids: Erdmans, 1999) 11.

3. Ibid.

4. Ibid., 15.

5. Peter L. Berger, *The Sacred Canopy: Elements of a Sociological Theory of Religion* (New York: Anchor Books, 1969) chapter 3.

Introduction

After the Holocaust no religion laying claim to moral standing is entitled to assert a cognitive monopoly on theological truth or on salvation.

The 9/11 attacks underscored two important points about religion and interfaith trialogue. First, religious pluralism and modernity itself are under deadly assault from religious absolutists who have no interest in dialogue. Just as secular culture run amok yields tyranny and fascism, so too does fanatical religion whose adherents are convinced that they have a theological monopoly on the truth. This results in supersessionary and triumphalistic teachings. Fanatics are convinced either that they are acting in the name of their God or, worse, that they themselves have displaced their deity.

The second point involves the foundations of interfaith exchange. The dialogue between Judaism and Christianity, engendered by the horrors of the Holocaust and formalized by the Second Vatican Council's promulgation of *Nostra Aetate* (1965) set in motion a dramatic change in the relationship between the Church and the Jewish people.[6] In the ensuing decades several implementing documents extended the liberalizing element embodied in *Nostra Aetate*. The interchange between Judaism and Christianity crystallized a set of criteria for authentic dialogue: the need for trust, the necessity for each dialogue partner being permitted the right of self-definition, the importance of learning to listen, the requirement of honesty in the dialogue, rejection of seeking to convert the Jewish people, the importance of recognizing plural truths, and the necessity of continuing the dialogue despite fundamental disagreements. Following 9/11 there is an urgent need to expand the dialogue to include Islam, whose worldwide adherents are more numerous than the global Christian population. The future of the human community may well hang in the balance.

Apart from scholarly interest, Islam as a religion attracted scant attention prior to 9/11. Now the situation is quite different. Unhappily, much of the attention paid Islam on the popular level comes through unfiltered and poorly informed blog sources. The lack of a basic knowledge of the religion, and ignorance of the teachings of the religious other, are both self-defeating and dangerous. This situation, however, in no way mitigates Küng's call for a self-critical theological reflection on the part of the various religions. Islam no less (and these days arguably more) than the other

---

6. Prior to *Nostra Aetate* there had been an International Conference of Christians and Jews in Seelisberg, Switzerland (July 30th–August 5, 1947) that dealt with the causes of Christian antisemitism. Those delegates were concerned with the extent of Christian culpability in preparing the soil for the Shoah. The issuance of the 10 points of Seelisberg, while crucial, lacked the widespread impact of the Vatican document.

Abrahamic traditions needs to engage in this type of reflection. Apologists for Islam who refuse to unambiguously condemn terrorism undermine trust and harm efforts at genuine interfaith trialogue. While Samuel Huntington's *clash of civilizations* thesis concerning Islam and the West may or may not be completely valid, it is the case that Islam and the West have been frequently, and often violently, at cultural, political, and theological odds. The Christian Crusaders of the Middle Ages and the contemporary Islamic jihadist murderers bear witness to this situation. Seen from this perspective, 9/11 is a continuation, albeit the most dramatic, of a civilizational clash. Unlike Christianity, however, Islam has undergone neither a Second Vatican Council nor a widespread rejection of the use of exclusionary and hateful terms such as *idolater* and *infidel*.

The historical record reveals that the path to Jewish-Christian dialogue has a long, tortuous, and frequently tragic background. Replacing 1900 years of the "Teaching of Contempt" for Jews and Judaism is a new and complicated post-Holocaust undertaking. While the years since 1965 have ushered in a progressive era, one unimaginable a century ago, it is impossible to ignore the binary tensions created by the positive reforms instituted by *Nostra Aetate* and the more recent conservative push-back against the liberal openings of the Second Vatican Council. It is important to be cognizant of the divergent voices within the Church, and within the Christian world as a whole; liberal theologians speak out strongly in favor of continuing authentic Jewish-Christian dialogue, while conservative elements advocate on behalf of retrenchment. Nevertheless, Jewish-Christian dialogue continues. It is noteworthy that the dialogue, while appearing sclerotic at the institutional level, is more vibrant and productive within the academic and interpersonal realms.

Judaism is based on a dialogue with God that encourages interrogation of the deity by humans . . . no less than vice versa. Moreover, the Talmud—one of the tradition's oldest postbiblical sacred text—not only allows for diverse points of view, it enshrines them as normative. *Elu v'elu divrey elohim chaim* [both these and these are the words of the living God], the Talmud insists. This does not imply a lack of religious boundaries. Rather, it is meant as a reminder, as it were, that a given issue may be seen from a variety of perspectives. "The Torah has seventy faces," asserts rabbinic wisdom.

Islam, like Judaism and Christianity, is composed of a variety of schools of thought. While Sunni and Shia are the major religio-ideological branches of the tradition, they are by no means exhaustive. Two extremes reveal this fact. There is, on the one hand, the rejectionist Salafist movement, which, in turn, spawned Wahabism—an antimodernist movement ironically viewed by Salafists as being insufficiently reactionary. Both groups reject the humanity of any non-Muslim while advocating terrorism against all—including Muslims—whom they consider infidels. Sufism, the mystical branch of Islam, on the other hand, embraces nonviolence and is committed to religious coexistence and accommodation. Moreover, the Sufi movement has produced some of the world's most sublime poetry celebrating peace and coexistence.

It is important to note that historically there has been much cultural contact on the individual level between Muslims and Jews. Moreover, Moses Maimonides—arguably the most influential of the premodern Jewish philosophers—wrote in Arabic. However, the frequently referenced Golden Age of Spanish Jewry requires nuanced understanding. It is certainly the case that Jews fared better under Islam than in Christian society. But it is a mistake to believe that the Golden Age had anything in common with religious pluralism. Jews, as well as Christians, living in Islamic lands were second-class inhabitants referred to as *dhimmis*. Islam accommodated minorities provided that they remained minorities and acknowledged the supremacy of Islam. Following 9/11, Islam faces the challenge of separating mosque from state while heeding the call of moderate voices within the tradition.

Religion is not monochromatic. As the deadly results of 9/11 reveal, the danger that extremists will dictate the behavior of the rest of the Islamic community continues to exist. Ten years after 9/11, reflecting on his experiences with Christianity and Islam, Yossi Klein Halevi writes: "I shared with Christianity a shattering past but a promising present [whereas] my relationship with Islam was essentially the reverse. The past offered inspiring examples of Muslim-Jewish cooperation, especially among mystics, but the present state of dialogue was abysmal."[7] Not much has changed since this pointed observation was made. Although it is unclear at this point whether the horror of 9/11 will birth a meaningful trialogue, it is a religious and political necessity to listen, and to speak, to one another for the sake of the dignity and survival of humanity. And this is precisely what the contributors to this volume are doing; they are respectfully listening and speaking to one another.

---

7. Yossi Klein Halevi, *At the Entrance to the Garden of Eden: A Jew's Search for Hope with Christians and Muslims in the Holy Land* (New York: Perennial, 2002) 7.

one

The Interreligious Golden Age

Has It Ended?

A. JAMES RUDIN

For the global Jewish community, three major events—the September 11, 2001, Al-Qaeda terrorist attacks on the United States; Pope John Paul II's death on April 2, 2005; and the vote by the General Assembly of the Presbyterian Church (USA) on July 1, 2004, to support a selective divestment of holdings in multinational corporations doing business in Israel—ended the modern interreligious Golden Age. September 11, 2001, fundamentally altered Islamic–Jewish relations, the end of an extraordinary twenty-seven-year pontificate profoundly changed Catholic–Jewish relations, and the call by a major liberal church body to economically punish Israel represented a major shift in Protestant–Jewish relations.

The Golden Age began in 1965, when, at the conclusion of the three-year-long Second Vatican Council in Rome, the world's Catholic bishops overwhelming adopted (2221 for, and 8 against) the historic *Nostra Aetate* (*In Our Time*) Declaration on the Relation of the Church with Non-Christian Religions.[1] The Declaration specifically called for Catholics to engage Jews in purposeful dialogue built upon "mutual respect and understanding."

Nostra Aetate also "decries hatreds, persecutions, and manifestations of anti-Semitism directed against Jews at any time and by anyone." It rejected the deicide charge: collective Jewish responsibility for the death of

---

1. Pope Paul VI, *Nostra Aetate*. Online: http://www.vatican.va/archive/hist_councils/ii_vatican_council/documents/vat-ii_decl_19651028_nostra-aetate_en.html/.

Jesus. Some Catholics had hurled the odious deicide charge against the Jewish people for centuries and helped create a Christian "teaching of contempt" towards both Jews and Judaism.

Although the bishops spent many hours vigorously debating the precise wording of the Declaration before its final adoption, *Nostra Aetate* is less than 1600 words in length, and the section on Jews, Judaism, deicide, and anti-Semitism numbers only 675 carefully crafted words.

Despite its brevity, *Nostra Aetate* is not a piece of arcane or esoteric literature whose few sentences can easily be forgotten. Rather, it is one of the most important documents of the twentieth century and holds a significant place within modern religious history. The Declaration sparked an enormous number of positive contacts between Christians and Jews. Indeed, there have been more constructive Catholic–Jewish encounters since 1965 than there were in the first nineteen centuries of Christianity.

While the interaction between Christians and Jews was the main component of the Golden Age, it is often forgotten that the establishment of a nascent set of Islamic–Jewish relationships was underway especially in the United States before 9/11. Hope was expressed by many Jews that extraordinary, even historic, gains might also be achieved with the Islamic community.

The American Jewish Committee sponsored two national conferences on Muslim–Jewish relations at the University of Denver during the mid-1990s, and there were similar meetings in other American cities. Jews quickly discovered that like them, many Muslims in the United States were deeply concerned about assimilation, indifference to the faith, quality education, religious discrimination, and fears that young Muslims were losing their Islamic identity. It all had a familiar sound to American Jews, and those issues were often the pre-9/11 topics for the dialogue.

Although the themes had to be carefully chosen—one of the meetings in Denver focused on Islamic and Jewish perceptions of families—there was a sense that Muslims and Jews were developing positive relations akin to the older set of constructive Christian–Jewish interactions. Such was the hope.

But those encounters (I was a participant in many of them), sometimes public and sometimes "off the record," became much more difficult and highly problematic following 9/11. Once-trusted Islamic colleagues frequently turned out to be public apologists for terrorism, or they employed a form of doublespeak: professing support in their English-language communications for Muslim–Jewish dialogue, while at the same

The Interreligious Golden Age

time verbally assailing Jews and Judaism in Arabic, Farsi, and other "insider" languages.

The lethal attacks of 9/11, carried out by nineteen al-Qaeda members, drained much of the energy, enthusiasm, and commitment from those Jews who had been slowly and carefully building a positive set of relations with their Islamic partners. The news that shortly after the terror attacks Mohamed Gemeaha, the imam of a prominent mosque in Manhattan who had participated in pre-9/11 interreligious dialogues, had fled to Egypt added to the dismay. A few days after September 11, the Egyptian-born imam gave an interview to an Arab newspaper claiming that the U.S. government was persecuting Muslims, that Jewish doctors in New York were poisoning Muslim children, and that Jews, not Muslims, were responsible for the attack on the World Trade Center.

In Ohio, Fawaz Damra, the imam since 1991 of the state's largest mosque, the Islamic Center of Cleveland, had by 2001 emerged as a significant interreligious figure and appeared to many Jewish and Christian leaders as an irenic and valued interlocutor.

However, when Damra's pre-2001 Arabic-language tape-recorded messages intended for his congregation in which he called Jews "the sons of monkeys and apes" were made public after 9/11, Muslim–Jewish relations suffered a severe body blow from which they have not yet fully recovered. In June 2004 Damra was convicted for failing to disclose his links to three Islamic terrorist organizations when he applied for U.S. citizenship, and he was recorded on FBI wiretaps discussing funds for the families of Muslim suicide bombers. The Cleveland imam was also named an unindicted co-conspirator in the terrorism trial of Palestinian Jihad leader Professor Sami al-Arian of the University of South Florida.

When Damra was deported from the United States in January 2007, he left behind a deeply divided mosque and an enduring residue of bitterness among the Jews and Christians who had worked in good faith with the disgraced imam.

However, even before 9/11 , I can personally attest how difficult it was to discover an appropriate Islamic organization to participate in authentic Muslim–Jewish dialogue. In the days before the 2001 attacks, Islamic organizations in the United States—many controlled by religious and political extremists—never unequivocally condemned Muslim suicide bombers who killed Israeli civilians.

However, after the World Trade Center and Pentagon assaults, eleven leading Islamic and Arab groups did issue a joint declaration denouncing "the cowardly acts of terror against innocent American civilians."[2] But the Islamic/Arab coalition failed to call for U.S. action against the terrorists and the nations that sheltered them.

One of the serious problems in Islamic–Jewish relations remains a lack of a significant moderate Islamic community voice in the United States. Even before 9/11, several organizations with a radical political agenda, such as CAIR (the Council on American–Islamic Relations), the AMC (the American Muslim Council), and MPAC (the Muslim Public Affairs Council) refused to condemn by name the terrorist perpetrators of hostile actions against both the United States and Israel, including the 1993 bombing of the World Trade Center, the 1996 attack on U.S. military barracks in Saudi Arabia, the 1998 attacks on two U.S. embassies in Africa, and the 2000 assault in the USS Cole in Yemen's harbor.

In addition, since 9/11 many Islamic religious and political leaders, including President Mahmoud Ahmadinejad of Iran and prominent imams, have unleashed a constant stream of obscene verbal attacks on the United States, the West, Christianity, Judaism, and the State of Israel. Nonetheless, some Jewish leaders in Europe, Israel, and North America have continued their encounters with Muslims in the hope of establishing meaningful dialogue based upon the important principles enunciated in *Nostra Aetate*: "mutual respect and understanding." However, before inaugurating even a modest effort to develop constructive relations with Islam and Muslims, it is necessary to understand some of the key issues on this important agenda.

1. *Territorial conflict*: The Arab–Israeli conflict has great significance for both Jews and Muslims. For most Jews, the creation in 1948 of the State of Israel is an ancient promise fulfilled—the ingathering of exiles from more than 120 countries and the creation of a vibrant nation-state based upon Jewish values that would finally guarantee physical and spiritual security.

Yet, for many Muslims, the permanent existence of an independent Jewish state in the Middle East is a religious and political aberration that must eventually be eliminated, for it is built on *dar al-Islam*, the "abode of Islam"—territory that was once under Islamic rule and law. Most devout Muslims believe their rule and law must be returned to the territory, and the Jews who live there must submit to Islamic authority—a concept that

---

2. Islamic Society of North America, "ISNA Condemns Terrorist Attacks." Online: http://www.islamicity.com/articles/Articles.asp?ref=AM0109-335%20/.

delegitimizes Israel, not merely politically, but theologically as well. Such a position attacks a core belief of mainstream Judaism.

2. *Theological differences*: Although similarities do exist between Judaism and Islam—both peoples profess monotheism, speak Semitic languages that share many word roots, follow prescribed rituals for daily prayer, and practice dietary laws that include the prohibition of pork—the significant differences in theology, custom, and religious law exceed all these commonalties. Theologically, perhaps the most significant difference is the Muslim belief that Islam represents the ultimate fulfillment of both Judaism and Christianity: the "Final Seal" of the Prophet.

3. *Lack of authentic knowledge*: I know from years of interreligious work that in many cases Muslim academics and religious leaders know practically nothing about authentic Judaism. Some years ago in New York City a visiting group of prominent professors of Islamic studies from Arab countries was asked which books or articles on Judaism they had read that were written by Jewish authors. Without exception, their startling answer was "none."

The professors all admitted their perceptions and knowledge of the Jewish religion derived exclusively from other Muslims, many of whom are hostile to Jews and Judaism. Using such biased volumes as primary source material in any dialogue runs counter to a fundamental principle of interreligious relations: each faith group has the right to define itself in its own terms.

So too most Jews know little about the Islamic faith and community. How many know that approximately two million Muslims reside in the United States? (There are no exact figures, but Muslim organizations tend to greatly inflate the numbers in order to bolster their claim—for political purposes—that Muslims now outnumber Jews in America.)

The American Islamic community is composed of three diverse groups—African Americans (many of them converts from Christianity), Arabs, and Indo-Pakistanis and others from Southeast Asia. Approximately 40 percent of U.S. Muslims are African Americans, including sports figures Mohammed Ali and Mike Tyson, who follow the spiritual leadership of the late Warith Deen Mohammed, and his father, Elijah Mohammed. Another African American Muslim, Louis Farrakhan, the Nation of Islam (NOI) leader, has for decades attacked Jews and Judaism in the vilest language. However, most African American Muslims are not NOI members, but follow instead the teachings of W. D. and Elijah Mohammed.

Trialogue and Terror

The Indo-Pakistani community is composed of many immigrants to the United States from Pakistan, Bangladesh, Indonesia (the nation with the largest number of Muslims), India, and Sri Lanka. Most engaged in the Middle East conflict are Arabs, mainly immigrants from that region. Arab Muslims seek to enlist African American and Indo-Pakistani support for the Palestinian cause, and they frequently impart toxic anti-Israel and anti-Jewish messages in the process.

But when Jews and Muslims do meet, the latter group often employs several well-known phrases to highlight the positive side of relations between the two communities.

Children of Abraham: Because Jews, Muslims, and Christians claim a spiritual connection to the first patriarch, all three groups consider themselves "children of Abraham." Jews revere Isaac, the son of Abraham and Sarah; Muslims trace their heritage to Ishmael, the son of Abraham and Hagar, even though Islam did not come into existence for another two thousand years.

Although Jews and Muslims jointly claim Abraham/Ibrahim as their own, including his burial place in Hebron, they symbolically and permanently part company with the births of Isaac and Ishmael—a separation that has had momentous consequences for both faith communities, as the divine covenant is linked to Isaac and his progeny. Although the Bible promises that Ishmael's descendants will be numerous and become a great nation, once Sarah casts away Hagar and Ishmael, little more is heard from them except for the Genesis account that Ishmael's twelve sons became tribal chieftains—a parallel to Jewish history one generation later. Unfortunately, some Muslims use the ancient story to buttress their modern anti-Israel position by linking Ishmael's fate with that of the Palestinian refugees.

The Golden Age in Spain: The second phrase points to an earlier idyllic Golden Age that existed for Jews and Muslims in Spain starting in 711, with the Islamic invasion of the Iberian Peninsula, until the Christian reconquest on January 2, 1492, and the expulsion of the Jews the same year. While Jews living in Islamic Spain were frequently better off than their co-religionists residing in Christian-controlled lands, the Golden Age was nevertheless very restricting for Jews.

They were forbidden to serve in public positions of authority (this rule was not uniformly followed), to carry weapons, or to ride horses. Their only means of transport were mules and donkeys, from which they were required to dismount in deference to any Muslim on foot. They also were subjected to occasional violent attacks from Muslim mobs. Nonetheless, Jews in Spain produced important and enduring works in theology, poetry, philosophy, science, and philology. Classic works by Moses Maimonides, Hasdai Ibn Shaprut, Yehudah Ha Levi, and Solomon Ibn Gabirol, among others, attest to the extraordinary richness of Jewish intellectual and spiritual life during the Golden Age.

People of the Book: Muslims often use this to mean that Jews and Christians, monotheistic minorities living within Islamic societies, must be respected and not harmed because of their identification with texts that are also sacred to Muslims. In practice, however, Jews and Christians, the "Peoples of the Book," lived highly restrictive lives or "dhimmitude," as "protected people" under Islamic rule, beginning in the eighth century and continuing into modern times. As preeminent nineteenth-century Jewish historian Heinrich Graetz has noted, Jews and Christians could not build new houses of worship, had to sing in subdued tones in synagogues and churches, and were required to wear distinguishable marks.[3]

Each of these three phrases is filled with ambivalences, ironies, and paradoxes that require careful analysis. Clearly, the history of Jews living as a minority under Islamic rule is uneven. In some places and eras, Jews were tolerated, albeit with severe restrictions; but in times of war or societal stress, Jews were mistreated and killed by Muslims. In addition, many scholars note that the Quran includes both hostile references to *Yahud*, meaning the Jews of Muhammad's day, as well as favorable references to *bani Isra'il*, or the children of Israel, who believe in the One God. The paradoxes that underlie our commonalities need to be examined in interreligious dialogue—as does the entire historical scope of Jewish-Islamic relations.

Despite the challenges and the shattering of friendships, associations, and trust following 9/11, Islamic–Jewish relations will necessarily form a key component of future interreligious relations in the United States and in other parts of the world. But they will take place in an atmosphere and public arena far different from the unrealistic hopes that were often expressed before 9/11.

Because of the horrific anti-Zionist, anti-Israel, and ultimately anti-Jewish poison currently being spread by Muslim leaders in the world, a post-Golden Age dialogue based upon reasonable expectations with reliable and authentic partners is no longer a luxury but a necessity.

---

3. Heinrich Graetz, *History of the Jews* (Philadelphia: Jewish Publication Society of America, 1956) 3:87–88.

Trialogue and Terror

A successful encounter will initially require a series of small achievements that can later lead to incremental gains. There is no "quick fix" in Islamic–Jewish relations for many reasons: the 9/11 negative fallout, the Arab/Iranian conflict with Israel that is of central concern and meaning for both Jews and Muslims, the Hamas and Hezbollah foundational documents calling for the physical destruction of the Jewish state, and the justifiable sense of betrayal many Jews who were engaged in Islamic–Jewish relations experienced after the 2001 attacks.

Positive Catholic–Jewish relations were the chief beneficiary of the recent interreligious Golden Age. Before the death of Pope John Paul II, many Catholic and Jewish leaders, especially in North America and Western Europe, worked closely together for nearly forty years in a systematic effort to reverse the lachrymose history that has poisoned relations between those two faith communities for two millennia. Their clear goal was to replace the dismal past with new sturdy human bridges of solidarity, mutual respect, and understanding.

Catholic–Jewish relations during that time were on a "fast track," spurred on by a blizzard of positive Vatican and other Church statements and declarations, and especially by John Paul II's leadership. Many of the post-1965 documents focused on an acknowledgment of Christianity's taproots within Judaism; self-critical examinations of Catholic teaching materials as they related to Jews, Judaism, and the Holocaust; an official repudiation of all forms of anti-Judaism and anti-Semitism; a painful admission that the Shoah took place within "Christian Europe"; and, especially after Egypt and Jordan signed peace treaties with Israel, a more sympathetic perception and appreciation of modern Israel as a vital component of authentic dialogue.

The beginning of a healing and reconciliation process between these two ancient faith communities is one of the great success stories in recent intergroup history. Yet that relationship, so filled with promise, became more complex and difficult with the death of Pope John Paul II, a larger-than-life, world religious leader who made the improvement of Catholic relations with Jews and Judaism a centerpiece of his pontificate.

Before the mists of legend (and possible sainthood) envelop the late pope, it is important to recall why his reign was both the catalyst for and the crowning achievement of the interreligious Golden Age.

The Interreligious Golden Age

Because Karol Joseph Woytyla was Polish-born, his election as pope on October 16, 1978, was met with widespread skepticism within the Jewish community. There was concern that the new pope would reflect the traditional anti-Semitism that marked much of Jewish history in Poland. But John Paul II proved the skeptics wrong. His extraordinary contributions to building mutual respect and understanding between Catholics and Jews are historic in nature, and he will be remembered as "the best pope the Jews ever had."

On the eve of World War II in 1939, when the future pope was nineteen, the Polish Jewish community of 3.5 million was a center of rich spiritual, intellectual, and cultural resources, and represented 10 percent of that country's total population. In his native Wadowice, a quarter of young Karol's schoolmates were Jews.

Woytyla was a young man during the German occupation of Poland and was a personal witness to the Shoah, in which six million Jews were murdered throughout Europe. But Poland was the Nazis' chief killing field, and the monstrous Auschwitz-Birkenau death camp was not far from Woytyla's own hometown. By war's end, over three million Polish Jews had been killed.

After that horrific experience, Pope John Paul II needed no academic seminars or scholarly papers to instruct him about the radical evil of the Holocaust. The tragedy was indelibly etched in both his head and his heart. During his first papal visit to Poland in June 1979, John Paul II knelt in prayer before the stone marker that had been set up in memory of the Jews murdered at Auschwitz-Birkenau. In later years he called the Shoah "an indelible stain on the history of the [twentieth] century."[4]

In his travels, the pope actively sought visits with the Jewish communities in many lands, and he repeatedly condemned anti-Semitism as a sin against God. John Paul II's visit to Rome's Great Synagogue on April 13, 1986, was the first visit by a pope to a Jewish house of worship since the days of the Apostle Peter.

In his synagogue address, the pope reminded Catholics that Jews are "our elder brothers in faith" and that the Jewish covenant with God is "irrevocable." On April 7, 1994, the pope hosted a historic Vatican concert to commemorate the Shoah. I was present at that occasion and vividly remember John Paul II's poignant plea never to forget the Jewish victims

---

4. Pope John Paul II, "Letter of His Holiness Pope John Paul II on the Occasion of the Publication of the Document 'We Remember: A Reflection on the Shoa.'" Online: http://www.vatican.va/holy_father/john_paul_ii/letters/1998/documents/hf_jp-ii_let_19980312_shoah_en.html/.

of the Holocaust—among whom were many of his childhood friends and classmates.

A few months earlier the Holy See and the State of Israel had established full and formal diplomatic relations. This important action, combined with the pope's public denunciations of anti-Semitism and his reverent remembrance of the Holocaust, changed the initial Jewish perception of John Paul II. His personal intervention in 1995 satisfactorily resolved the decade-long crisis over the location of a convent in Auschwitz. As a result, the Carmelite nuns finally left the death camp building where the Germans had stored the poison gas used to kill Jews.

On March 12, 1998, the Vatican released *We Remember: A Reflection on the Shoah*. Although there was much criticism from both Catholics and Jews about the document itself, John Paul II's brief introductory letter was universally praised. In it, the pope urged Catholics to "examine themselves on the responsibility which they too have for the evils of our time."[5]

In March 2000 the pope visited Israel. Once again I was privileged to be present at an important event in his pontificate. Unlike Pope Paul VI's brief visit to Israel in the mid-1960s, when the pontiff never once mentioned the name of the Jewish state, during his stay John Paul II was an honored guest at the official residence of the Israeli president and in the offices of the Chief Rabbinate. The pope's sorrowful visit to Yad Vashem, the Israeli Holocaust Memorial, where he met with Polish Jewish survivors, was televised around the world.

The most lasting image of the entire pilgrimage—perhaps of his entire pontificate—was John Paul II's slow walk to the Western Wall in Jerusalem, Judaism's holiest site, and his insertion of a prayer of reconciliation into one of the Wall's many crevices.

Although there were serious Catholic–Jewish flashpoints during John Paul II's long reign, many of them were ultimately overcome or solved because both sides did not want the positive dialogue to weaken or die. In June 1987 the Holy See accorded full diplomatic honors to President Kurt Waldheim of Austria during a visit to the Vatican. At the time of the visit, the United States had placed Waldheim on its "watch list" and had forbidden him entry into the country because of his wartime activities in the Balkans.

After years of hiding his record, Waldheim was accused of participating in war crimes against Jews and other groups. The intense negative reaction to the Waldheim visit nearly caused the cancellation of the pope's

---

5. Ibid.

scheduled meeting a few months later with American Jewish leaders in Miami.

But the meeting took place, and the pope electrified his audience by declaring, "Never again!" in reference to the Shoah. John Paul II had another highly successful meeting with Jewish leaders during his visit to the United States in October 1995.

Toward the end of his long pontificate, however, some serious problems arose in Catholic–Jewish relations, most notably around the question of making the appropriate wartime records of the Vatican available to a team of Catholic and Jewish historians. It is an issue John Paul II's successors must confront if those relations are to grow in strength. While the Vatican document *Dominus Iesus*, issued in 2000, did not specifically mention Jews or Judaism, questions were raised whether the Holy See had abandoned the pope's strong commitment to positive interreligious relations.

In early 2004, there was another flashpoint when the pope appeared to offer an endorsement for Mel Gibson's controversial film, *The Passion of the Christ*. John Paul II was reported to have seen it at a private screening and commented, "It is as it was." Vatican sources were quick to deny any papal approval of the film, but the contretemps remained. A year later the pope's new book, *Memory and Identity: Conversations between Millenniums*, drew criticism from some European Jewish groups. They charged that John Paul II unfairly compared the "evil" of abortion with the horrors of the Shoah. Vatican officials claimed that this was a misinterpretation of the pope's words.

But despite these flashpoints, the Catholic–Jewish encounter actually became stronger as it became clear that Pope John Paul II was leading his Church, and by extension all of Christianity, into a new historic relationship that had begun at the Second Vatican Council. The pope, then a young bishop, attended the Council, and it had a lasting positive influence upon him and his teachings.

When he died in 2005, he had earned an imperishable place in Jewish history, because his gifted revolutionary leadership had dramatically strengthened the long-overdue process of Christianity's reconciliation with its Jewish "elder brother."

The concern today is that Karol Woytyla and his extraordinary achievements in interreligious affairs and the high priority he placed upon them may fade as the Catholic Church faces new challenges and issues, many of them internal. There is a sense that the Catholic Church faces a myriad of serious problems—a shrinking number of seminarians in the West, the rapid growth of secularism in Europe and North America that negatively impacts upon Roman Catholicism, continuing clergy sexual abuse scandals, a resurgent ultraconservative element that seeks to mitigate or even negate the reforms of the Second Vatican Council—that demand the time, talent, and attention of the pope.

I have also heard some Catholic leaders declare the task in developing positive relations with Jews and Judaism is nearly complete, allowing energy and attention to be turned elsewhere, i.e., toward improving relations with Muslims and addressing the serious internal problems of the Church. I strongly disagree with such a view, believing instead that our joint work has just begun. Nearly two thousand years of religious anti-Judaism cannot be eradicated in less than a half century. The Christian "teaching of contempt" toward Judaism and its adherents took centuries to develop, and it will require a serious and systematic effort lasting many more years to overcome that tragic legacy of the past.

Despite Pope Benedict's XVI's strong public professions and acts of support for the Catholic–Jewish enterprise, many Jewish and Catholic observers believe that those interreligious relations, while highly meaningful to the pope, do not appear to have the same sense of urgency as they did during the previous pontificate.

Let me be clear. While he lacks his predecessor's enormous charisma and compelling personality, Benedict XVI has, however, publicly reaffirmed and reinforced John Paul's positive record regarding Catholic–Jewish relations, anti-Semitism, the Shoah and the commitment to the security and survival of Israel as a Jewish state. Visits to synagogues in his native Germany and in the United States, and a series of important meetings with Jewish leaders in Rome and the United States were widely reported and warmly welcomed by the Jewish community. In addition, Benedict's visit to Israel in May 2009, combined with a keen awareness of his own biography—growing up in an anti-Nazi German family during the Shoah—is very much a part of the pope's personal outreach to Jews.

Yet on Ash Wednesday 2008, *L'Osservatore Romano*, the official Vatican newspaper, published the revised text of a 1962 Latin-language prayer that is permitted to be used on Good Friday.

Normally, such an article would attract little attention, despite its placement in the Vatican paper. But this was no ordinary prayer; its Latin title is "Pro Conversione Iudaeorum," or "For the Conversion of the Jews."

And Pope Benedict XVI, the author of the new text, which still retains the prayer's original title, is no ordinary liturgist.

The original Latin prayer urging the conversion of the Jewish people to Christianity contains a negative description of both Jews and Judaism: "Let us pray also for the Jews . . . May our God and Lord remove the veil from their hearts; that they may also acknowledge our Lord Jesus Christ . . . Almighty God . . . you drive not even the Jews away from your mercy, hear our prayers, for the blindness of that people, that acknowledging the light of your truth, which is Christ, they may be rescued from their darkness."[6]

Benedict eliminated some of that offensive language, including "veil from their hearts," "the blindness of that people," and the mention of the "darkness" of the Jews. But the new Latin version, while clearly an improvement, is deeply disappointing because it still seeks the conversion of the Jews to Christianity at the "End of Time."[7]

Also dismaying was the weakening of the positive theological language vis-à-vis Jews in the revised adult Catechism, and, of course, Benedict's January 2009 action in lifting the ban of excommunication on the followers of the late Bishop Marcel Lefebvre created a firestorm.

In 1988 Pope John Paul II had excommunicated Lefebvre and members of his Sacred Society of Pius X (SSPX), a group soaked with highly toxic anti-Jewish and anti-Semitic teachings, some of them stemming back to the French Revolution. One of the four Lefebvre bishops whose excommunication was lifted was Richard Williamson, a public denier of the mass murders that took place during the Holocaust.

The negative reaction to both Benedict's action and Williamson's obscene denial of the Holocaust's radical evil was both swift and fierce, much of it coming from Catholic clergy and laity. As a result of the backlash, the pope was compelled to write an unprecedented letter to the world's bishops that explained the mistakes he and other Vatican officials had made regarding the SSPX.

Benedict's actions in lifting the excommunication of SSPX members created a sense of bewilderment mixed with anxiety among many Jews and Catholics. Despite Benedict's positive statements and policies, the question remains: will John Paul II's stunning achievements and teachings about Jews and Judaism be strengthened, or will they be marginalized,

6. *Roman Missal* (Chicago: Canons Regular of St. John Cantius, 1920) 221–22.

7. This is reflected in the language of the Christian-Jewish Dialogue of Montreal, "Resolution on the Revised 1962 Good Friday 'Prayer for the Jews,'" January 12, 2009. Online: http://www.jcrelations.net/en/?item=3054/.

perhaps deemphasized, as the Catholic Church confronts its serious internal problems and an increasingly negative encounter with the world's Muslims. Will sufficient attention be paid to Catholic–Jewish relations? Or will a sense of exhaustion—or worse still, ecclesiastical atrophy—set in after the past four decades of exuberance and extraordinary advances?

⁌

During the recent interreligious Golden Age, many Protestant church bodies both in North America and in Europe followed the lead of the Catholic Church and adopted a series of statements, policy positions, and declarations denouncing anti-Semitism and recognizing Christian culpability for the Shoah.

On many domestic social justice concerns, much of the organized American Jewish community was a coalition partner with liberal mainline Protestant denominations as well as the National Council of Churches (NCC). The NCC is an umbrella organization comprising thirty-five Protestant and Eastern Orthodox churches, with headquarters in New York City.

The issues that brought about partnership included support for church-state separation; opposition to anti-Semitism, racism, ageism, and sexism; opposition to Christian conversion campaigns aimed at Jews; opposition to mandated prayers and Bible reading in public schools; a pro-choice position on abortion; opposition to South African apartheid; and opposition to the Religious Right's agenda in the United States, including any effort to legally define the United States as a "Christian nation."

At the same time that Jews and liberal Protestants began to relate, Jews and evangelical Christians had entered into a wary but vital relationship prior to 9/11. Jews perceived years ago that the strongest Christian public support for the survival and security of Israel came from evangelicals. During the decades'-long campaign to free Soviet Jewry, the evangelical community was a strong, vocal ally of the American Jewish community.

Yet most American Jews differed with many evangelicals on a myriad of issues that included gun control, abortion, passage of the Equal Rights Amendment, embryonic stem cell research, gay rights, and prayer and Bible reading in America's public schools.

During the Golden Age, the American Jewish community intensified its contacts and shared concerns with both liberal Protestant and conservative evangelical church bodies. It was a delicate balancing act fraught with pitfalls and often-confusing responses to specific issues: joining with liberal Protestants against evangelicals on church-state issues, but also welcoming evangelical support for Israel while many liberal Christian leaders were cool, at best, or hostile, at worst, to the Jewish state.

In addition to the flashpoints mentioned above, there were other serious controversies with Protestant Christians during the Golden Age. However, the sincere and usually effective efforts made by leaders in both communities mitigated or overcame the difficulties. I personally lived through many of those storms, and remember them even as combat warriors proudly recount the skirmishes and battles they survived.

But the 2004 action of the Presbyterian Church (USA) General Assembly (GA) urging economic divestment from firms doing business in Israel shattered the coalition between liberal Protestants, on the one hand, and Jews, on the other. The GA meeting in Richmond approved the divestment initiative by a vote of 431–62. Subsequently, the United Methodist Church and the Episcopal Church also explored divestment from Israel as a means of pressure that would somehow "promote peace" in the Middle East.

Happily, all such efforts were ultimately thwarted and, in some cases, rescinded because of the dedicated leadership of many Presbyterian, United Methodist, and Episcopal clergy and laypeople who worked closely with their Jewish counterparts.

But enormous damage was done. The 2004 Presbyterian action followed by the United Methodist and Episcopal divestment campaigns radically changed the fundamental Jewish perception of liberal Protestant leadership and sharply increased the complexities and difficulties of an already highly ambivalent relationship.

In the post-Golden Age environment, liberal Protestant churches continue to experience a severe membership decline, and even the once "upward and onward" membership climb of the evangelical churches has stalled. The latter community has also been plagued by a series of ugly clergy sex scandals that has shaken public confidence.

Recent religious surveys indicate that a growing number of Americans are turning away from all forms of organized religion. These factors are creating a serious problem for every faith community. Unfortunately, many economically stressed clergy and laypeople are concerned with basic existential questions of institutional survival and view the development of positive Christian–Jewish relations as a luxury, an activity best pursued by a few "ecumaniacs."

But, of course, those relations will continue even in a difficult financial environment, but perhaps with less public enthusiasm. The end of the Golden Age means much harder work for those who labor in the interreligious vineyard. The halcyon days when all things seemed possible among Jews, Christians, and Muslims are over.

I would paraphrase Bette Davis's famous line in the award-winning film, *All about Eve*: "Fasten your seatbelts, it's going to be a bumpy night." But Hollywood must not have the last word on future interreligious relations. That honor goes to Zechariah, the Hebrew prophet who urged us to be "prisoners of hope" (Zech 9:12).

two

Salvation Jewish Style

GILBERT S. ROSENTHAL

I was a student of both Professor Mordecai M. Kaplan and Professor Abraham Joshua Heschel at the Jewish Theological Seminary in the 1950s. Kaplan was the great iconoclast and religious naturalist; Heschel was the neo-Hasid and mystic. On Monday mornings, Kaplan would describe his concept of religion as guarantor of salvation, and he defined God as the power or process that makes for human salvation. On Tuesday, we would report to Heschel on Kaplan's notion of salvation, to which Heschel would reply: "Salvation is a Christian, not a Jewish concept." The following Monday we would relate to Kaplan Heschel's critique. Kaplan fairly exploded, retorting, "When was the last time he prayed? The prayers are full of references to salvation!" Who was right? They both were right: salvation of the *individual soul* is really a Christian concept; but *salvation of the group or nation or people* is genuinely a Jewish ideal. True, Judaism—unlike Christianity—is not primarily a salvational religion. In my long rabbinate, Orthodox rabbis have never condemned me as a heretic who will burn in hell and lose salvation for my views on Jewish theology or law. They may have criticized some of my legal or theological positions, but they never defined their criticism in terms of salvation.

At the same time, *group or national salvation* is, indeed, an important Jewish notion. The paradigmatic example of national salvation of Israel has been and still remains the exodus from Egypt. That theme recurs innumerable times in Scripture, in rabbinic literature, and the liturgy, and on every festive occasion including Sabbaths, festivals, and, of course, preeminently

Passover.[1] Jews never cease to remember those distant events in Egypt and at the Sea of Reeds; they immortalize the redemption of the Israelites at every possible occasion and in every liturgy: "From Egypt You did redeem us; from the house of bondage You did rescue us," runs one prayer.[2] And this is but one small example of the many that stud the liturgy. The Song of the Sea of Reeds, celebrating the miraculous victory over Pharaoh's armies, is recited in every morning service, as the congregation chants, "The Lord is my strength and power, and He has become my salvation . . . You led in Your love this people whom You have redeemed."[3] That ancient, defining redemption has always served as an inspiration and still is the eschatological hope of the Jewish people.[4]

The Bible offers a view of salvation that is unmistakably this worldly and does not deal with "salvation of the individual soul." The blessings for which we pray are the blessings of the earth and soil, of the crops and herds, of the wind and rain, of the family and home: "If you will listen to these laws and keep them and abide by them, then the Lord your God will keep the covenant with you and the kindness He swore to your ancestors. He will love you and bless you with the fruit of your womb and the fruit of your soil, your corn and your wine, your oil and the increase of your herds and the young of your flocks . . . and remove from you all sickness and disease that you encountered in Egypt, but He will inflict them on your enemies." And perhaps most importantly, the Bible describes the ultimate salvation as victory in wars against the inevitable enemies of the people of Israel: "You will consume all the peoples the Lord your God delivers to you."[5] Conversely, sins against God will lead to dire punishments against individuals and the nation, the crops and herds, the family and tribes, the ultimate punishment being exile from the land: "If you do not listen to Me and keep these commandments, I will afflict you with terror and disease

---

1. Exod 20:2; Num 24:8; Deut 4:34; 20:1, 30; Jer 11:1–10; 23:7; 31:10; Hos 13:14; Pss 107:1ff.; 114:1ff.; 136:10ff.

2. In the prayer that begins, *Ezrat Yisrael*, and is formally known as, *Geulah*: "You have been the help and redeemer of our people from of old," recited before the *Amidah*. The prayer utilizes the verb or noun form of *yeshua*, *geulah*, and *pidyon* no less than thirteen times.

3. Exod 15:2. Significantly, this verse is quoted in Isa 12:2 and Ps 118:14.

4. 1 Kgs 8:51–53; Ps 135:8, 9, 14; Mic 7:15; Isa 11:15–16. Invariably, salvation in the Bible is for the nation or the community. In the Psalms, individual salvation is often alluded to but generally that refers to salvation of the individual from the hands of an enemy (e.g., David from the hands of Saul). See 2 Sam 22:1ff.; Ps 18:1ff. Also see Pss 27:1ff.; and Hab 3:8, 13, 19.

5. Deut 7:12ff.; 11:13ff.; 22:6–7; 28:1–14.

... You will sow seeds and your enemies shall eat them ... you will be smitten by your enemies and they shall rule over you ... And I will scatter you among the nations and draw the sword against you; your land shall be desolate and your cities shall lie in ruin."[6]

Furthermore, the Bible is clearly on record as rejecting a notion of an afterlife. Now ancient Israelites surely knew of the idea of an afterlife: they lived in close proximity with great civilizations such as the Egyptians, the Assyrians, the Babylonians, the Canaanites—all of whom affirmed such a belief, and in the case of the Egyptians made it a centerpiece of their religion. But time and again, the Bible rejects that ideal. "There is hope for a tree; if it is cut down, it will renew itself ... If a person dies can he live again?" ponders Job, responding to his own question in the negative.[7] The Psalmist insisted in a number of psalms that death is the end of a human being's existence. "What is to be gained from my death, from my descent into the Pit? Can dust praise You? Can it declare Your faithfulness?" "The dead cannot praise God, nor can those who descend into the grave."[8] "For it is not *Sheol* that praises You, nor the land of death that extols You; nor do they who descend into the Pit hope for Your grace ... The living, only the living can give thanks to You as I do this day," pleaded the gravely ill King Hezekiah, as he begged God to heal him.[9] It was only very late in the biblical era that the notions of resurrection and an afterlife took root, most notably in the book of Daniel, in what is presumably the final book of the Hebrew Bible: "Many of those who sleep in the dust of the earth will awake, some to eternal life, others to reproaches, to everlasting abhorrence."[10]

For reasons that are not clear to us, the Pharisees made the belief in resurrection of the body and immortality of the soul in an afterlife a basic dogma of Judaism. Perhaps they were refuting the pagan claims that there are deities who reign over the living and other deities whose realm is the world of the dead. In a rare theological statement in the Mishnah, the sages ruled that, "Whoever denies that the concept of bodily resurrection

---

6. Lev 26:14–45; Deut 28:15–68.
7. Job 14:7ff. Cf. Kohelet 3:18, 22; 12:7.
8. Pss 30:7–10; 115:17.
9. Isa 38:18–19.
10. Dan 12:2. Cf. 2 Macc 7:9 & 12:43; Wis 3:1–4.

derives from the Torah or that the Torah was given at Sinai loses his or her portion in the afterlife."[11] Their view prevailed over the Sadducees who denied resurrection but may have accepted the concept of spiritual immortality. As such, the rabbis incorporated these Pharisaic notions as normative in theology and liturgy. They consisted of several elements: *atid la-vo*, the coming future; *yemot ha-mashiah*, the days of the messiah; *tehiat ha-metim*, the resurrection of the dead; *din ve-heshbon*, final judgment; *olam ha-ba*, the next world or afterlife; *Gan Eden*, paradise for the virtuous; and *Gehinnom*, hell for the wicked.[12] But these concepts were refined and interpreted by two very different schools of thought. One school of thought regarded the afterlife in literal, sensuous, even crass terms of what heaven and hell would be like. For example, in Heaven, the righteous will feast on the flesh of the mythical bull, the great fish Leviathan, and drink a wine prepared by God from the days of creation.[13] As to hell, the wicked will burn eternally in fire or boiling manure or be subjected to all manner of torture.[14] This passage from the Midrash sums up the literal school of theology:

> Ten things the Holy One, blessed be He, will renew in the next life. He will illumine the world; He will cause running water to issue from Jerusalem; He will cause the trees to bear fruits every month and people to eat them and be healed; He will rebuild all the ruined cities so that no waste places will remain on earth; he will rebuild Jerusalem with sapphires; peace will reign throughout nature; he will assemble all the beasts, birds and reptiles and make a covenant between them and Israel; weeping and wailing will cease in the world and there will be no more sighing, groaning or anguish—but all will be happy.[15]

The other school adopted a spiritual or metaphorical approach to the entire question. Rav maintained that there will be neither eating nor drinking nor copulating in the *olam ha-ba* but the righteous will sit around

---

11. Mishnah *Sanhedrin* 10:1.

12. See Gilbert S. Rosenthal, *What Can a Modern Jew Believe?* (Eugene, OR: Wipf & Stock, 2007) 233–44.

13. *Avot* 3:20; *Baba Batra* 74b–75a; Louis Ginzberg, *Legends of the Jews*, trans. Henrietta Szold, 7 vols. (Philadelphia: Jewish Publication Society, 1954) 1:27–28; 5:43–44, 48, notes 127, 139.

14. Mishnah *Eduyot* 2:10; *Rosh Hashanah* 16b–17a; *Shabbat* 152b; *Midrash Psalms* (ed. S. Buber) Ps 31, p. 120a; *Yerushalmi Sanhedrin* 10:3, 29b.

15. *Exodus Rabbah* 15:21.

a table with garlands in their hair and bask in God's *Shekhinah* (glory).[16] Samuel insisted that there would be no difference between this world and the days of the messiah except that political tyranny and oppression will disappear.[17] Resh Lakish reinterpreted the literal notion of hell, bestowing on it a totally ethereal interpretation: "There is no Hell in the next life but the Holy One, blessed be He, will remove the sun from its sheath. The righteous will be healed by its rays while the wicked will be judged by it."[18]

The liturgy codified the rabbinic views of salvation, and in fact there are many mentions of *geulah* or *yeshuah*, redemption and salvation, in the prayers.[19] But more: the prayers that deal with salvation are invariably in the plural, only rarely singular, and they refer to the salvation of the community, the nation and the people of Israel. The prayers that contain references to salvation generally refer to God's salvation of Israel from Egypt and from their enemies at the Sea of Reeds—the paradigm of all redemptive interventions of God. The prayer that precedes the *Shema* articulates the hope that God will "bring us from the four corners of the earth and lead us erect to our land, because You are a God who works salvation and chose us from among the nations." Similarly, the so-called *Geulah* prayer before the *Amidah* speaks of God "who redeemed us from Egypt and saved us from the house of bondage," and it then shifts into the present and future expectation that "the Rock of Israel will arise to aid Israel and redeem Judah as He promised," concluding, "Praised be You God, who redeemed Israel." The first blessing in the *Amidah* refers to God as "the King and helper who is a savior and shield." The seventh blessing in the *Amidah*, titled *Geulah*, reads, "Look at our affliction and plead our cause. Redeem us speedily for Your name's sake because You are a mighty Redeemer. Praised are you, O God, who redeems Israel."[20] The *Hoshanah* service on the seventh day of Sukkot says not a single word about the salvation of the soul or individual redemption: it is a prayer for all the people, that God may save them and bless their crops and herds and grant

---

16. *Berakhot* 17a.
17. *Berakhot* 34b.
18. *Nedarim* 9b.
19. Other verb or noun forms that are utilized in the liturgy include *p-d-h*, redeem, and *p-r-k*, rescue. But they are basically synonyms for the more common *g-a-l* and *y-sh-a*.
20. Mishnah *Taanit* 2:4; Yerushalmi *Berakhot* 2:4, 5a; *Pesahim* 117b. The switch to the present tense of the verb *g-a-l* ("save") in the liturgy is deliberate, states the Talmud, and includes the eschatological hope that God will save His people in the future as in the past.

them a new year of plentiful blessings. And it is always in the plural form: "Save us, O God!" The prayer concludes, "Save Your people and bless Your inheritance."

How did Judaism perceive of salvation for other nations and religions? That is an intriguing question that is fraught with much significance for today, especially. Two great rabbis debated the issue in the second century: do Gentiles have a portion in the world to come or not? Rabbi Eliezer ben Hyrcanus argued that they do not. But Rabbi Joshua ben Hananiah insisted that the righteous (*tzadikkim*) of all nations do have a portion in the world to come. Rabbi Joshua's view was accepted as the normative one.[21]

☙

In a similar vein, the Talmud records a conversation between the Roman Emperor Antoninus (his identity is uncertain) in which Antoninus queried Rabbi Yehudah Ha-Nasi, the Prince and head of the Jewish community in Eretz Yisrael and editor of the Mishnah, whether he would have a portion in the age to come. "Yes indeed, you will," replied Rabbi Yehudah. "Only the wicked who behave like Esau of old will be denied that privilege; but you are a righteous person and for you, therefore, a portion in the afterlife has been reserved."[22]

Maimonides (1135–1204) ruled in his authoritative law code, the *Mishneh Torah*, that the pious people of all nations (*hasidei umot ha-olam*) have a portion in the afterlife. And he explained that this includes those non-Jews who abide by the seven laws given to Noah after the flood. The seven commandments consist of six negative and one positive *mitzvot*: You shall not worship idols; you shall not blaspheme God's name; you shall not murder; you shall not steal; you shall not commit sexual immorality; you shall not be cruel to animals; you shall establish courts of justice in every community. This became the normative Jewish view on salvation for the non-Jews.[23]

---

21. Tosefta *Avodah Zarah* 11:2, p. 434 (ed. M. Zuckermandel); *Sanhedrin* 105a.

22. *Avodah Zarah* 10b on Obad 1:18. Cf. *Hullin* 13b: "Gentiles outside of Eretz Yisrael are not really idolaters; they are merely following the customs of their ancestors."

23. *Mishneh Torah, Teshuvah* 3:5; *Melakhim* 8:10–11; *Edut* 11:10. The Noahide laws are derived from Gen 9:1–17 in the Talmud *Sanhedrin* 56aff. Earlier versions of the Noahide laws are found in *Jubilees* 7:20ff. and Acts 15:19–21. Cf. *Tosefta Avodah Zarah* 8:4–8, pp. 473–74.; *Genesis Rabbah* (ed. Julius Theodor-Hanoch Albeck) 34:19, pp 316–17; *Mishneh Torah, Melakhim*, 9:1 and 10:1–10. See Louis Jacobs, *Principles of the Jewish Faith* (New York: Basic Books, 1964) 437ff. In *Melakhim*, Maimonides seems to limit salvation to those *hasidei umot ha-olam* who accept the seven laws of

Various sages and philosophers built on the foundation laid by the Talmud as explicated and codified by Maimonides. The most daringly dramatic step toward equalizing the status of non-Jews in halakhah was taken by Menahem Meiri of Perpignon (d. 1316). Meiri created a new category of non-Jews: *umot ha-gedurot be-darkei ha-datot ve-nimusim*—peoples regulated by the norms and laws of religion. Although he does not deal with the theological implications of this notion, limiting himself to a discussion of the *legal* status of Christians and Muslims, the implications are profound: they stand on a higher level than those who merely abide by the Noahide rules and are thus accorded even greater rights—indeed, equal rights—in legal matters such as torts, civil law, business relations, etc. In effect, Meiri abolished legal distinctions between a Jew and a Christian or Muslim.[24]

༄

Other medieval sages built on this foundation a new legal and theological approach to the non-Jew. Yehudah Aryeh Leone Modena (1571–1648) and Simone Simhah Luzzatto (c. 1583–1663) agreed that Christians and Muslims are monotheists; consequently, they have a portion in the world to come.[25] Rabbi Isaac Lampronti of Ferrara (1679–1756), in his path-breaking talmudic encyclopedia, *Pahad Yitzhak*, ruled that when the Talmud refers to a *goy* it implies a pagan of ancient times, not a Christian or a Muslim. "Today's Christians among whom we dwell and to whom we turn for protection, believe in the creation of the universe out of nothing, and in the exodus from Egypt, as well as other basic principles of religion. When they pray, their intention is to the Maker of heaven and earth, as many of our decisors have written." Lampronti had in mind Polish scholars such as Rabbi Moses Isserles of Krakow whose glosses on Joseph Karo's

---

Noah as a divine revelation rather than the fruits of their intellectual and spiritual pursuits. His source seems to be an obscure Midrash, *Mishnat Rabbi Eliezer*, which was first published in the twentieth century. Moreover, he is evidently articulating his own opinion.

24. See Jacob Katz, *Exclusiveness and Tolerance*, Judaica Scripta 3 (London: Oxford University Press, 1961) 114–28; Moshe Halbertal, *Ben Torah le-Hokhmah* (Jerusalem: Magnes, 2001) 80–108.

25. Yehudah Aryeh Leone Modena, *Magen VaHerev*, ed. Shlomo Simonsohn (Jerusalem: Mossad Bialik, 1968) 250, 256–57, 266, 268–69, 273, 276, 280–81; Modena, *Historia de 'riti hebraici* (Venice, 1638) Book 2, chap. 5, par. 4 & Book 2, chap. 8, par.1; Simhah Simone Luzzatto, *Maamar al Yehudei Venezia*, ed. and trans. Dan Lattes, Ricardo Bachi & Moshe Shelves (Jerusalem: Mossad Bialik, 1950) chap. 13, pp. 113–16.

Shulhan Arukh are authoritative for Ashkenazic Jewry, as well as Rabbi Moshe Rivkes, author of a widely cited commentary on Karo's great law code.[26]

Turning to German Jewry, we find that the views of Rabbi Jacob Emden, Moses Mendelssohn, and Franz Rosenzweig are instructive and somewhat revolutionary. Rabbi Emden (1697–1776) was an Orthodox rabbi who certainly opposed any liberal trends that were cropping up in West European Jewry. Yet his views on Christianity are remarkably liberal. He wrote that, "The Nazarene brought a double blessing to the world. On the one hand, he strengthened the Torah of Moses majestically, and on the other he did much good for the gentiles . . . by doing away with idolatry." Both Christianity and Islam recognize the Creator of the world and abide by the basic laws of Noah, believe in the difference between good and evil, and look forward to an afterlife. Consequently, Emden assured non-Jews that they, too, would enjoy the blessings of the *olam ha-ba*.[27]

The famous Jewish philosopher Moses Mendelssohn (1729–1786) was a literary friend and admirer of Emden and shared many of his attitudes towards other faiths. Mendelssohn recorded his appreciation of the goodness of Jesus on the condition that he never regarded himself as equal to the Father or a divinity, and that he never intended to subvert the faith of his fathers. He wrote: "Since the Creator intended all humans for eternal bliss, an exclusive religion cannot be a true one. I venture to state that this is a criterion for truth in religious matters. No revelation purporting to be alone capable of saving man can be the true revelation if it does not harmonize with the purpose of the All-Mighty Creator."[28]

The third German voice articulating a theology of other faiths was that of the brilliant philosopher Franz Rosenzweig (1886–1929). He

---

26. Isaac Lampronti, *Pahad Yitzhak*, 4 vols. (Jerusalem: Mossad Harav Kook, 1976), introduction, 1:38–39 and repeated verbatim in the entry for *goy* in 4:438ff. I have analyzed these and other Italian Jewish rabbis and philosophers and their views of other faiths in my essay, "Jewish Attitudes towards Other Faiths: The Italian Model," *Journal of Ecumenical Studies* 44 (2009) 203–25, esp. 203–5.

27. On Emden, see Jacob Katz, *Exclusiveness and Tolerance*, 167; Alexander Altmann, *Moses Mendelssohn: A Biographical Study* (Philadelphia: Jewish Publications Society, 1973) 210, 217. Emden expressed his views on Christianity in a letter of 1757, *Sefer Olam Rabbah ve-Zutah*, and in several other works, including his *Sefer Shimush* and *Leshem Shamayim* on *Mishnah Avot* 4:11. The letter has been translated and published by Harvey Falk in his, *Jesus the Pharisee* (Mahwah, NJ: Paulist, 1985) 17–23. Cf. Blu Greenberg, "Rabbi Jacob Emden: The Views of an Enlightened Traditionalist on Christianity," *Judaism* 27 (1978) 351–63.

28. Altmann, *Moses Mendelssohn*, 262.

suggested that before God, "Jews and Christians labor at the same task. He [God] cannot dispense with either. The truth, the whole truth, thus belongs neither to them nor to us. Just for this reason we remain. Thus, we both have but part of the truth. Only God has the whole truth." Consequently, Jews and Christians now await and hope "only for the great reconciliation on the very last day."[29]

In sum, as early as the second century, Judaism acknowledged that "salvation" was available to all peoples who accepted the basic rules of civilized living, or what we term, "natural law." Some theologians and sages, particularly those who were attracted to the doctrines of the Kabbalah, rejected this position.[30] But the mainstream thinkers in Spain and Germany, Italy, and Poland were convinced that salvation is not an exclusive Jewish gift but is open to those who adhere to the basic rules of decent and moral living.

Nevertheless, for some religions, personal salvation of the single soul is what really matters. Moreover, there are those faiths that are not content with saving their own souls—they are intent on saving others as well, and they view it as a positive commandment, a *mitzvah*, to go out and proselytize the world and convert the outsiders. So it was that zealous Christian missionaries, including both Catholics and Protestants, went to the faraway lands, to darkest Africa, to exotic Asia, to the New World, and sought to bring the light and blessings of salvation to the pagans—with all the blessings, as well as all the dreadful and bloody consequences. And if the natives or locals rebuffed their efforts, they viewed them as "infidels" so that all means, both fair and foul, might be applied to lead the benighted ones to the light and the truth and save their souls from eternal damnation. Much the same tactics were applied by the Muslims who spread their faith by the sword from North Africa to Indonesia, from Spain to Mongolia. One of the bizarre applications of this doctrine is the behavior of the Mormon Church that insists that all but Mormons are damned and that posthumous baptism, even without the knowledge and permission of the deceased and the family, is meritorious. Thus, the Mormons have been

---

29. Franz Rosenzweig, *Star of Redemption*, trans. William Hallo (Notre Dame: University of Notre Dame Press, 1985) 380–417.

30. For opinions of the *Kabbalah* concerning non-Jews, see *Zohar* 1:28b, 46b–47a; 2:37a; 3:14b, 40a–b; Isaiah Tishby, *Mishnat Ha-Zohar*, 2 vols. (Jerusalem: Mossad Bialik, 1961) 2:285ff.

busily baptizing millions of people who have died, including thousands of Holocaust victims, much to the outrage and bitterness of the survivors.[31]

Often, alas, in the process of spreading their blessings and saving souls from "eternal damnation," forceful and even lethal measures are applied. In religion, fanatics too often seize the reins and cause untold suffering. Winston Churchill defined a fanatic as someone who can't change his mind and won't change the subject. I remind my readers that Gandhi was assassinated by a Hindu fanatic, that Muslim fanatics gunned down Anwar Sadat, that Yitzhak Rabin was murdered by a Jewish fanatic, that the killers of three thousand people on September 11 were Muslim fanatics. Fanatics have murdered over a word, a law, a ritual, a doctrine, a deed, and an old historical event. The Crusades, the Inquisition, the various wars of religion are bloody proof of that depressing fact. "We have just enough religion to make us hate one another but not enough to love one another," mused Jonathan Swift. The gruesome history of the wars of religion in Europe between Catholics and Protestants in the sixteenth and seventeenth centuries is proof of that observation. By the time of the Treaty of Westphalia in 1648, ending the brutal Thirty Years' War, about one-third of Germany's population had been killed or had died of famine or disease, not to mention by the slaughter in Sweden, the Netherlands, Austria, France, and other lands. "Men never do evil so completely and cheerfully as when they do it from religious convictions," suggested Blaise Pascal.

As I survey the world situation today, as I contemplate the lethal conflicts raging between religious and ethnic groups in Asia, Africa, and the Middle East, I have the uneasy feeling that Samuel Huntington was on target, that we are witnessing "the Clash of Civilizations" (to borrow the title of his important and frightening book analyzing the conflicts that have replaced the Cold War in our world). In Iraq, Sunnis and Shiites slaughter one another in the cruelest and most grisly fashion—and they are both Muslims! And the internecine slaughter in the Balkans a few years ago highlighted the sad fact that Europe hasn't learned very much from the tragic history of the twentieth century, the century described by Isaiah Berlin as the "bloodiest in human history." At the base, I detect that same old original sin that has plagued humanity since time immemorial. I refer

---

31. The Church of Jesus Christ of Latter Day Saints (Mormons) agreed to discontinue posthumous baptism of Holocaust victims and signed a pledge to that affect in 1995 with the Conference of Presidents of Major American Jewish Organizations—a ceremony I personally witnessed. Sadly, the Mormons have violated their pledge and have continued to "convert" Jewish victims of the Holocaust despite the outrage of Jewish groups, especially of Holocaust-survivors organizations.

to the toxic and malignant notion: "I have a monopoly on truth. I possess the keys to the kingdom. I'm saved—you are damned! I'm in—you are out! My way or the highway."

Oceans of blood have been spilled because of this attitude. When one believes that he or she is saved and others are damned; that his or her way is right and the others are wrong, then any means may be employed to achieve a "righteous goal." So Shiites slaughter Sunnis; Hindus kill Muslims; Muslims and Christians wage war—and, of course, everybody slaughters Jews.

This uneasy feeling has deepened and sharpened since the tragedy of September 11 when nineteen religious fanatics murdered in cold blood three thousand innocent civilians in the worst domestic terrorist violence in America ever. The killers were fanatical Islamists who were indoctrinated with the notion that non-Muslims are damned and undeserving of paradise whereas *jihadists* or *shahadeen* are martyrs for the true faith, whose acts of homicide and suicide will bring them the eternal reward reserved only for the faithful. The fact that fifteen of the nineteen killers were Saudis was no accident, in my opinion. They had been infected by the fanatical Wahhabi version of Islam that teaches that non-Muslims are damned and that anything is legitimate in dealing with infidels such as Jews and Christians, Bahais or Buddhists, Hindus or Sikhs. This poison has been disseminated by the fundamentalist *madrassas* (Muslim schools) that "educate" Muslim children in Saudi Arabia and Iraq, Pakistan and Indonesia, and are generally funded by Saudi money. The philosophy of such schools was aired publicly in a documentary special hosted by Barbara Walters that dealt with the issue of heaven and hell. Walters interviewed a Muslim suicide bomber who stated bluntly, "Of course you Christians and Jews will go to and burn in hell." And then I watched in dismay as an American evangelical preacher said exactly the same thing about non-Christians. Is it any wonder that people go around murdering others in the name of religion or of God? The recent resurgence of the Taliban—a ruthless band of religious fanatics and murderers who think nothing of cutting off the heads of "infidels" and splashing acid in the faces of young schoolgirls who dare to seek an education—has only added to our sense of concern and fear. It seems that the predictions of Samuel Huntington about a clash of Muslim and Christian civilizations have come true. The eminent Muslim political scientist, Professor Fouad Ajami, of Johns Hopkins University, who had criticized Huntington's thesis several years ago, was compelled to concede that Huntington was right: we are witnessing the clash of those two civilizations.[32]

The events of these past years since that fateful September 11 have increased our suspicion of the Muslim world. As one eminent Muslim put it, "Not every Muslim is a terrorist but these days it seems that every terrorist is a Muslim." The European Muslim population in places such as France and Holland, England and Denmark are restive, rebellious, and even murderous. A Muslim fanatic slaughtered the Dutch filmmaker Theo Van Gogh in a public street because he dared to criticize Islam and the Prophet. Muslims in France have rioted and injured, murdered and burned Jews and other non-Muslims and their property and houses of worship in the name of Islam. Synagogues all over western Europe have been desecrated and torched by Muslim fanatics. Muslims in Denmark and elsewhere have rioted and injured scores because a cartoon in a Danish paper lampooned the Prophet. And to insult the Prophet Muhammad is a capital offence in the Islamic world. Europeans are deeply uneasy about the enormous growth of the Muslim population from about a million in 1945 to over 15 million in western Europe today. They tremble when they hear certain Muslim leaders talk of the reconquest of Europe from the Christians and the restoration of the Caliphate. And the more we read of the implementation of *Shaaria* law and the stoning of women accused of adultery or the whipping of women who refuse to marry an unworthy suitor, the more nervous we all become. I cannot fathom how the archbishop of Canterbury suggested that the British government recognize the legitimacy of *Shaaria* law for British Muslims just as the government recognizes the Jews' Bet Din (ecclesiastical court). What kind of comparison is that? The Bet Din enjoys no legal standing in the civil law; it confines its jurisdiction to Jewish ritual matters and the issuance of a *get* (religious divorce). And to the best of my knowledge, no Bet Din stones adulterers or flogs young women who refuse to marry a prospective husband.

As all of this unfolds, the image of Muslims deteriorates in the mind of the Western world. Things have gotten so bad that people look askance at Muslim women who cover their heads and the suspicion of anything related to Islam grows and becomes more prevalent. In the face of all of the acts of terror and suicide-homicide, most eminent Islamic scholars, imams, and kadis remain silent: they surely have failed to issue a *fatwa*

---

32. Samuel P. Huntington, *The Clash of Civilizations and the Remaking of World Order* (New York: Touchstone, 1997); Fouad Ajami, "The Clash," *The New York Times Book Review*, January 6, 2008, 10.

(decree) condemning suicide bombings when the victims are Israelis or Jews, although they had no problem issuing *fatwas* and death warrants against Salman Rushdie and Ayan Hirsi Ali for their "heretical" writings.

It seems that the doctrine that my faith is the only true faith and all others are false is still prevalent. The ancient teaching, *extra ecclesiam nulla salus*—no salvation outside the true church—is very much alive and with us these days. Consequently, it is legitimate to employ any and all means to lead sinners to the "light and truth." The latest Pew survey of American religious attitudes (December 2008) indicated that 53 percent of Americans believe that other religions can gain eternal life (salvation)—a decline of 11 percent since 2002. White Evangelical Protestants are the most exclusionist of all groups: 64 percent cite *their* faith as the only key to salvation. Now if this is the reality in America, we can just imagine how things fare in Asian or African or Middle Eastern lands. If we fail to reject this malignant doctrine, we'll be waging religious wars for all eternity. I know that all religions extol the virtue of *humility* as one of the cardinal principles of ethical behavior. How can one square that notion with the idea that "my way is the only right way"; that those who do not accept my faith are doomed? Such hubris and overweening pride lead eventually to the slaughter of those of different faiths, as we have learned from the tragic history of humanity. Huntington writes of "the bloody borders of Islam"; but there have been and still are plenty of "bloody borders of Christendom," as we all know only too well. And all of this is the inevitable result of that hubris that insists so resolutely, "My way is the only way!"

Consequently, let me put the question to my readers very clearly and simply: Do you believe that God drew up a covenant only with Catholics or Protestants or evangelicals or Muslims or Jews? Do you really believe that an omnipotent Deity cannot draw up more than one covenant? He drew up covenants with Noah and Abraham and Israel at Sinai and Joshua at Gilgal; is He incapable of drawing up additional covenants as He purposes? And is God incapable of more than one love? Is not God, the all-loving, compassionate, merciful One, able to love more than just one people or tribe or religion? We might recall that, "there are many rooms in my Father's house" (John 14:2). There are over one billion Muslims in the world; over one billion Catholics; over a half billion Protestants and Eastern Orthodox; 14 million Jews; untold numbers of Hindus and Buddhists. Are they all damned because one group of believers has gotten it in their heads that they alone are the elect of the Deity; that they alone are saved and all others are damned? Such foolish arrogance defies all logic, in my opinion.

If we are ever to have world peace, we need peace between religions. If we are ever to witness an end to religious strife, we must agree with Dr. Abraham Joshua Heschel that "religious pluralism is the will of God."[33] If we are ever to end bloodshed between faith groups, we have to engage in peaceful dialogue, in the spirit of Isaiah (1:18), "Come now, let us reason together." Nations that don't talk shoot, and it is the same phenomenon in interreligious relations. To put it differently, when people do not speak to one another, they do unspeakable things to one another. It is vital that we engage in interreligious dialogue, remembering always that *dialogue means consultation not confrontation, conversation not conversion.* If we are ever to witness messianic fulfillment on earth, we must tear down walls of hatred and suspicion and build in their places bridges of understanding and respect.

I leave my readers with three brief thoughts for reflection:

> Beware the person who says, "Brother, sister, I want to save your soul." He's apt to take your body in the process.

> A Hasidic master once taught, "A person should worry about his own soul—and his neighbor's stomach."

> And finally, a lovely quatrain by the American poet Edwin Markham:

> He drew a circle to shut me out:
> Heretic! Rebel! A thing to flout!
> But love and I had the wit to win:
> we drew a circle that took him in![34]

---

33. Abraham Joshua Heschel, *Moral Grandeur and Spiritual Audacity: Essays*, ed. Susannah Heschel (New York: Farrar, Straus and Giroux, 1996) 272.

34. Anthologized in *Best Loved Poems to Read Again and Again*, compiled by Mary Sanford Laurence (New York: Galahad, 1979) 42.

three

Life and Afterlife

Judaism's Contribution to the Jewish–Christian–Muslim Trialogue

DAVID PATTERSON

"I am the Way, the Truth, and the Life; no man comes unto the Father except through me." (The Gospel according to St. John 14:6)

"As for those who do not believe in my teaching, they are the inmates of the Fire, and in it they shall abide." (Quran, The Cow 2:39)

"The stranger [non-Jew] who dwells among you shall be as one of your own, and you shall love him as yourself. For you were strangers in the land of Egypt: I am the Lord." (Leviticus 19:34)

Most religious traditions have their metaphors for what the afterlife is like, and most metaphors of the afterlife are rooted in how we understand this life. Just as our conception of life is tied to our conception of afterlife, so is our conception of the afterlife tied to our conception of life—and how it ought to be lived. Indeed, the afterlife is the source of that *ought*. Understood as the eternal, the afterlife is not later but always: it lays claim to us *prior* to time and summons us *from the midst of* time. At once *ever after* and *always already*, the afterlife is, was, and ever shall be.

For this reason our understanding of life is rooted in our understanding of the afterlife. Life is rooted in time, and time is made of change, which in turn defines the *yet-to-be*. As the defining feature of time, the *yet-to-be*—the horizon that imparts meaning and direction to our every movement—unfolds not only as future but as future perfect, not only from what has been before but from what will have been—after. And the afterlife is *forever* after, *eternally* after, the dimension of the eternal itself, as it devolves on time. Without this dimension of the eternal we merely kill time and thus have no time. Thus we race like Alice and the Red Queen, always in a rush, only to remain where we are, until we tumble into oblivion. As the dimension of the eternal, however, the afterlife returns us to life. For it returns us to the task and the testimony that we have *yet* to engage. The afterlife announces the one responsibility *more* that we have *yet* to meet, one summons *more* that we have *yet* to answer. Life is made of the *yet*; the afterlife is made of the *more*. In the *yet* we have our responsibility for the other human being; in the *more* we have the commandment from the Holy One concerning that responsibility.

Our understanding of the afterlife, therefore, shapes our relation not only to the Holy One but also to the human one. To have time is to have time *for another*, both as God and as person, in an abrogation of the self. And to have time for another in this life is to have space for another in the afterlife, both as God and as person, in an abrogation of self. If our religious tradition allows no room in the afterlife for one who is not part of our tradition, then we allow no room for her in this life, both as God and as person. Such an exclusionary stance characterizes traditions that insist on the adherence to a creed as the key to the kingdom, for the sake of the self. If the exclusion of another from the afterlife also excludes him from this life—*both as God and as person*—then an afterlife purchased with faith or belief alone, and not with deeds of loving kindness, is an afterlife empty of God and person. It is made only of the gratification of the self, which is the emptiness of the self in which, like Midas, we finally have what we always wanted. But in the confusion of being and having—when having amounts to self-gratification—there is no hell more hellish than having what we always wanted.

I have suggested that a creed-based religion that allows no place for the nonbeliever in the World to Come also excludes him or her from this world. From such a religious stance, then, there can be no dialogue with nonbelievers. At best, a tradition that sees the creed alone as the ticket to the World to Come can only seek converts, and seeking converts is never a dialogical process. For dialogue requires the presumption not only of good intentions but of an intention for the sake of the Good on the part of the other. It requires the assumption that I may learn something from another that is essential both to life and to the afterlife, without the stipulation that I abandon the foundations of my tradition in order to have a place in the afterlife. It requires, moreover, the assumption that there is wisdom in other person's tradition. It requires, then, situating the other person in a position of height, in a position of righteousness, that I myself have not yet attained. It requires, in short, room for the nonbeliever in the afterlife.

Because Jewish teaching does not insist that a person embrace a belief in Judaism in order to have a place in the World to Come, it allows room for the nonbeliever in this world as well. Basing its notion of righteousness much more on deeds than on belief, Judaism is in a better position to dialogue with "the stranger" than traditions that insist on belief as a necessary condition for salvation. In the pages that follow we shall consider (1) Jewish teachings with regard to the stranger (*ger*) or non-Jew, (2) Jewish teachings on what becomes of the soul in the afterlife, and (3) the implications for a Jewish-Christian-Muslim trialogue.

Jewish Teachings with Regard to the Stranger

Before going further, it must be acknowledged that the Talmud contains teachings on non-Jews such as the following: "A Jew must not associate with the Gentiles because they are shedders of blood" (*Avodah Zarah* 22a). The context of such teachings, however, must be kept in mind: the Gentiles referred to here are the Romans, who were notorious shedders of blood. At various times in Jewish history, non-Jews have been either betrayers or murderers of Jews, so that one might understand why the Jews might develop a certain suspicion of non-Jews. Wherever the stranger has not desired the death of the Jews, however, Jewish teachings from the Torah, as well as from talmudic and midrashic sources, have treated him or her as a child of God; generally speaking, this is where the term *ger* applies.

So what does Judaism teach with regard to the *ger*? The teaching from the Torah is as familiar as it is fundamental: "You shall not wrong a stranger, nor shall you oppress him; for you were strangers in Egypt" (Exod 22:20). Indeed, there is nothing strange about the stranger: a child of the Holy One, he is our *brother*, not "the other," if *other* is taken to mean alien or unfamiliar. And so it is written: "You know the soul of a stranger, for you were strangers in Egypt" (Exod 23:9). The phrase "you know the soul of the stranger" is *yedaatem et-nefesh hager*. Recalling that the word for "know," *daat*, also means to "be joined together with," we realize that, as an emanation from the Holy One, each soul, Jewish and non-Jewish, is joined with the other both *essentially* and *physically*. All souls are *benei Adam*, children of Adam, who emanate from the Source, like beams of light emanating from a star, so that, through the Source each is connected to the other. In that connection (*tzavta*)—and not in any ethnic, cultural, or sectarian circumstance—lies the commandment (*mitzvah*) not to wrong the stranger.

Hence "the stranger who dwells among you shall be as one of your own, and you shall love him as yourself. For you were strangers in the land of Egypt: I am the Lord" (Lev 19:34). That is, you shall love him *k'mokha*, "as yourself," an echo of the commandment to love your neighbor, your fellow Jew, "as yourself," *k'mokha* (Lev 19:18). What does it mean? A better rendering of *k'mokha*, "as yourself," is, "that is what you are like." In other words, "you shall love the stranger, because your love for the stranger *is* your self," is your very soul: that loving is the *who* that you are in the depths of your being. And to be who you are is to have a place in the World to Come, as the Chasidic master Zusia of Onipol reminds us: "When I shall face the celestial tribunal, I shall not be asked why I was not Abraham, Jacob or Moses. I shall be asked why I was not Zusia."[1] To be Zusia—to be who I am—means treating the stranger with the loving kindness that only I, and not another, can offer. It means answering to my name when I am called by name: "Here I am for you."

Chasidism teaches that the commandment to love the other human being, both as neighbor and as stranger, is the foundation of all of Torah (see, for example, *Toledot Yaakov Yosef, Korach* 2). Oriented toward Torah, we are oriented toward the other human being. And, oriented toward the other human being, we are oriented toward Torah, that is, toward God Himself, as the Koretzer Rebbe taught: "God and Torah are one."[2] So we see why the commandment to love the other person is followed by the phrase "I am the Lord": it means that we can have no connection to God without this fundamental connection with the *ger*. Because the *ger* is not an alien other but one to whom the Jew is connected in the depths of his or her soul, we also have this commandment: "You shall not pervert the justice due to a stranger or to the fatherless, nor take a widow's clothing as a pledge. But you shall remember that you were a slave in Egypt, and the Lord your God redeemed you" (Deut 24:17–18). Here we have a revelation

---

1. See Elie Wiesel, *Souls on Fire: Portraits and Legends of Hasidic Masters*, trans. Marion Wiesel (New York: Summit, 1982) 120.

2. Louis I. Newman, trans. and comp., *The Hasidic Anthology: Tales and Teachings of the Hasidim* (New York: Schocken, 1963) 147.

of the *absolute* responsibility each of us has for those who have nowhere to turn, as exemplified by the widow, the orphan, and the stranger; the matter of whether they are believers or nonbelievers is irrelevant to the responsibility. These commandments, moreover, are revealed both in the singular and in the plural: they apply to you both as a community and as an individual.

While Judaism understands the Jews to be a "people apart" (see Lev 20:24), their distinction among the nations lies in their singled-out mission to transmit certain teachings concerning, among other things, the treatment of the stranger. Indeed, if we want to understand how a community views the human being, we should look not to how it treats its kin but to how it treats the stranger. In Judaism, a human being, unlike an animal, is above all a speaking being—that is what it means to be created in the image and likeness of the Holy One.[3] Therefore the most basic bond between one human being and another lies in the word. For this reason the Mishnah teaches that the prohibition against wronging someone in buying and selling also applies to wronging someone, including the stranger, *with words* (*Bava Metzia* 4:4). And chief among the words that a Jew must utter to another human being, both believer and nonbeliever, is the word *you*, as in, "here I am for you." Hence the teaching from the Zohar: "In the beginning G-d created the 'you' [*Bereshit bara Elokim at* (rather than the usual *et*)]" (Gen 1:1). Or: "In the beginning G-d created the letters from *alef* to *tav*, the stuff of the word, which is *at*: You" (*Zohar* I, 15b). In the beginning G-d created the avenue through which we may enter into a relation to Him. For "in every You," as Martin Buber has said, "we address the eternal You."[4] The trace of the divine in my fellow human being is the You in my fellow human being.

Further, the Talmud teaches, "Do not taunt the *ger* with the same blemish you have" (*Bava Metzia* 59b). Simply stated, with regard to the treatment of others, we have this dictum: do not judge. Let God be the judge of who is righteous and who is not, of who believes and who does not, of who acts and who does not, of who has a place in the World to Come and who does not. Again, inasmuch as we determine that our fellow human being has no place with God, we can have no relation with our fellow human being. Contrary to those traditions that declare theirs is the only path to God, thus dividing humanity into believers and nonbelievers,

---

3. See, for example, Maimonides's *Moreh Nevuchim* 1:51.

4. Martin Buber, *I and Thou*, trans. Walter Kaufmann (New York: Scribner, 1970) 57. See also Emmanuel Lévinas, *Outside the Subject*, trans. Michael B. Smith, Meridian: Crossing Aesthetics (Stanford: Stanford University Press, 1994) 34.

the Talmud teaches that the non-Jew has a place in the World to Come; indeed, the non-Jew has such a place even more readily than the Jew, since the Jew has a much greater responsibility to fulfill (see *Sanhedrin* 105a). The stranger has a place in the World to Come because he or she has an *indispensable* place in this world: since God's purpose in creation is to create a dwelling place for Himself, it is to create a dwelling place for one another, Jew and non-Jew alike. And every soul sent into this world has an *indispensable* role in accomplishing the divine purpose.

And so the gates to God's kingdom "are at all times open" to the stranger, as it is written in the Midrash (*Shemot Rabbah* 19:4). "Beloved are the strangers," says the Midrash, "or Scripture in every instance compares them to Israel" (*Bemidbar Rabbah* 8:2). Beloved by whom? Beloved by God, as taught in another Midrash: "'I have loved you' (Malachi 1:2) refers to the stranger" (*Bemidbar Rabbah* 8:2). According to Jewish teaching, each time a Jew encounters a stranger, he or she encounters one of God's beloved, one of God's children, a concept that falls outside the consciousness of any tradition that does not view God as a Father. Because the Jews cry out to God, "Father!" they can cry out to the stranger, "Brother!" Here we recall yet another teaching from the Midrash: "If you will estrange those who are distant [the strangers], you will ultimately estrange those who are near [the Jews]" (*Bamidbar Rabbah* 8:4). Which means: recognition of our essential connection to the most distant of human beings (nonbelievers) rests upon our realization of a connection to those who are nearest (believers). And each connection is connected to the other, both here and hereafter.

Because Judaism allows room to count adherents of other traditions among the righteous, we have in Jewish teaching the ancient concept of the *chasidei umot haolam*, or the Righteous among the Nations. In Abraham's story this concept is illustrated in his encounter with the King of Salem, Melchitzedek, the non-Hebrew who went out to offer Abraham bread and wine on his way home from saving Lot, who had been kidnapped during a battle among the kings of the region (see Gen 14:18). The lesson? It is this: the stranger, the non-Jew, may well be among the righteous whom God has sent into the world to elevate creation. Thus, in his first conversation with God after sealing the Covenant, Abraham argues for the sake of the righteous—not for the sake of the Hebrews—in Sodom and Gomorrah (Gen 18:20–32). Biblical figures regarded as the Righteous among the Nations include Batya, the daughter of Pharaoh who rescued Moses (Exodus 2); Hiram, King of Tyre, who sent help to Solomon (1 Kings 5); and Evedmelech, who rescued Jeremiah from the cistern (Jeremiah 38). So highly regarded are these Righteous Gentiles, the Midrash counts them among the nine people who, like Enoch and Elijah, entered the afterlife without having to endure the throes of death.[5] But what does Judaism teach about the afterlife?

What Becomes of the Soul in the Afterlife?

While Judaism and the God of the "Old Testament" have been labeled as "judgmental" and "vengeful," it was not Judaism but other traditions that came up with the notion of "the fire" or eternal damnation. Because its understanding of righteousness is based more on our actions in this world than on a belief in another world, few Jewish texts among the mainstream biblical and talmudic writings address the matter of what becomes of the soul in the afterlife. Even in the mystical tradition, where such matters are discussed, the teachings are scattered, and at times confusing. But a few general points can be made.

According to Kabbalah, there are four stages in the life of the soul after it passes through the gates of death. These stages are associated with four worlds, which in turn parallel the four lower levels of the soul.[6] Associated with *nefesh* or the physical aspect of the soul, the first stage in the life of the soul after death is called the *Olam Hadimyon*, the "World of Imagination" or "World of Illusion." It corresponds to the *Olam Asiyah* or the "World of Action," which is the physical realm of matter and energy. As the soul goes through its departure from this realm, it is at first overwhelmed with memories and images of its physical life. It lingers in this world, and it may linger for a long while or a short while, for any number of reasons.

For example, a soul might not at first realize that it has shed the body. It may be troubled about tasks left undone or worried about loved ones left behind. It may visit loved ones either to comfort them or to seek comfort from them. This is one reason why in Judaism we sit for a period of mourning called *shiva*: for seven days we comfort the departed soul and thus assist it along its ascent into the upper realms. It may happen too that a soul has become too attached to the illusory pleasures or pains of this

---

5. See Moshe Weissman, ed., The Midrash Says (Brooklyn: Bnay Yakov, 1980) 1:73. The other four are Abraham's servant Eliezer, Asher's daughter Serach, Yehuda Hanasi's son Yaavetz, and the Messiah; other sources say there are only seven.

6. See Adin Steinsaltz, *Simple Words: Thinking about What Really Matters in Life*, ed. Elana Schachter and Ditsa Shabtai (New York: Simon & Schuster, 1999) 114–21.

world and that those illusions hold it here. Hence the idea of the *Olam Hadimyon*, the World of Illusion: just as the nefesh can easily become trapped in a confusion of what is real and unreal, so can the soul become trapped in this stage of its afterlife. The Zohar, in fact, suggests that the *nefesh* remains attached to the *Olam Hadimyon* for as long as the body is in the grave (see *Zohar* II, 141b). Hence the custom of visiting the *kever*, the "grave," of a holy person.

In the Midrash it is said that "the soul does not go out of the body until it beholds the *Shekhinah* [the Divine Presence]" (*Pirke de Rabbi Eliezer* 34). This vision may come either at the instant of death or long after the body has been in the grave. The vision of the Shekhinah is a vision of the living truth of the living Torah, a vision of what is meaningful and dear. As the soul moves beyond the *Olam Hadimyon*, it undergoes a replay of its life, now measuring itself not according to the ways of the world but according to the truth and the will of God. Here we come to a deeply emotional realization of what is truly dear in life—and of how we have betrayed the other, both as God and as human. With our emotions racing from one extreme to another, this stage in the soul's ascent beyond death is the *Kaf Hakela*, which literally means the "Cup of the Slingshot."[7] It corresponds to the *Olam Yetzirah*, the "World of Formation," a realm where the soul begins to assume its true form, both in its descent and in its ascent. Associated with the level of soul called *ruach* or "spirit," the *kaf hakallah* presents us with a view of our life in the four-dimensional material realm from outside that realm. Thus seeing "the whole picture" and attaining a clear vision of the truth of Torah, the soul experiences an intense longing and, in most cases, a profound regret for what might have been—what should have been—but was not.

Coming to this realization brings into play the level of soul called *neshamah*, which is the level of intellect and insight. Here, as the soul ascends further, it enters into a process of purification or of healing the wounds it has inflicted upon itself through its neglect of the commandments; undergoing this purification or healing opens up an even deeper understanding of its own essence as an emanation of the Holy One. Although the soul knows that this cleansing is excruciating, it also knows that it is necessary,

---

7. This is a biblical phrase from the first book of Samuel, where Abigail says to David, "The Lord thy God shall sling out the souls of your enemies as from the cup of a slingshot" (1 Samuel 25:29). Invoking this verse, the Talmud says that the souls of the righteous are gathered beneath the Throne of Glory, while two angels sling the souls of the wicked from one end of the universe to the other (see *Shabbat* 152b), prior to their entering Gehinnom.

as when a person who has been badly burned knows that his wounds must be cleansed if he is to be healed. Thus the pain associated with this third stage in the afterlife: it is *Gehinnom*, which corresponds to the *Olam Beriah* or the "World of Creation," where the soul undergoes a kind of re-creation or a rebirth, with all the pangs of birth. Often mistranslated as "hell," Gehinnom comes from God who, like a Father, loves every soul as His child and wants every soul near Him. If Gehinnom is a state of total darkness, as it is written in the Midrash (*Shemot Rabbah* 14:2), it is also a realm in which the light of its divine spark is restored, so that the soul may enter the Presence of the Holy One.

In Judaism, then, the soul is subject to purification, but not to eternal damnation (see Tosefta *Berakhot* 6:7). As a manifestation not of divine wrath but of divine love, Gehinnom is not "down there"; rather, it is part of the upper realms, "above the firmament," as the Talmud states it (*Tamid* 32b). It is a depth from which we cry out, deep unto deep, to attain the ultimate height. Because the purpose of Gehinnom is to add to our understanding at the level of neshamah, Rabbi Adin Steinsaltz describes it as something like "deep therapy."[8] The greater the attachment of the soul's thinking and understanding to the illusion of the ego, the greater the pain of attaining the new, purifying understanding that comes in Gehinnom. How long does this agonizing process go on? According to the Talmud, it depends on the person's life (*Shabbat* 33b). Symbolically, it takes no more than a year.

Once it has been purified in Gehinnom, the soul enters *Gan Eden* or the "Garden of Eden," the realm associated with the level of soul called *chayah*, which is the soul's source of life. Hence the association of this stage of the afterlife with the *Olam Atzilut*, the "World of Emanation," the realm from which the soul and the Torah of which it is made emanate into creation. As in the case of the other dimensions of the afterlife, the metaphors for imagining what *Gan Eden* is like are elusive at best. The Talmud says that the Sabbath is one-sixtieth of this paradise (*Berakhot* 57b). Indeed, there may be moments of reflection, love, prayer, or joy, when we have a faint intimation of this immortality. Once in *Gan Eden*, the soul may approach an ever-increasing intimacy with the Holy One, as the fifth level of the soul, *yechidah* or "oneness," is increasingly intensified. This ascent, and not the torment of hell, is what is eternal in kabbalistic teaching.

In Judaism these metaphors for what becomes of the soul in the afterlife apply to all souls. According to the Talmud, the nature of the soul's

---

8. Steinsaltz, *Simple Words*, 118.

ascent through the upper realms in the afterlife is determined by how we are able to answer four questions pertaining to this life: Were you honest in your business dealings? Did you make time for Torah study? Did you strive to have children? And did you await the coming of the Messiah? (*Shabbat* 31a). Every soul, in other words, must account for (1) its day-to-day, ethical treatment of other people, whether they are believers or nonbelievers, (2) its effort to attain a deeper, spiritual understanding of the Creator, (3) its affirmation of life, which is most profoundly expressed by bringing life into the world, and (4) its waiting as a witness, which is a *working* as witness, for the time when the divine teaching will be inscribed in every heart, that is, when each human being treats the other with loving kindness. God does not ask us about our belief in this creed or that. Nor does He ask about our effort to make everyone follow the same religion we follow. In a word, He asks about our love for human life.

Implications for a Jewish–Christian–Muslim Trialogue

While Jews, Christians, and Muslims may not agree on theological matters, surely we can agree on the importance of living ethically, affirming the dearness of life, and working for a time of peace on earth—all for the sake of attaining a greater nearness to God and to our fellow human beings. If our understanding of the fate of the soul in the afterlife rests upon this view of life, then the doors to dialogue will be open. If, however, we insist upon the theological truth over the existential demand—if we insist upon a division of humanity into believers and nonbelievers—then genuine dialogue will be impossible. History has proven nothing if it has not proven this: whenever a tradition insists upon its own theological truth to the absolute exclusion of others, it quickly finds a theological justification—even a theological imperative—for murder. One thing that a Jewish-Christian-Muslim trialogue must seek to restore, then, is the absolute, divine prohibition against murder. In the end, that is what the trialogue is about. It is not a question of whether my tradition keeps me from being murdered; no, it is a question of whether my tradition keeps me from becoming a murderer.

All three traditions share the teaching concerning the Ten Utterances of Revelation at Mount Sinai. According to Jewish teaching, God gives Moses two tablets, and not one, in order to articulate two realms of relation: the first tablet pertains to the relation *ben adam leMakom* and the second to the relation *ben adam lechevero*, "between human and God" and "between human and human" respectively.[9] And yet *there is only one relation*. In order to drive home the definitive connection between the two tablets, we have the teaching that says the commandments should be read not just top to bottom but also right to left (see, for example, *Zohar* I, 90a). Thus, the Sixth Utterance parallels the First: "Thou shalt not murder" is an expression of "I am God," so that he who murders denies God. For a religiously observant Jew, Christian, or Muslim, we must affirm God in everything we do. If the ultimate aim of a trialogue is to affirm God, we do that most fundamentally by refusing any teaching that would sanction murder.

Here too we have a teaching from the Jewish tradition that may be of some help. It concerns *Kiddush Hashem*, the "Sanctification of the Holy Name." According to this talmudic teaching, we may violate any of the 613 commandments in order to save our own lives, except three: murder, idolatry, and adultery (see *Pesachim* 25a–25b; *Sanhedrin* 74a; *Ketuvot* 19a). We must allow ourselves to be murdered rather than commit murder, for committing murder is the most radical form of denying God. In that way we offer all that we are, our very lives, to affirm the holiness of the Holy One in a *Kiddush Hashem*. Wherever the Holy One is used as an excuse to murder—wherever we understand martyrdom, for example, in terms of killing other people—we commit a desecration of the Name. Any genuine Jewish-Christian-Muslim trialogue must come to terms with this point and account for the occasions when the adherents of these traditions have viewed piety in terms of killing other people, rather than in terms of dying in a refusal to kill others. Any "piety" that is expressed in murder—even if we murder ourselves in the process of murdering the "nonbelievers"—is a thinly disguised idolatry, in which people are slaughtered on the altar of power, possessions, and other false gods.

Assuming such a stance in Jewish-Christian-Muslim trialogue is much more a matter of pursuing justice than of forgiveness or reconciliation. To be sure, the pursuit of justice, Jewishly understood at least, is essential to affirming the divine prohibition against murder. Just as we are commanded to refrain from murder, so are we commanded to pursue justice or *tzedek* (Deut 16:20), a word that also means "righteousness." What sort of righteousness? Not the sort that amounts to nothing more than self-serving piety. Rather, it is the sort that is at the root of *tzedakah*,

---

9. See, for example, Abraham ibn Ezra, *The Secret of the Torah*, trans. H. Norman Strickman (Northvale, NJ: Aronson, 1995) 64–65.

or a giving to the other human being without expectation of reciprocation, without conditions or ulterior motives. It begins with each participant in the trialogue saying to the other what we are summoned to say to God: "*Hineni!*—Here I am for you!" And to say it to the human other is to say it to the divine Other. Viewed within the contexts of the religious traditions, a Jewish-Christian-Muslim trialogue has a fourth participant: the Holy One Himself, who prohibits murder and commands us to seek justice. And He does so by putting to us the questions He put to the first murderer: "Where is your brother?" (Gen 4:9) and "What have you done?" (Gen 4:10). Not, what is your doctrine? or, what do you believe?

The scriptural basis for the accent on the prohibition against murder, the pursuit of justice, and answering for our fellow human being brings us to another implication, one regarding our Scriptures. There are, after all, Scriptures in all three traditions that may seem harsh. In the Torah, for example, there are many transgressions for which the penalty is death, ranging from cursing one's parents (Exod 21:17) to desecrating the Sabbath (Exod 31:14). Equally aware that the Torah commands us to choose life (Deut 30:19), however, the sages of the Talmud set so many conditions for invoking a death penalty that it is virtually impossible to do so (see *Sanhedrin* 40a–43a). Indeed, it is written in the Mishnah: "In the measure with which a man measures, it is meted out to him" (Mishnah *Sotah* 1:7). In others words, the sword hangs over the judge who pronounces sentence. What the talmudic move teaches us is this: choosing life does not mean choosing life for oneself but choosing life for the other person. As we have seen, my life and well-being lie in the life and well-being of the other person. Here too Jewish tradition may have something to offer the trialogue that could benefit the other two partners.

As far as I understand it, neither Christianity nor Islam has anything comparable to the Talmud. Islam has the Hadith, which is a collection of teachings regarding the words and deeds of Mohammad, but it is not exactly an "Oral Torah" that tends to mitigate the harsh teachings of the Scriptures. Indeed, some of the most hate-ridden teachings on the Jews and Christians come from the Hadith (for example, *Sahih Bukhari*, Book 8, No. 427; Book 23, No. 414; Book 23, No. 472). Like the Talmud, the Hadith all but has (or perhaps has) the authority of Scripture. It at least has the authority of the teachings of the Christian saints, among whom we find many hate-filled diatribes against the Jews. Based on Paul's teaching that the Jews are "children of the devil" (Rom 8:44), there are the examples of Justin Martyr,[10] Tertullian,[11] Origen,[12] Cyprian,[13] Gregory of Nyssa,[14] Ambrose,[15] John Chrysostom,[16] Jerome,[17] Thomas Aquinas,[18] and others. If the Protestants among our partners in trialogue should say, "Well, they were Catholics," I refer them to Martin Luther.[19] While the commentaries from the oral traditions and saintly writings of Islam and Christianity have considerable authority, they do not contain the scriptural commentary that would promote the affirmation of life and the embrace of compassion for the stranger in the way the Talmud does. Yes, the Talmud has some harsh teachings with regard to those who inform on the Jews, betray the Jews, and murder the Jews. But it has nothing comparable to the Hadith or the Christian saints with regard to those who choose not to follow Judaism; it does not teach that the "nonbelievers" are doomed to eternal damnation.

Here too the example from Judaism—the much older tradition from which Christianity and Islam emerged and to which both are already indebted—may have something to teach its offspring. Given the fundamental teaching that our love of God finds its expression in our love for the other human being—*any* other human being—Judaism has an oral tradition that embraces any non-Jew who is not out to kill us. A Jewish-Christian-Muslim trialogue has the unprecedented opportunity of establishing something akin to an extension of the oral tradition that may ultimately take on the authority of a new oral tradition. But here lies the challenge:

10. See Marvin R. Wilson, *Our Father Abraham: Jewish Roots of the Christian Faith* (Grand Rapids: Eerdmans, 1989) 93.

11. "Christian Jew Haters"; online: http://www.sullivan-county.com/identity/jew_haters.htm

12. Ibid.

13. See Cyprian, "Three Books of Testimonies against the Jews," quoted in Franklin H. Littell, *The Crucifixion of the Jews: The Failure of Christians to Understand the Jewish Experience*, ROSE 12 (Macon, GA: Mercer University Press, 1986) 27–28.

14. Quoted in Mark R. Cohen, *Under Crescent and Cross* (Princeton: Princeton University Press, 1995) 171.

15. "Christian Jew Haters."

16. See James Parkes, *The Conflict of the Church and Synagogue: A Study in the Origins of Antisemitism* (New York: Jewish Publication Society, 1934) 163–66. Chrysostom's first homily is reproduced in Parkes's volume.

17. See Robert S. Wistrich, *Antisemitism: The Longest Hatred* (New York: Pantheon, 1991) 19.

18. See Edward H. Flannery, *The Anguish of the Jews: Twenty-Three Centuries of Anti-Semitism* (New York: Paulist, 1965) 95.

19. See Martin Luther, *Von den Juden und ihren Lügen*, ed. Georg Buchwald, Luthers Flugschriften für unsere Zeit 3 (Dresden: Landesverein für Innere Mission, 1931).

we must glean from our Scriptures and from our sages precisely those teachings that would promote an embrace of the other, allowing above all a place for the other in the afterlife. And each of the three traditions must help the other in that process, beginning with how each understands the place of the non-believer in the afterlife. Otherwise there can be no trialogue worthy of the name.

Closing Remarks

In Judaism the realm of the afterlife is called *Olam Haba*. We have referred to it as it is commonly referred to in English, "the World to Come." This, however, is not a precise translation. The *Olam Haba* is literally "the World That Is Coming," here and now, a world already in our midst. That is why a teaching that excludes the "nonbeliever" from the *Olam Haba* also excludes him or her from this world as well. That is why, Jewishly speaking, any trialogue that has hidden between the lines such an exclusion is sheer wind. And if it is sheer wind, we shall inherit the wind.

Learning from the teachings of their parent religion, Christianity and Islam may—must—learn to include in their thinking about the *Olam Haba* a place for the "nonbeliever." This lesson they can learn from their very roots, from Judaism. They can do so first by allowing a Jewish reading of the Jewish Scriptures, rather than twisting those Scriptures into something that would suit their own creed. Next, the attempts at the trialogue can be written and recorded and disseminated, as illustrated by the example of this volume. Finally, we can support one another for taking this risk, especially as we meet with pressure from our co-religionists. While there are Jews who simply frown at Jews who attempt such a trialogue, I personally know of Christian scholars who risk their careers for taking the steps necessary to enter into a true dialogue with Jews. And I know of Muslims who risk their lives. Of the three of us, then, the Jews generally take the least risk. The Christians committed to trialogue are to be counted among the truly courageous, but the Muslims are among the most courageous of all.

While some of what I have said here may seem harsh, I end with an expression of gratitude and admiration for the Christians and Muslims who participate in this effort. Theirs, I think, is the much more daunting task. In their actions they attest to a teaching that includes the other, both as God and as person, both in this world and in the World That Is Coming.

four

Pride without Prejudice

Towards a Dialectical Education for Religious Identity

DEBORAH WEISSMAN

Since that fateful morning on September 11, 2001, religion and religions have been in the public eye, under intense scrutiny. For years, many social scientists had considered them a relic from some premodern past. But they seem to have bounced back—one could even say, "with a vengeance." Or, perhaps they never really faded away.[1] The appearance of decline may have been an optical illusion caused by focusing too much on the Western European experience. Both academically and in terms of popular culture, it is clear that religion is a major force in the contemporary world. Hardly a day goes by without some major news item involving religion somewhere in the world. Yet, much of the press that religions receive is far from complimentary.

Throughout the world, religions are involved in violent conflicts. Often these conflicts have political, national, ethnic, social, and economic aspects, as well. Still, the image of religion in the world today—and, especially in the Middle East—is often an image of extremism, xenophobia, and violence.

It is difficult to argue that this image has no truth to it. In the name of religion, atrocities have been committed. Religion has, in many cases,

---

1. See, for example, *The Economist*, Nov. 3–9, 2007, an eighteen-page report on faith and politics, "The New Wars of Religion."

fanned the flames of extremism. What is it about religion and religions that accounts for this unholy alliance between faith and extreme violence? First, many people of faith seem to have absolute faith that allows no questioning of authority and that makes no room for other truths. When we interpret present-day reality through ancient Scriptures, we may lose touch with those around us and their human needs. And when we expect reward for our actions in the world to come, it may impel us to be violent to others in the world that is.

But, beyond that, it may be more a question of the extremist, violent forms of our religions being given a great deal more exposure than the rest of us. After all, a bombing, an attack on worshipers, the language of incitement—these are more newsworthy than peaceful dialogue and coexistence. Harmony among groups doesn't sell newspapers.

Still, the question remains whether religious education that inculcates a particular identity and belief system does not by its very nature encourage a kind of triumphalism, which in its extreme forms may incite to violence against the Other. Most pointedly, the three great monotheistic religions have been accused of claiming to possess the ultimate truth and allowing less room for pluralism than the pagan or polytheistic cultures. Can we educate children and young people to be committed adherents to one faith, without denigrating another? In short, is it possible to educate for "pride without prejudice?"[2]

A Tough Balancing Act

There is sometimes a suggestion in liberal circles, either tacit or explicit, that one of the main problems in the world lies in the very process of "othering." It is in the very nature of our boundary setting, our division of the world into in-groups and out-groups, that we can find the root of all evil. If only we would see our various religious and ethnic identities as secondary and our common humanity as primary, then we could reduce the level of hatred and abuse in our troubled world. There is a basic mistrust of the phenomenon, often pejoratively known as tribalism. It is to that argument that we will now address ourselves.[3]

---

2. With obvious acknowledgements to Jane Austen, the immediate reference is to a booklet published in 1977 by the Israel Interfaith Association: Hildegard Mohr and Michael Krupp, eds., *Pride and Prejudice—An Inter-religious Approach* (Jerusalem: Israel Interfaith Association, 1977).

3. Some of what follows is an updated reworking of material I have previously published in two other frameworks: "Jewish Religious Education as Peace Education:

The argument does seem at first compelling. So many of the conflicts in the post-cold war global reality seem to be along either religious or ethnic lines, or perhaps even both. Furthermore, the seemingly intractable conflict in the Middle East, between the Israelis and the Palestinians, has on occasion been described as an updated version of tribal warfare. If only the two sides would relinquish their tribal identities and/or their tribal claims to the land, then perhaps peace could be achieved.

One of the great musicians and songwriters of the twentieth century, the late, lamented John Lennon, wrote in his song "Imagine," and here I paraphrase: what would happen if there were neither national borders nor any religion?[4] The kind of utopian vision represented in the song has much appeal, particularly to young idealists. It is, however, not only impractical but even dangerous educationally.

⁓

An important book on the subject of group identities is Harold R. Isaacs's *Idols of the Tribe: Group Identity and Political Change*. Isaacs quotes from Aleksandr Solzhenitsyn's undelivered Nobel Prize lecture in 1970: "Nationalities are the wealth of humanity, they are its crystallized personalities; even the smallest among them has its own special colors, hides within itself a particular facet of God's design."[5]

Indeed, for many, the cultural diversity of humankind is one of the main things that make our world interesting. The contemporary environmental movement has heightened our awareness of endangered species of flora and fauna. We are (justifiably) supposed to be concerned with the preservation of every kind of insect, for example, not to mention the whales and many other creatures. Some would argue that this sensitivity should extend as well to human cultures, languages and tribes on the verge of extinction.

From Crisis to Opportunity," *British Journal of Religious Education* 29/1 (January 2007) 63–76; and "What We Are and Who We Are: Educating for the Universal-Particular Dialectic in Jewish Life," in *Śafot ve-sifruyot ba-ḥinukh ha-Yehudi: Meḥḳarim li-khevodo shel Mikha'el Rozenak*, ed. Jonathan Cohen, Studies in Jewish Education 11 (Jerusalem: Magnes, 2006) 79ff.

4. I owe a debt of gratitude to my former student at the Kerem Institute in Jerusalem, Amiad Meltzer. In 2002, he called my attention to a pamphlet put out by the Shalem Institute, in which Lennon's lyrics are analyzed.

5. Harold Isaacs, *Idols of the Tribe: Group Identity and Political Change* (New York: Harper & Row, 1975) 183.

But the religions and identities of human groups or tribes are necessary for reasons that far outweigh interest and variety. Michael Walzer suggests that moral discourse that attempts to posit a common denominator devoid of particular cultural nuances and complexities is "thin"—it becomes, in fact, the lowest common denominator.[6] He contrasts this with "thickness," grounded in human particularity. To this, we can add that human beings grow and develop in particular cultures, nurtured by families and communities.[7] The cultures are the carriers of moral and ethical values, taught through texts, stories, parables, proverbs, examples, practices of the particular tribe into which the child was born. Without the primary ties to family and community, it is unlikely that we could produce moral human beings, socialized into the norms of human behavior. As Walzer suggests,

> Societies are necessarily particular because they have members and memories, members with memories not only of their own but also of their common life. Humanity, by contrast, has members but no memory, and so it has no history and no culture, no customary practices, no familiar life-ways, no festivals, no shared understanding of social goods. It is human to have such things, but there is no singular human way of having them.[8]

The discipline of anthropology is founded largely on the insight embodied in the last sentence of Walzer's statement.

Wipe out "tribal" identities and you wipe out the cultural anchoring of such imperatives. Without the stories different peoples have of their own suffering, what identification will they develop with the suffering of others? Without a sense of tribal honor, what motivation will they develop for decent behavior? Indeed, "the members of all the different societies, because they are human, can acknowledge each other's different ways, respond to each other's cries for help, learn from each other and march (sometimes) in each other's parades."[9]

Or, as Walzer has put it: "The crucial commonality of the human race is particularism."[10]

---

6. In Michael Walzer, *Thick and Thin: Moral Argument at Home and Abroad* (Notre Dame: University of Notre Dame Press, 1994).

7. Two Jewish thinkers who have especially developed these concepts are Rabbi Yitzhak (Irving) Greenberg in the United States and Professor Eliezer Schweid in Israel.

8. Walzer, *Thick and Thin*, 8.

9. Ibid.

10. Ibid., 83.

A universalized human being is, in a sense, a dehumanized one.

At the same time, an exclusively particularist approach is also potentially dangerous. We can perhaps paraphrase the famous dictum of Hillel: "If we are not for ourselves, then who will be for us? But if we are for ourselves alone, what are we?"[11]

It is not intended here that we ignore or even minimize the intense danger posed to world peace by many people who claim to be acting in the name of their religions and ethnic or national causes. But two salient points ought to be made: First, we must strive to emphasize within each of our cultures those elements that promote a more open and compassionate attitude to other human beings. The major faith traditions have resources from which they can draw to nurture such an approach.[12] In his book *Longitudes and Attitudes*,[13] journalist Tom Friedman, citing Middle East expert Stephen P. Cohen, suggests that the true clash in today's world is not "between civilizations" (as argued by Samuel Huntington) but within each civilization or religion—a clash between the forces of extremism and those of moderation, tolerance, or what might be called "religious humanism." Particularism ought not obscure the universal nature of God and God's creatures. Particularism is not synonymous with chauvinism. The task of ridding our own particular traditions of their elements of chauvinism or xenophobia is best done by the members of the groups themselves, but doing it within the presence of the Other can be especially challenging and meaningful.

Second, sometimes it is precisely when people feel that their own identity is under attack that they respond violently. Again, a quotation from Walzer: "When my parochialism is threatened, then I am wholly, radically parochial . . . and nothing else . . . Under conditions of security, I will acquire a more complex identity than the idea of tribalism suggests."[14]

The contemporary phenomenon of global terrorism is undoubtedly exacerbated by feelings of insecurity as described above. Our goal, then,

---

11. The actual quotation, from Mishnah *Avot* 1:14, is "If I am not for myself, who will be for me? And if I am for myself alone, what am I? And if not now, when?"

12. See, for example, the book by the chief rabbi of the British Commonwealth, Jonathan Sacks, *The Dignity of Difference: Avoiding the Clash of Civilizations* (London: Continuum, 2002).

13. Thomas Friedman, *Longitudes and Attitudes: Exploring the World after September 11* (New York: Farrar, Straus & Giroux, 2002).

14. Walzer, *Thick and Thin*, 82.

should not be the eradication of group identities but their empowerment through ensuring the safety and security of the different groups.

Thus, we are faced with the serious educational challenge of developing a model for religious education that is dialectical—that strengthens the particular identity and commitment of the group and its members and, at the same time, tries to inculcate within them a respect for the Other and the Other's faith, an openness to different cultures, an awareness that we are all human beings, of equal worth. How can this be done?

Since the author of the present chapter is a Jewish educator, the examples will be drawn from that tradition. It is hoped that this model will have implications for religious educators within other traditions, as well.

Probably the most important principle with which to begin is that one must search for resources within one's own particular tradition. A secular human rights discourse, for example, may in some situations be counterproductive. For Jews, the search should be based on biblical as well as rabbinic-talmudic and other traditions and should begin at the beginning, with the creation of Adam.

Our Common Humanity

The Hebrew Bible (known to Christians as the "Old Testament") begins with eleven chapters about the creation of the world and the origins of humankind, much before coming to the first Hebrew, Abraham. Before the covenant made with Abraham's descendants (Genesis 17), we read about the rainbow covenant made with the children of Noah (Genesis 8:21—9:17). The Jewish theological basis for universalism is the belief that all human beings were created in the image of God (Genesis 1:26–27). In the Mishnah we find the following very important passage:

> Therefore but a single person was created in the world, to teach that if anyone has caused a single soul to perish, Scripture imputes it to him as though he had caused a whole world to perish; and if anyone saves a single soul, Scripture imputes it to him as though he had saved a whole world. Again, but a single person was created for the sake of peace among humankind, that none should say to his fellow, "My father was greater than your father"; ... Again, but a single person was created to proclaim the greatness of the Holy One, blessed is He; for people stamp many coins with one seal and they are all like one another; but the King of Kings, the Holy One, blessed is He, has stamped every person with the seal of the first man, Adam, yet none of them is

like his fellow. Therefore every one must say, "For my sake was the world created." (Mishnah *Sanhedrin* 4:5)

Thus, the biblical story of the creation of the human being in the image of God is the basis for the ultimate worth, equality and uniqueness of all people.

Some readers may be familiar with a different formulation of this passage. In later (and more widely known) manuscripts, the words "from Israel" are added, as in "a single soul from Israel." Twentieth-century Jewish philosopher Leon Roth in an article titled "Moralization and Demoralization in Jewish Ethics"[15] points out that in terms of the context—namely, the creation of Adam—the extra words do seem to distort the simple meaning of the text. Roth refers to the process by which a more universal text became "particularized" as the "demoralization" of the text. He writes: "The addition of the word *me-Yisrael* produces a sudden, and ludicrous, deflation."

Anyone conversant with the strictures of traditional Judaism knows that in addition to the belief in our common humanity, Jewish law sets the Jewish people apart and demands of the Jews various behaviors not demanded of others, for example, the strict dietary laws. Yet even within this separation, we can find an intimation of unity, as in the following Rabbinic homily:

Twice in the Torah—once in Leviticus 11 and once in Deuteronomy 14—we find a list of nonkosher birds. Among those listed is the *chassida*, the stork. It would appear that the name of this bird is derived from the word *chessed*, "loving-kindness." Our great medieval biblical commentator Rashi, following the *Midrash*, asks, "Why is the bird called *chassida*? Because it performs acts of *chessed* by sharing its food with other storks."

It took hundreds of years for the next logical question to be addressed; namely, then why isn't it kosher? This question was asked in the nineteenth century by a Chassidic rebbe, the Gerer Rebbe, known as *Chiddushei HaRim*. The answer he gave: "Because it performs acts of *chessed* by sharing its food with other storks. Only with other storks."

In this short parable we have the strength and the weakness of communities; we have the dilemma of particularism and universalism. Strong particularistic communities do *chessed* towards members of their own group, but the true challenge is: how do they relate to outsiders, who may

---

15. *Modern Jewish Thought: Selected Issues, 1889–1966*, The Jewish People: History, Religion, and Literature (New York: Arno, 1973).

be members of other communities? (Or who may not be members of any particular community.)

On a number of occasions, Jewish spiritual teachers have attempted to reduce the many laws and commandments within the Jewish tradition to a basic set of core principles. Perhaps the two most famous of the attempts were that of Hillel,[16] and of Rabbi Akiva.[17] Hillel stated that the essence of Torah[18] is the principle, "What is hateful unto you, do not do unto your fellow."[19] (To be fair, he also added: "The rest is commentary; now go and study it.") Rabbi Akiva formulated a Golden Rule in a slightly different fashion: He said the major principle of Torah is, "Love your neighbor as yourself."[20] Arguing with him[21] was another sage, Ben Azzai, who said that an even greater principle than that is, "This is the book of the generations of Adam" (the Hebrew could also mean "man" or "human being").[22] The argument may revolve around whether it is preferable to base an ethical system on a subjective standard (i.e., "as you love yourself") or on the more objective foundation of our common human origins. Some commentators have suggested that in Rabbi Akiva's formulation there are really two commandments—to love your neighbor, but also to love yourself.

In another section of rabbinic literature[23] there appears a discussion in which a number of rabbis attempt to take the 613 commandments and reduce them to fewer, more basic ones. Several interesting texts from the Prophets are referenced this regard. For example, it is mentioned that the prophet Micah reduced the hundreds of commandments incumbent upon a Jew to three: "It has been told you, O man, what is good, and what the Lord does require of you: Only to do justice, and to love mercy, and to

---

16. First century, Land of Israel.

17. Second century, Land of Israel.

18. Although we mentioned earlier that in its narrow sense this refers to the first five books of the Bible, in its broad sense it can mean the entire corpus of Jewish religious literature.

19. Babylonian Talmud, *Shabbat* 31a. A similar formulation had appeared earlier in (for Jews) the noncanonical book of Tobit.

20. Leviticus 19:18.

21. The controversy is recorded in several places in rabbinic literature, including Jerusalem Talmud, *Nedarim* 30b and *Midrash Sifra* 7:4.

22. Genesis 5:1–2. The full text says, "This is the book of the generations of Adam, in the day that God created Adam; in the likeness of God made He him, male and female created He them, and blessed them, and called their name Adam, in the day when they were created."

23. Babylonian Talmud, *Makkoth* 24a.

walk humbly with your God."[24] Isaiah reduced these further to just two: "Thus says the Lord, 'Keep you justice, and do righteousness.'"[25] Finally, the prophet Habakkuk said simply, "The righteous shall live by his faith."[26]

It should be noted that all of the attempts to distill Jewish beliefs or commandments into their basic core, emphasize the ethical commandments, or what the Jewish tradition characterizes as interpersonal commandments (the others being commandments between people and God).

In a number of sources[27] Jews are commanded to "walk in the paths of the Lord." This is interpreted as *imitatio dei*, imitating the attributes and deeds of the Almighty. It has been understood as being compassionate and merciful, clothing the naked, visiting the sick, burying the dead, and comforting the mourners. The law, as codified by Maimonides and others, mandates such behavior toward non-Jews, as well, using the rabbinic phrase, *mipnei darkei shalom*. The phrase means "in the interests of peace." This is often interpreted as a social precaution, enjoining the Jewish community for its own good to be charitable toward the Gentiles, so that there will be no uncomfortable consequences of their overly parochial behavior, including, perhaps, violent reprisals.

Yet many commentators have suggested that the phrase can be interpreted more literally. The literal meaning is "because of the ways of Peace." Peace is one of the names of the Almighty, and thus Jews who are compassionate towards all human beings are indeed walking in the paths of God.[28]

The Problematic Texts

But not all the biblical and rabbinic texts present such a positive, humanistic approach; many are xenophobic. It may often seem as though many, if not most, traditionally Orthodox Jews are more influenced by the narrow, parochial texts than by the ones we have cited above.

Professor Moshe Greenberg, the great Bible scholar and teacher at the Hebrew University, in a number of seminal works, has pointed out the tremendous educational challenge we have today, particularly in

---

24. Micah 6:8.
25. Isaiah 56:1.
26. Habakkuk 2:4.
27. Most prominently in Babylonian Talmud, *Sotah* 14a.
28. For this insight I am indebted to Professor Moshe Halbertal of the Hebrew University in Jerusalem.

Israel, in dealing with these questions in our study of traditional Jewish culture. Greenberg is a member of an interfaith dialogue group in Jerusalem known as the Rainbow.[29] Several years ago the theme for the group's discussions was "Embarrassing Texts in our Respective Religious Traditions." Greenberg opened the year's discussions with a presentation on the embarrassing texts in the Jewish tradition that relate to non-Jews in a negative light. His views appear in a Hebrew book published in 1984, *Al HaMikra v'Al HaYahadut* [30] and an English article published in 1996, "A Problematic Heritage: The Attitude towards the Gentile in the Jewish Tradition—An Israel Perspective."[31]

In a later essay, Greenberg gives us a wonderful way of dealing with these problematic texts: "Even the choicest vine needs seasonal pruning to ensure more fruitful growth."[32]

One of the techniques of "pruning" would be to contextualize the problematic text within Jewish history. Jews, who were a persecuted minority in most periods and in most places, sometimes treated violently by the surrounding societies, developed defensive, insulating postures. They often engaged in polemics with the outside world, particularly within medieval Christendom. The victimhood of Jewish history, of course, reached its tragic climax in the Holocaust in Europe, from 1933 to 1945. If many Jews today are mistrustful of the outside world, it is not without cause.

But some important and far-reaching changes have taken place in the post-Holocaust world. The changes that seem most dramatic began in the Roman Catholic Church with Vatican II, but similar changes have been noted in other denominations as well. In recognizing the sincere transformation that has been undertaken by many Christians, we should undertake our own process of going through classical Jewish texts and teachings regarding the Other. Some of these teachings may be contextualized historically or reinterpreted; others should be seen as part of an ongoing internal debate, in which we take sides. In our own day, we must, I believe, take the side of rejecting racism and sexism,[33] two phenomena

---

29. I am also privileged to be a member of this group. Editor's note: Professor Greenberg passed away May 2010.

30. Edited by Avraham Shapira, *Am Oved*, Tel Aviv.

31. "A Problematic Heritage: The Attitude towards the Gentile in the Jewish Tradition—An Israel Perspective," *Conservative Judaism* 48/2 (Winter 1996) 23–35.

32. As quoted in Seymour Fox et al., eds. *Visions of Jewish Education* (Cambridge: Cambridge University Press, 2003) 145.

33. For the latter, see: Tamar Ross, *Expanding the Palace of Torah: Orthodoxy and Feminism*, Brandeis Series on Jewish Women (Hanover, NH: Brandeis University Press, 2004).

that take away from the dignity of human beings, created in the Divine Image.

As an amateur theologian, I would like to add one additional consideration. Racism and xenophobia are widespread—indeed, almost universal—phenomena in human societies. As a student of anthropology, I learned that in many tribes, the words for "human being" are the same as the name of the tribe. We did not need divine revelation to be narrow and chauvinistic. What we needed revelation for was the revolutionary insight that all human beings are created in the Divine Image. Thus, it would appear, at least to me, that the universalist hermeneutic is the more authentic. For those of us who see the Torah as having some transcendent source—whether divinely revealed or inspired—a humanistic message may ultimately be the more religiously authentic of the two approaches.

Can There Be Plural "Truths"?

It could be argued that religions that make claims to represent ultimate truths (a more apt phrase, I believe, than "absolute truths") leave no room for other faiths and *their* truths. However, this might be an overly glib or superficial presentation of the nature of religions in reality. Another approach may be grounded in classical Jewish sources:

A *Midrash*[34] relates that when God created Adam, the "angel" of truth argued against this move, saying that human life would be full of lies. God responded by throwing "truth" down to the ground. Some commentators have extended the metaphor by suggesting that on earth, truth has been shattered into millions of little pieces. Different people possess pieces of the truth.

The Jewish tradition of Oral Torah can be important here in a certain way: It helps to create a culture of discourse and debate, with room for alternate truths. Dr. Shlomo Fischer, who has been associated with the Van Leer Institute in Jerusalem, and Professor Suzanne Last Stone, of Yeshiva University in New York, have suggested that there are several "characteristics of Judaism that support pluralism and acceptance of diversity." [35] One of these is, in their words, "the tradition of intellectual pluralism within

---

34. *B'reishit Rabba* 8:5.

35. *Guidelines for Teachers: Tolerance and Principles of Religion* (Sarajevo: International Forum Bosnia, 2004) 85.

the normative *halakhic* community fostered by its skeptical approach to truth-claims."[36]

Another is "the internal structure of Judaism—its limitation to one nation—which has led to a positive valuation of the role of other collectivities in the divine plan."[37] I would simply amend that to read, not necessarily that it *has* led to a positive valuation, but that it *could*.

Let us focus for a moment on their first point. The Oral Torah is based on endless discussions that compel the participants to look at the objects of their inquiry from many possible perspectives. Questions are raised about most assumptions. Students are rewarded for asking difficult questions. In the event that a student asks an especially interesting question that was heretofore asked, for example, in a relatively obscure rabbinic or medieval source, he[38] will offer a blessing to God.

It is well known that the houses—in modern parlance, schools—of Hillel and Shammai were constantly arguing over points of Jewish law. The Talmud in *Eruvin* 13b records that finally, a Divine Voice came down from heaven and declared, "These, and also these, are the words of the Living God, and the Law is according to the house of Hillel."

That passage is interesting in three ways: first, it seems to support the notion of plural truths. Another rabbinic passage makes this point perhaps even more sharply: "These are the sages who sit in assemblies and study the Torah, some pronouncing unclean and others pronouncing clean, some prohibiting and others permitting, some declaring unfit and others declaring fit. But a person might say: How, then, shall I learn Torah? Therefore the text says, all of them 'are given from one shepherd.' One God gave them, one leader proclaimed them from the mouth of the Lord of all creation, Blessed be He."[39] One divine source—the source of Truth with a capital *T*—many truths on the human level.

Second, even when plural truths are recognized on a theoretical plane, a decision must be taken regarding lawful behavior in the real world. Otherwise, there would be no sense of community and society would degenerate into chaos.

---

36. Ibid.

37. Ibid.

38. Here I am using the male pronoun purposely to indicate that, regrettably, for most of history, women were not involved in this kind of Jewish discourse. The situation, fortunately, began to change in the last quarter of the twentieth century.

39. *Hagigah* 3a–b, as quoted in Barry Holtz, *Finding Our Way: Jewish Texts and the Lives We Lead Today* (New York: Schocken, 1990) 23.

Third, the passage seems to fly in the face of another equally well-known passage from another tractate, *Baba Metzia* 59b:

> Again R. Eliezer then said to the Sages, "If the *Halakhah* agrees with me, let it be proved from heaven." Sure enough, a divine voice cried out, "Why do you dispute with R. Eliezer, with whom the *Halakhah* always agrees?" R. Joshua stood up and protested: "The Torah is not in heaven!" (Deut. 30:12). We pay no attention to a divine voice because long ago at Mount Sinai You wrote in your Torah at Mount Sinai, "After the majority must one incline." (Ex. 23:2) R. Nathan met [the prophet] Elijah and asked him, "What did the Holy One do at that moment?" Elijah: "He laughed [with joy], saying, "My children have defeated Me, My children have defeated Me."

So, do we listen to Divine Voices or do we not? Perhaps we can say that in general, we do not. Rational discussions are held on the basis of texts, and the majority rules. But at one point in talmudic "sacred history," it became necessary for a Divine Voice to lend its sanction to the idea of plural truths.

Now, someone might claim that the plural truths being referred to in all of these talmudic passages are representative of a fairly narrow form of pluralism; they all come from "dead male" rabbis within the normative Jewish tradition. Could this still be a basis for a Jewish appreciation of the Other, who is truly other?

Medieval rabbis have made it reasonably clear that Islam is a "true," nonidolatrous, and monotheistic faith. Christianity is more controversial, because of the belief in the Trinity, the use of icons, and the like. But many authorities would see it too as a religion of truth. For example, the twelfth-century Tosafists, in their commentary on *Avodah Zarah* 2a, state, "we are certain that the Christians do not worship idols." Even more unequivocal was Menachem ben Solomon HaMeiri of Provence (1249–1316). He averred that both Christians and Muslims were "peoples disciplined by religion" and that the theological problem of *shittuf* (believing in one God, together with other divine manifestations) was not applicable to non-Jews, thus allowing for Trinitarian Christianity.[40] More controversial than that would be the status of the Eastern religions, although some authorities have concluded that these too can be seen as true faiths.[41] In any case,

---

40. See *Beit HaBechirah*, his commentary on the Talmud, particularly, *Baba Kamma* 113b and *Avodah Zarah* 20a.

41. For a comprehensive study of the questions involved, see: www.innerjew.com/Teshuvah.html

it might perhaps be argued that once you have a philosophical basis for the notion of plural truths, the parameters of those truths is a secondary question.

A twentieth-century Jewish philosopher and mystic Rabbi Abraham Isaac HaKohen Kook wrote, "Some err and think that world peace can be built only through total consensus ... But the truth is that real peace, on the contrary, can come to the world only through precisely the multiplicity of peace, and this is when all sides and opinions come to light, and are proven to each have their own place."[42]

We should bear in mind that Rabbi Kook died in 1935, before the Holocaust. Had he lived longer, he might have amended his position to exclude certain sides and opinions; I don't know. *I* believe that there *are* limits to pluralism, and I'm certainly not arguing for a nihilistic relativism. But I *am* arguing, using social scientific terminology, that what we need in society is not "the replication of uniformity," but "the organization of diversity."[43]

A Vision and a System

The Prophets gave us visions of a better world in the future, both on the macrolevel—"Nation shall not live up sword against nation"[44]—and on the microlevel—"But they shall sit everyone under his vine and under his figtree, and none shall make them afraid."[45] In this vision of redemption, "For let all the peoples walk each one in the name of its god,"[46] and the world will be full of righteousness, equity and harmony.[47] In Jewish thought, this vision is often called the Messianic era. It can be brought about by human action, abetted by divine intervention. The belief that it can come though human action is a bulwark against despair; the belief in the need for divine intervention, a shield against hubris.

But how can such a lofty vision be translated into a human program for living? Jewish culture, like Islam and some of the Eastern traditions—but unlike Western Christianity—emphasizes a legal system for the

---

42. Abraham Isaac Kook, *Olat HaRa'ayah*, 330.

43. The terms are taken from Anthony F. C. Wallace, *Culture and Personality* (New York: Random House, 1961) 26–27, 84–92.

44. Isaiah 2:4, Micah 4:3.

45. Micah 4:4.

46. Micah 4:5.

47. See, for example, Isaiah 11:1–9, 12:2–5, 35, 52, etc.

regulation of everyday life. That system, called *Halakha* (from the root "to walk") is like a *tao*, a path, which Jews are summoned to walk on a daily basis. The laws govern everything from eating to marital relations to business or medical ethics. The ideals embodied in the Prophetic visions are concretized through incremental steps on a day-to-day basis.

The educational philosophy underlying the *Halakha*[48] emphasizes habituation, but not blindly. The biblical source for this approach is in Exod 24:7, when the people tell Moses, "All that the Lord has spoken, we will do and we will hearken." In other words, the doing precedes the hearkening. Sometimes, as an educational strategy, especially with children, one has to encourage and develop in them patterns or habits of good behavior, even before they understand all the reasons for it. But as they grow and mature, their understanding has to be developed, along with these behaviors. An ethical human being can not simply be a blind, unquestioning conformist, as new situations will arise in which he/she will have to exercise reasoned judgment in making ethical decisions. The issue of obedience to authority vs. autonomous judgment is a classic question in Jewish thought.[49] Except for some ultra-Orthodox sects that might require consulting a rabbi before making any decision in one's life, most Jews would maintain that the ideal would be faithfulness to the Law with understanding, intentionality, and a commitment to critical thought.

Some Practical Suggestions

How can such a challenging and ambitious program of education be accomplished? The approach suggested above would have important curricular implications for Jewish education. Rather than stressing, for example, the biblical book of Joshua, with its military conquest of the land, Jewish education would do well to stress the first eleven chapters of Genesis, as well as the books of Isaiah, Micah, Jonah, and Ruth, for more universalistic texts.

Studying the Oral Torah is important, not only for the specific texts, but primarily for the methodology of the discourse. Older students and adults should be exposed to Jewish philosophical approaches to the questions of universalism and particularism.

---

48. See Michael Rosenak, *Tree of Life, Tree of Knowledge: Conversations with the Torah* (Boulder: Westview, 2001).

49. See David Hartman, *A Living Covenant: The Innovative Spirit in Traditional Judaism* (New York: Free Press, 1985).

Beginning with early childhood, educators should encourage each child to develop a healthy sense of self-esteem, without denigrating the other. Each child should be helped to develop a sense of pride in their family, community, and culture, while valuing others' families, communities, and cultures. Traditional stories, parables, aphorisms, songs, and so forth should be used to inculcate a language of discourse about ethical behavior vis-à-vis the Other.

It is important that teachers model respectful behavior towards their students and towards each other. If all human beings are created in the image of God, then enhancing human dignity is a way of serving God. Examples of ethical behavior on the part of others—from "Lives of the Saints" to today's newspaper—can be brought in for analysis and discussion. The teacher should try to developing group norms of behavior and even hold disciplinary discussions when these norms are violated. The outstanding educator who used these techniques most notably was Janusz Korczak in twentieth-century Poland.

Jewish history has been characterized variously as "lachrymose" or as "the history of literature and of suffering."[50] Persecution has been a major part of the history of the Jewish people, to be sure. No Jewish school's curriculum should omit the expulsions, pogroms, Crusades, Inquisition, blood libels, and so on, leading up to the horrors of the twentieth-century Holocaust. But these should not be taught as exhausting the entire story. There have also been significant periods in which Jews and Jewish culture thrived, both within the Land of Israel and in the Diaspora. The history of anti-Semitism should be part of the curriculum but should include, for example, the significant changes that have taken place within the Catholic Church since Vatican II.

Also, even the painful memories can be used in such a way as to develop sensitivity toward the suffering of all people. Holocaust courses could devote significant attention to the role of the Righteous among the Nations. As an example of this, I would like to relate the story of the French Huguenot town of Le Chambon-sur-Lignon. During the Second World War, five thousand Christians there saved approximately the same number of Jews. Pierre Sauvage, an American Jewish filmmaker hidden in the town as an infant, went back in the early 1980s to research the motivation for this impressive rescue operation. In his outstanding documentary, *Weapons of the Spirit*, he reached the conclusion that several factors were

---

50. One of the historians most disturbed about this presentation of Jewish history was Salo Baron of Columbia University.

responsible, including the inspired leadership of the local pastor, Reverend André Trocmé.

The townspeople, a fierce, mountainous lot, had a long tradition of resisting the central authority in Paris. But, ultimately, the main reason for their resistance, he maintained, was the collective historical memory they shared of having themselves been persecuted as a religious minority in the seventeenth century. This, to be sure, was an echo of the biblical injunction, "And you must understand the soul of a stranger, for you were strangers in the land of Egypt."[51]

We can draw an analogy with a statement by Eliezer Berkovits. In discussing the issue of faith after the Holocaust (in his book by that name), he wrote: "We are not Job . . . We are only Job's brother. We must believe, because our brother Job believed; and we must question, because our brother Job so often could not believe any longer."[52]

Analogous to that would be the text read on *Pesach* (Passover) at the *Seder*. We must recite, "Pour out Your wrath on the nations that do not know you," because of the Nazis and their accomplices. But because of the Righteous among the Nations, perhaps we should add the following: "Pour out Your love on the nations who have known you and on the kingdoms who call upon Your name. For they show loving-kindness to the seed of Jacob and they defend Your people Israel from those who would devour them alive. May they live to see the *sukkah* of peace over Your chosen ones and to participate in the joy of Your nations."[53]

Having mentioned *Pesach*, we will digress briefly into a discussion of teaching the Jewish festivals. There is a well-known and oft-told joke that says that Jewish holidays can be summarized in three sentences: "1. They wanted to kill us. 2. We survived. 3. Now, let's eat."

As amusing as that might be, it is simply not true. First, of the seven major festivals—(not to mention the weekly celebration of *Shabbat*) *Rosh Hashanah, Yom Kippur, Sukkot, Sh'mini Atzeret-Simchat Torah, Chanukah, Purim, Pesach,* and *Shavuot*—only three fit into that mold at all: *Chanukah, Purim,* and *Pesach*.

51. Exodus 23:9
52. Eliezer Berkovitz, *Faith after the Holocaust* (New York: Ktav, 1973) 5.
53. Noam Zion and David Dishon, *A Different Night: The Family Participation Haggadah* (Jerusalem: Hartman Institute, 1997) 142.

The other festivals, as well as, for example, *Tu Bishevat*, the Jewish Arbor Day, celebrated in the winter, have different themes. Why have those three festivals left such an imprint on the Jewish imagination?

First, for Jewish schools in the Northern Hemisphere (where the majority of the world's Jews reside), the first four festivals generally occur at the very beginning of the school year, and there is not much time to deal with them in a meaningful way. *Shavuot*, on the other hand, takes place at the very end of the year and sometimes gets lost in the rush. The other three happen during the course of the year and the teachers have plenty of time to deal with them in the classroom.

But more than that, *Chanukah* is fortunate enough to occur around Christmas, and *Pesach* around Easter. Jewish communities seeking to compensate their children for not being part of the majority culture sometimes overcompensate by stressing festivals that, with the exception of *Pesach*, are minor.

Still, even those three are far richer and more multidimensional than the joke would indicate. The way those three festivals are taught could be a powerful tool in developing our educational dialectic of pride without prejudice. For example, *Chanukah* could be presented—without negating its historical meaning—within the more universal framework of festivals of light during the winter solstice. Even the Talmud[54] recognizes that *Chanukah* has a strong link to this important natural occurrence and the existential need of human beings for light as a symbol of hope within darkness.

Similarly, one of the major customs on *Purim* is dressing up in costume. On a certain level, the festival is really about identity—personal, as well as group[55]—and the relationship with the Other. One of the ways to relate to the Other is, quite literally, by getting into his or her shoes. Or, perhaps by confronting the Other within us.

The tradition of *Purim* provides us with a wonderful model of how aggression, even when justified, can be channeled in a nondestructive way. There is a biblical commandment to "blot out the memory of Amalek" (see Exodus 17 and Deuteronomy 25:17–19). At first glance, this seems to be, God forbid, a prescribed genocide. Haman was a descendant of Agag, the Amalekite (see Esther 3:1 and 1 Samuel 15:8). The way we fulfill the commandment of wiping out the memory of Amalek is that when the book of

---

54. *Avodah Zarah* 8b.

55. Identity—and mistaken identity—are also a major theme within the book of Esther, read on Purim. See, for example, Esther 2:20; 6:1–11; 7:5; 8:17—9:1; etc.

Esther is read in the synagogue on *Purim*, we make noise at every mention of Haman's name. What a wonderful way to sublimate feelings of anger and aggression. If only all of us could find such creative ways of dealing with frustration!

Finally, *Pesach* surely celebrates the Exodus from Egypt of the Hebrew slaves. Yet it is also a general festival of freedom and liberation from many forms of oppression, and on that level, has more universal significance.[56] Even the particular memory can be a spur for action directed outwardly: These are the words of Rabbi Yitzchak Halevi Herzog, Chief Rabbi of the Land of Israel, in his testimony before the English-American investigative commission in 1946:

> False claims have been heard that a Jewish majority would act cruelly to a non-Jewish minority living amongst it. It has also been claimed that the non-Jewish religions would be hurt by the change of the present status of the Land of Israel and its becoming a Jewish community. Claims like these can be sounded only by those who forget that more than 3000 years ago, God could think of no better rationale for His commandment to the Jews to love the stranger than the memory of the injustice that was done to them in Egypt out of hate for the stranger. True, our exile has taught us to hate—to hate hatred.[57]

Once the festivals are perceived as multi-dimensional, and are taught on a level that is appropriate for older pupils, and even adults, their reality becomes more complex.[58] Indeed, we might say that the kind of Jewish education we are advocating can be summarized as four developmental *c*'s, that is: *community, commitment, complexity,* and *critique*. First, the pupil should be socialized into a sense of *community* with a series of ever widening concentric circles: her or his friends, class, local community, the Jewish people. Other communities are to be respected for their uniqueness, without adding value judgments. Once there is identification with a

---

56. For a wonderful exploration of the universal significance of *Pesach*, see Jonathan Sacks, *The Chief Rabbi's Haggadah: Hebrew and English Text with New Essays and Commentary* (London: HarperCollins, 2003) esp. 1–7, 21–26.

57. From "The Land of Israel and the State of Israel," by Professor Uriel Simone, of Bar-Ilan University; can be found on the Netivot Shalom website: http://www.netivot-shalom.org.il/judaism/land-sta.php/.

58. For approaches to the festivals that treat them on a more mature and complicated level, see Irving Greenberg, *The Jewish Way: Living the Holidays* (New York: Summit, 1988); Arthur Waskow, *Seasons of Our Joy: A Celebration of Modern Jewish Renewal* (Toronto: Bantam, 1982).

community, there can develop a sense of *commitment* and responsibility. Gradually, the student is exposed to the *complexity* of the subject. At that stage, it is appropriate to allow for, and even encourage, a *critical approach*.

In addition to theoretical learning, Jewish students should be exposed to actual encounters and dialogues with people from different religious and cultural backgrounds. Once people begin to see each other as human beings, prejudices will break down. Educational institutions should consider possibilities for joint intergroup social action projects.

Perhaps the biggest problem facing Jewish educators is the lack of adequate opportunities to accomplish these complex and ambitious educational goals. Not enough young Jews are exposed for enough hours to Jewish educational experiences over enough years of their lives. The recent growth of successful adult education programs is most gratifying, but all too often it simply points to the paucity of Jewish education during childhood and youth. Thus, the dialectical approach outlined here may be too much for the Jewish educational system to handle, particularly in the Diaspora, already challenged by a duration of all too few years and hours within the years, not enough trained educators, and so on. This describes the supplementary educational system, of once, twice, or even three times a week. But the program we have tried to propose should become a priority for Jewish day schools throughout the world and for schools in Israel.

Priorities for Dialogue

Scholars have reached back as far as the Bible for examples of interreligious dialogue (see, for example, Malachi 3:16). And there are examples of meetings between religious leaders of different faiths in medieval Europe—some were hostile disputations, but some were actually friendly colloquia. Interreligious dialogue began in an organized manner as far back as 1893, at the first World's Parliament of Religions, held in Chicago. Serious, ongoing dialogue involving Jews and Christians has been more a product of the post–World War II era. Still many issues remain to be discussed further, including the need to engage with Islam, but not at the expense of bilateral dialogue. In a shrinking world, cognizant of ecological emergencies, bloody intergroup conflicts, changing centers of power, and so on, it is hoped that the model offered in this paper can contribute to a dialogue that will help build peace and mutual respect.

five

Jewish–Christian–Muslim Dialogue after 9/11

RICCARDO DiSEGNI

The Challenge of 9/11

The Babylonian Talmud relates a discussion between the rabbis of the schools of Shammai and Hillel, which lasted a long time, but was not concluded because it was suddenly interrupted by a political crisis: "They were not able to finish, since the hour became crazy (*lo hispiqu ligmor ʿad shenitrefa hashaʾa*)" (*Yevamoth* 15a).

This source is related to the war under Roman Emperor Trajan or the beginning of the Bar Kochba Revolt (132–135 CE), the wars that finished with the destruction of the land of Israel, the end of any hope of Jewish political independence, and the killing of hundreds of thousands of Jews. Obviously during this war there was not any possibility for a pacific gathering of the Sanhedrin and normal decisions. Compared with the tragic war results, the rabbinical discussions interrupted by the war, although elegant and in some way essential in the development of Jewish law, appear in a different light and maybe much less important.

This is a good example of the fact that the harsh reality of history compels people to reevaluate the meaning and the importance of their behavior, mainly of their intellectual activities. In our times the beginning of the third Christian millennium has been singed by a chain of tragic events, the most important and symbolic of them being the 9/11 attack on the Twin Towers and the Pentagon.

Trialogue and Terror

There is widespread discussion with different opinions on the historical meaning of these events;[1] some interpreted them as the beginning of a new dramatic era of war, while others consider them the last episode of a failed attempt to change the world by terrorism.

Without choosing either of these interpretations as valid, it seems at the very least that these events mark a passage in the recent history of the Western world, in its relationship with the rest of the world. In particular what has changed is the relation of the West with Muslim culture, and the strong impact of the religious factor in political controversies. At least from the time of the French Revolution, in the past two centuries wars have been fought among states, and religious factors were marginal. In more recent years, after the fall of Communism, new ways of strong identity developed, and religion again became again a model of cohesion and self-definition among the masses. Opposition to Western civilization has complex roots, religion being only one component, but in the collective imagination of both sides it appears as the main element of definition and opposition.

In light of these developments, it is clear that the religious worlds are now involved in a new responsibility. Their role is no longer simply internal, intimate, limited to personal conscience, but has become consequential in the wider area of political conflicts. This is understood clearly by great political leaders who continuously appeal to religious leaders to find ways of communication and, if possible, reconciliation among themselves. Peace and dialogue among religions is no more a simple matter of theology or historical and social discussion, but becomes a fundamental key in the political assessment of the world in this century. The hour "became crazy."

For this reason it seems that all previous and even fundamental discussions among religious leaders are a little thing in comparison with contemporary responsibilities. But in order to focus the agenda of our times, it is necessary to evaluate all previous experience, with either its positive or negative results. The following pages present a Jewish evaluation of the state of the question.

---

1. Editor's note: There were three terror planes on 9/11. The third crashed in a field near Shanksville, Pennsylvania, when passengers resisted the terrorists.

Dialogue and Communication

The term "religious dialogue" is quite new when used with some definite meaning in the context of relations between religions. Trying to describe the actual implications of this expression, it can be said that this term comprises exchanges of information on doctrine, rites, customs, private or public discussion on all these issues, reciprocal teaching, social and political cooperation in practical purposes, personal knowledge of the Other by means of official and unofficial meeting, opening of "hot" direct lines between leaders especially for moments of crisis. The purpose of all these exchanges can be different, ranging from simple knowledge to friendship and respect to an attempt to use communication in order to bring the Other to one's own universe. All this seems a quite new phenomenon. However, communication between different religions often existed. The prevalent image of permanent conflict, hatred, or persecution has to be critically discussed, as does the romantic portraits of times or areas of beautiful coexistence, that from time to time are offered in contrast with some other, less sanguine, situations. For instance there is a predominant belief that the conditions of Jews under Christianity were much worse than in the Islamic world, which is portrayed as tolerant in opposition to a Christianity systematically involved in murder and inquisition trials. Surely the number of Jewish victims of Christianity far exceeds those who died under Islam. But this is only part of the story and represents a risky simplification.

Closer to the historical truth is the fact that there were many different patterns of coexistence and communication, depending on place and time. First of all, Jews lived in the same places where Christians and Muslims used to live, and even when they were closed in ghettos, there was always direct daily contact, resulting in a reciprocal knowledge not only of differences but also of commonly shared principles, values, and holy texts and traditions. The communication of uneducated people had its high-level parallel in the studies of scholars from both sides interested to know and discuss the Others' texts, even when they were moved by polemical or apologetic purposes. In order to convert people, or to resist conversion, one needed to know the Other, his culture, and his way of thinking. Public medieval debates organized by kings are quite isolated and dramatic episodes, but they show the level of reciprocal knowledge. "Hotlines" of communication for crisis management often existed and were open, not simply to grant Jews a way of defending themselves, but also for some way of reciprocal benefit, e.g., asking the Jews to use their international connections to assist various rulers.

The Dialogue as a New Form of Communication

What then is new in the contemporary "dialogue"? We are not talking about the philosophical definition of the concept, something related to the I-Thou encounter of Martin Buber's thought, but about the specific connotation that this term started to have in the last sixty years in the field of interreligious relations. Since the world from where the concept developed is mainly Christian, either intra-Christian or in Christianity's relation to Judaism, it is the Christian meaning that we have to discuss, before talking about Muslims. In Christianity's relationship to Judaism there are several aspects that mark the difference from the ways of past communication. Let us consider the most important of them, from an optimistic perspective.

First, the dialogue is based on the assumption of the dignity of the counterpart who is no longer considered a hostile entity, to be kept apart with shame or horror, or as an archaeological residual of a glorious past but no longer of any actual value. Second, the dialogue is characterized by a constructive, positive approach; the main purpose of encounter being not the demonstration of superiority, or the moral or ideological defeat of an adversary, but a respectful way of knowledge. Third, the dialogue is for Christians a way of self-evaluation and rethinking their personal identity in two main directions: discovering the roots of their own history, culture, and faith; and replying to one of the greatest provocative questions of the twentieth century: how is it possible that a religion which identifies itself as based on the commandment of love could keep and let grow in its body hatred against the Jews? It is not a mere coincidence that the Christian dialogical revolution began in a consistent way just after the Second World War and Auschwitz. Requests from the Jewish side, as expressed in the commitment of Jules Isaac, were only a catalyst in a fertile field full of expectations.

Jewish Reply to the Christian Request for Dialogue

Ignoring the historical background, it could be possible to think the dialogue is a simple situation in which two different entities meet and speak. The reality is, however, much more complicated. In order to understand the sense of the religious dialogue, we could not do without knowledge of the historical and ideological conditions in which it developed. From this perspective the reasons for difficulties and the contradiction of the process will appear much more clearly.

Christian–Jewish dialogue was not, and still is not, a bilateral parallel movement of encounter. Even before the Nazi persecution there were Jews and Christians in search of a constructive and respectful way of communication and cooperation. But they were a small number of isolated personalities. Their number grew after Auschwitz, and their quest became urgent. But the main purpose was not the establishment and spread of an organized system of communications; the request from the Jewish side was not dialogue, but simply, stop teaching hatred. This appeal was finally received in the Christian world, but the way Christianity acted and reacted in those years went far beyond this request, was not necessarily connected to it, was quite surprising, and often inspired diffidence. Let us start with dialogue.

As explained above, contemporary Christians may feel an essential necessity to meet Jews, as a part of their process of autodefinition. Jews do not share this feeling. Jews and Christians are different not only in their beliefs, but in many other essential aspects. The two realities are not comparable. They are not as two men who struggle for a long time, then try to make peace; or two political parties; or two states; or two commercial companies in competition. They have other differences: the demographic factor (very small for the Jews); the role of religious hierarchy (fragmented if not totally lacking among the Jews); identity, which may not necessarily be religious, but national and historical; and probably the most important, the fact that Christianity derived from Judaism: in historical terms Christians cannot understand themselves without connecting to their Jewish roots. Jews don't need Christians for self-definition, apart from some quite marginal considerations, or within the frame of some unnecessary polemical opposition.

Another point is the weight of history: only for a very short time were Jews in power, and Christians were persecuted heretics; for the rest of their history Jews were a minority without power, subjected to and often persecuted by Christians. The result of this is that even when dialogue is possible, it is always in some ways asymmetrical. When the Second Vatican Council issued its *Nostra Aetate* document and opened a new era calling for dialogue, Jewish reactions were of all possible kinds: enthusiasm, skepticism, diffidence, coldness. Why should Jews engage in the dialogue? What have we to gain from this? How to trust a world that for more than nineteen centuries has been against us? Is this not a new way to attract and convert Jews to Christianity with smiles, after all violent attempts failed?

More deeply, at the root of diffidence, Jewish theology and understanding of Christianity played its part. How to consider the Christian religion? How could it be possible to be in discussion and confrontation at the same level with a faith that we always considered as extraneous and foreign (*zarah*) to our belief? There is also another important component, which is not merely theological: Jewish reluctance is also based on its closed social structure, supported by its religious laws such as those dealing with food and sex, whose aim or consequence is to preserve a whole priestly community from mixing with the outside. The boundaries and the rules to protect these boundaries, as they are fixed in Jewish tradition, are much stricter than in the contemporary Christian world. To lower the level of this border defense is considered to risk keeping the mission of holiness and therefore the continuity of the Jewish people. It is not a new problem; the Christian revolution started also with the request of *synesthein*, "eating together," no longer caring about dietary laws.

After decades of more or less experimental dialogue these questions still have their meaning and elicit different replies. Let us examine some of the main critical points.

The Open Critical Points

Jewish National Rebirth and the State of Israel

In the development of modern Jewish history the State of Israel came to represent, for the greatest majority of the Jewish people, the core and the center of Judaism and the fulfilment of the promises and hopes of two thousand years of Diaspora existence. In more recent years the State of Israel is the place where about half of the world's Jewish people live. Christian–Jewish friendship is therefore unthinkable, even on an abstract religious basis, if it omits a reflection on and a positive approach to this State. The behavior of Christian denominations has been different and variable. From one side, at the present moment there is strong support from right-wing evangelical groups for Israel, based on theological considerations. On the other side, based on different theological and also political considerations, the Catholic and Vatican opposition to the national rebirth of the Jewish people since the beginning of the Zionist movement is known and well documented.

During the pontificate of Paul VI, when already great developments had been introduced in Christian–Jewish relations, papal and Vatican hostility to the State of Israel was remarkable. Symbolic evidence of this approach was the behavior of the pope during his visit to the Holy Land, with his cold and detached relation to the Israeli president (the pope never even called him by this title) and the government. A revolution in this approach happened under John Paul II. He recognized the State of Israel, opened normal diplomatic relations, and visited the country making spectacular gestures of friendship, such as placing a prayer leaflet at the Western Wall, and visiting Yad Vashem, the memorial for victims of the Shoah. Behind these fundamental steps, however, a solid resistance and opposition persists, surfacing in moments of crisis. In the spring of 2002, during the siege of the Church of the Nativity in Bethlehem, the ancient repertoire of theological hostility resurfaced and was expressed in mixed religious-political terms.

Shoah

A reflection on the causes, the meaning, and the responsibilities of the Shoah and the risks of a new one was forcibly pushed on the agenda of official relations; it was unthinkable that all this could pass without comment. However, as careful Jewish observers could expect, the results of an analysis of the past were mixed. The churches expressed their horror at what happened, in terms which became even clearer with the passage of time (the initial responses were not so clear or strong). However, it is the question of responsibility that reveals deep differences between the two faiths. In the official 1998 Vatican document ("We Remember: A Reflection on the Shoah") there is only a modest recognition of the influence of the centuries-long religious education of hostility to the Jews, and a tepid contempt expressed for the religious leaders who did not oppose the murder of the Jews. Essentially, the greatest responsibility is relegated to Nazism, which is considered a pagan, anti-Christian movement.

In this view, the destruction of Judaism was only the first step in the process of a planned extermination of Christianity. In most Jewish eyes the idea of Nazism as paganism could be accepted; this extends even to its possible anti-Christianity. But the negation of the objective fusion of old (Christian) and new (Nazi) hostility, when the new one found its main source of energy in a never ending old river of hate, is absolutely unacceptable. It becomes a type of major religious self-absolution of whole populations who were, in spite of or due to their religious education, insensitive or cooperative or even enthusiastic in the destruction process of European Jews.

The behavior of Pope Pius XII during the persecution is a focal point in these discussions. On the one hand, he is considered, because of his silence, the most relevant evidence of Catholic indifference, if not complicity, in the face of the destruction of Europe's Jews. On the other hand, there is a strong tendency among conservative circles to push for his beatification and rehabilitation. Apparently only a minority of the Jewish people is ready to support this last opinion, while the majority thinks that at least a careful and objective analysis of all the documents could bring better clarity: every hasty or impulsive decision must be avoided at the present moment. What is possible to conclude on this point is that there is a relevant difference of interpretations between Jews and Christians on the Shoah. However, the Church is solidly committed to avoid the spreading of hate from now on. This is a good point of agreement for the future. All this is related to the more general problem of Anti-Semitism.

Anti-Semitism

In all official declarations of the past decades the commitment against anti-Semitism was expressed in a progressively clear way, starting from the weak *deplorat* (disapproval instead of condemnation) of *Nostra Aetate*. This point, however, needs radical clarification since there is still a possible distinction between anti-Semitism and anti-Judaism; the first term relates to the racial aspect, the second to the religious aspect. It is also clear that in Jewish religious thought, as well as in historical, political, and sociological analysis hostility against the Jews may be classified in different ways; but each possible form is condemned. The risk in Christian thought is that there is not only a historical or theological distinction but also a moral one in the sense that some kinds of hostility are absolutely immoral while others can be tolerated or even positive.

The famous sentence of Pope Pius XI, "we are all Semites," may be considered a claim to Christianity's Jewish roots; thus, any attack on these roots is an attack on Christianity itself. Racism cannot be tolerated in the official (recent, not in the Spain of *limpieza de sangre*) doctrine since the salvation of baptism is offered to any human being, from whatever "race" he/she is coming. But all this still leaves the door open to any kind of opposition to Jewish doctrine that developed after Jesus, and to the Jews' fidelity to this doctrine. Talking against Jewish rites and religion as they are now is progressively considered unfair behavior, and public manifestations of contempt are becoming even rarer.

Officially the definition of Jewish faith as *judaicam superstitionem* disappeared. Since 1959 the Jewish convert is no longer requested to reject his original "superstition" in a public declaration at the moment of baptism, as Edith Stein or Jean-Marie Lustiger did in their times (it is not a big consolation; it's the conversion itself that should be rejected). There is, however, still a spreading contempt, lack of understanding, and ironic approach against religious Judaism, but it seems like a residue of the past, and an overwhelming movement has succeeded in delimitating it. In fact, respect towards the Jews, as they are now, and for their religion, as it is now, is growing. The general atmosphere is dramatically changed. Some traditional polemics, such as residual Marcionism, namely, the distinction between a Jewish God of justice and revenge, and the Christian God of love, is always present and can surface at any occasion, as can the support of anti-Israeli opposition. But there is also a recent relevant doctrinal revision that opposes these ideas. The conclusion is that while there is strong commitment against anti-Judaism itself, resistance is still high.

Supersession, Salvation, and Conversion

The actual role of the Jewish people in the eyes of the churches is controversial. The famous words of Pope John Paul II in his 1986 visit to the Roman Synagogue, "you are our elder brothers," may symbolically be considered the expression of an ambiguous, clearly inexpressible approach to the question. In the book of Genesis and in Paul's letters to the Romans and Galatians the elder brother is the bad one who loses his privileges and primogeniture. This is the core of the traditional Christian theory of supersession; the believers in Jesus take the place of the Jewish people to bring salvation to mankind. The "elder brother" sentence is ambiguous because the average person understands only the positive message of brotherhood, which is of course extremely important. But from the theological point of view this is the affirmation of the substantial futility of contemporary Jewish vitality, in the terms of the old Augustinian theory of "witnesses."

Supersession also means that Jewish faith is incomplete; it must be fulfilled and filled with the Christian faith, and this is a positive aim. In other words, the Church does not give up its program of converting the Jewish people. The difference is this conversion must be achieved only in respectful and nonaggressive ways. The only problem is that it is embarrassing to declare this intention clearly, since the Jews could be offended and close themselves to any kind of dialogue. In fact at the very beginning of the dialogue season, in the decade of the sixties, the most prominent rabbis of the Orthodox world declared that the only purpose of this new approach was conversion, but in a new, friendly, way. The discussions among Jews concerning these declarations continue today. The Church is not easing the good intentions of those in the Jewish field who favor dialogue.

The specific story of the prayer for the Jews on the Holy Friday before Easter is very didactic on the development of the question. The original Latin text, titled *Pro conversione Judaeorum* ("For the Conversion of the Jews") was a prayer *pro perfidis judaeis*, to remove from their eyes and heart the *velamen* ("curtain") that kept them far from the achievement of the truth, namely salvation through Jesus. In 1962 the words related to the *judaica perfidia*, which literally meant "lack of faith," but is in modern languages a synonym of wickedness, were removed; but the prayer itself, asking for conversion, was maintained. It is interesting to note that many then and still now, are full of gratitude for the cancellation of the words, and forget that the main text with this title persisted.

In 1965 a new text, titled *Pro Judaeis* ("For the Jews"), was elaborated, to be used in the masses in local languages—talking no more about the *velamen*, but asking for the "full redemption" of the Jewish people. A note accompanying the text explained that full redemption means recognition of Christ. The Jews were first called as *populus acquisitionis antiquae* (literally, "people of the old purchase"). In 1970 and 1975 further versions *acquisitionis prioris* ("of the first purchase") that in some local translations was given as "un tempo fu il tuo popolo eletto" ("*once*[!] was your chosen people"). A new official Italian version of 1983 has the phrase "popolo primogenito della tua alleanza" ("firstborn people of your alliance"). The request for full redemption was always maintained, without explanatory notes.

The actual version in use is the result of this evolution, but in the *motu proprio* of Pope Benedict XVI of 2007 permission was given to use in the Latin missal the old, 1962, expression. Responding to waves of protest a new text has been prepared, but still not diffused. We learn from this story that the original basic request of conversion was never abandoned, and the actual formula of full redemption is preferred for its ambiguity, since the corresponding Jewish term, *geulla shlema* could mean, at least for the Jews, a totally different thing. In parallel the theme of election develops from a concept of a lost role to a more sophisticated expression; in fact we don't know if "*new* people of God" (or "of Israel") as the Church defines itself, means that the new is in place of the old or if the old can still be vital and vibrant together with the new. The first possibility, if openly affirmed, could close the doors of the dialogue; the second option is on the horizon but it is not supported by clear official statements.

Judaism's Relationship with Islam

From a Jewish point of view, and probably also from an Islamic point of view, the question of dialogue between the two faiths cannot be posed in the same terms as it is posed between Jews and Christians. There are deep differences. The structure of Islam is different from Christianity; its lack of religious hierarchy is much more similar to the structure of Judaism. The self-image of Islam in relation to Judaism is not that of a branch inserted into Jewish roots, as it is for Christianity, but that of an autonomous original revelation. This is true even if from the other side the affinity and "brotherhood" of the Jewish and Islamic traditions is clearly evident; from the main idea of monotheism to the use of a Semitic holy language to the ritual aspects of religious observance, and social solidarity. The Islamic world doesn't suffer a guilt complex toward Jews as Christianity does after Auschwitz; in their eyes the Shoah is a product of Christian Europe. This is true even if some Islamic religious leaders supported the Nazi program to exterminate the Jews. Nor does Islam seem to have complexes about all its polemic and religious traditions opposing Jews.

Muslims may show quite easily that beside these teachings there are others that speak in terms of tolerance and respect and, more important, the fact that under Muslim rule Jews never suffered as much as they did under Christianity. Islam does not need Judaism to verify its identity or goodwill in the third millennium (which for them, as for the Jews, who use different calendars, is not the third millennium). Islam does not feel the necessity of common prayer with the Jews; for them prayer has to be done in a definite ritual context. As previously stated, communications between Judaism and Islam always existed, and the new era of dialogue seems to be a specific problem for Christianity and not for Islam. Theological and critical studies, as well as social ways of meeting and cooperation are always welcome, but all this is neither especially new nor a specific necessity.

Trialogue and Terror

The dialogical problem with Islam stems from a totally different perspective. It is the problem of political-religious confusion, the consequence of the birth of the State of Israel. For Christians, and specifically for Catholics, as noted above, opposition started mainly from theological positions, complicated by political interests in the region, ranging from worrying about holy places to the destiny of Christian Arab minorities. For the world of Islam, and specifically for the Arab part of Islam, the problem of Israel itself is much more direct, from the tragedy of the Arabs living in that country to the shame of repeated defeats to the crisis of the ideal concept of an Islamic ruler which may also be tolerant towards the Jews, but only in the measure in which they submit. It is part of a more general crisis of Islam in its relations with the Western world.

In this crisis and in consequent ideologies, Jews, all Jews—not specifically the citizens of the State of Israel—are considered a unitary block, responsible for the evil suffered by Islam in recent decades, as the sword of the Western world against Islam. There is no distinction between nationality and religion. The only Jews who may be tolerated in this context are those, even ultrareligious, who dissociate themselves not only from the politics of the Israeli government but from the very idea of the State of Israel. There are quite a number of these kinds of Jews, as has been demonstrated in the Holocaust denial congress organized in Teheran by Mahmoud Ahmadinejad. But in fact these Jews are shunned by the great majority of the Jewish people, in spite of all its internal divisions.

A dramatic demonstration of this approach in the Islamic world is the recent declaration issued by Abdel Fattah Allam, from Al-Azhar University in Cairo, which is considered one of the most relevant doctrinal institutions in the Sunni world. When it was announced that a delegation from the Great Mosque in Rome and general Muslim organizations in Italy were planning an official visit to the Main Synagogue of Rome, the Al-Azhar sheikh declared that "we have a positive position about interreligious dialogue, but the dialogue between Islam and Judaism cannot begin until rights have been restored to those who properly should possess them." In other words, these rights may involve more or less the very existence of the State of Israel, and there is no possibility of a dialogue between Jews and Muslims until this critical situation is fixed. According to this view, the political conflict of Israelis and Palestinians must be exported far beyond the borders of the contested land. Every Jew is an enemy for every Muslim in the world.

It is clear that this conception is alarming for Jews, but it should not be ignored by any community of the Western world where populations of both Jews and Muslims live. It seems not only to deter dialogue but to assume a war of religion. It should be a primary interest for the Jewish people, but not only of the Jewish people, to counteract the spread of this conception. In these radical views Jews are not the only enemy, but they are put together with some allies, sometimes mythically identified as "Crusaders," sometimes identified with specific nations. The Jewish response is not simple, since the ways of Jewish identification are complex. As noted earlier, the link of the Jewish people living in Diaspora with the State of Israel is strong in all possible terms: political, historical, emotional, religious, and familiar. It could be very difficult to give up this link as the price to be paid to dialogue with Muslims. This very great price is considered an expression of an essential anti-Semitism which is obviously incompatible with the dialogue.

All this means that there is a challenging priority in the confrontation with the Islamic world, an attempt if not to eradicate then at least to limit and denounce the diffuse and possibly overwhelming wave of anti-Jewish feeling coming from some circles of that world.

Today's Agenda: From Dialogue to Trialogue

The previous remarks have shown the complex aspects of a reality that only superficially can be called dialogue. In the relations of Jews with Christians each party is looking for something different. The relations of Jews with Muslims, for their part, are heavily compromised and polluted by political elements. What is realistically possible to do? As I wrote initially, the events of 9/11 mark the beginning of an era of new relations, with a growing responsibility, which may be good or bad for the religions. What has been done, achieved or not achieved, until now, is only the premise of new tasks for each group. It could be possible that all the unresolved difficulties in the Jewish–Christian dialogue are a small and secondary thing in comparison with the duties of the day. Christians are still looking for the conversion of the Jews; Jews still consider the Christian faith as imperfect and "extraneous and foreign." So what? Is this today's main problem? To put the theological differences on the table immediately is a serious mistake, which may only poison the atmosphere and absorb energies that can be usefully employed in other arenas.

Christianity has the theoretical possibility, based on its hierarchical structure, to change some of its doctrinal aspects but probably is not ready for that or simply does not want to do it. Judaism, in all its components not only is not ready, but also has neither the interest nor the tools to do it. Religious confrontation is not comparable with political discussions and agreements where one may give territories in exchange for peace and so on. In religions changes and concessions require specific tools and long periods of time (often "biblical" in length), even if they are desired. Then why not push these radical and seemingly insurmountable principles beyond immediately achievable goals, as David Berger suggests, and instead concentrate on different aspects of our relations? (At any rate, this cannot be an excuse in the Orthodox Jewish religious world for a delay *sine die* of reflection on the role of the *other*; there is simply too much referring back to some medieval sources that obviously retain their importance, but there is a need for a dignified updated elaboration coherent with the Orthodox visions of history.)

Jewish–Muslim relations present a different context. Not only are the theological principles quite impossible to change, but neither party has an interest in doing this. There is an old tradition of communication, but this came to a dramatic crisis when Jews stopped being a tolerated minority within a Muslim majority. The core of the problem is the difficulty of some relevant components of the Arab Islamic world to see Jews as a free and powerful people, who even dominate some Muslim populations in what they consider an Arab country. This is part of a general difficulty of managing and interpreting the balance of strengths in our era, and is one of the components in the deadly cocktail that nourishes Islamic extremism. Theology is difficult or impossible to change, but political views can be changed even if they are connected with religion. So if the problem with Islam is political pollution, struggling against this pollution is the first aim.

Using the word *dialogue* for what has to be done or avoided in Jewish relations with the two other worlds means flattening the perspective; these are different realities to be managed in different ways. Similarly there are obviously different problems and specific difficulties in the communication between Christians and Muslims that are beyond the scope of this chapter.

There is, however, another important perspective on encounters of the three worlds which is sometimes indicated with the quite new term *trialogue*, a play on words that means a simultaneous meeting of three. The common denominators for this aim need to be identified, not only in order to avoid illusions but also to achieve some realistic results. First, the common nature of religions inspired by the same basic principle: God's discovery of Abraham, to whom each one of the three is connected; next, monotheism and revelation; then, moral imperatives in life; and the commitment to social activity of solidarity and education. These common roots create in spite of all the differences a kind of unity that is difficult if not impossible to find in other religions; in fact the world religions are very different not only in their beliefs but in their basic structure.

The homogeneity of the three religions derived from their common stem of Abraham is unique. They share also common basic ethical views and conceptions on the holiness of life that are often in conflict with other prevailing visions in today's society. History is the second point of contact: a dramatic demonstration of the possibility for self- and other destruction based on religious principles and differences, as well as of relatively rare but important positive developments that the exchange of experience produced, even where they were not pacific. There is a third element: the urgency of the moment, and the craziness of these years. It is not new in history to say that the world is crazy and full of violence, or that religion may nourish violence, but at least there is now a strong consciousness that something can be done by the religions in order to counteract violence. Simultaneous contact and communication between the three religions means working together to lower the level of hostility and the reciprocal lack of understanding, as well to identify commonly shared ethical values to be attested to the world in a pacific way. There is also a political necessity in this trialogue, as simultaneous meeting of the three, namely, the paradoxical diffidence and jealousy that may arise in the third party when the other two meet and exclude the third; each could feel excluded and under threat by an alliance of the other two. Putting all together may avoid this kind of suspicion.

Thinking about and programming these kinds of meetings is difficult, since we are entering into an experimental and dangerous field. There is a real risk of ritualism and rhetoric in this kind of encounter: putting together on a panel on any subject—as was customary in many countries—a priest, a rabbi, and an imam. Sometimes this can contribute to spreading knowledge and to respecting differences. But sometimes it becomes a sad competition to determine who is the seller of the best product, not to mention the risk of relativism. The urgency of the trialogue cannot be a parody of the old jokes about the priest, imam, and rabbi who meet on a train. It is not possible to give definite rules on this point, since local

Trialogue and Terror

conditions are decisive (subject, audience, speakers, general atmosphere, and so on). More probably our society needs fewer panels and more activities and testimonies of goodwill and positive examples of interfaith action.

It is the consciousness of new responsibilities and the need for new ideas and goodwill that must be spread.

six

9/11: Dialogue and Trialogue

EUGENE J. FISHER

9/11

September 11, 2001, was experienced a bit differently for those of us who live in New York, New Jersey, and the Washington area than for the rest of the country, or the world for that matter. In my case, I was halfway up a mountain outside Budapest, enjoying a respite from an extremely difficult summer in my life. In late June of 2001 my mentor, friend, and boss, Fr. Jack Hotchkin, died an untimely death from pneumonia. He was only in his mid-sixties but hated going to hospitals, so had resisted calling the doctor, even though he had had pneumonia before and knew the risks involved. I came back from a dinner with two of my good friends from the late, lamented International Catholic–Jewish Historical Committee, which I co-chaired on behalf of the Holy See, to receive a phone call from my colleague, John Borelli, that Jack was dead. I was devastated. He had, as the story came out, finally accepted to go to the hospital, but by the time his friend arrived to take him there, he was dead.

The second thing that happened in the summer of 2001, of course, was the demise of the aforementioned International Catholic–Jewish Historical Committee, which Jack had quite accurately prophesied from the beginning. The group of three Jewish and three Catholic scholars had, after several meetings in which each reported on the volumes they had undertaken to analyze, produced a preliminary report on the eleven volumes of Vatican archives published by the Holy See for the period of World War II.[1] Their joint conclusion was that the Jesuit scholars working on the

---

1. The series of volumes is titled *Actes et Documents du Saint Siege concernant la*

project had doubtlessly done a fair and objective job of selecting the key texts to publish. Indeed, a number of the texts held materials that could be embarrassing to the Holy See as it attempted, during the war, to save the Church from destruction at the hands of the Nazis, as well as to help as well as they could the millions of innocent victims of Nazism—Jews not least (but not at the beginning first) among them.

The scholars also jointly concluded, however, that they could not give a final verdict on the historical questions of the period without having access to the documents not included in the eleven volumes (see note 1), listing a series of historical questions raised by their studies of the *ADSS* volumes that they felt might be illuminated by other documents in the archives, beginning with the thousands of documents cited but not included in the volumes. Despite the willingness of Cardinal Jorge Mejia, then in charge of the Vatican dicastery, which included the Secret Archives, to allow the scholars access, the final decision by the Holy See was negative. So the scholars reluctantly put their efforts on hold until they could be given access to the documentation they felt they needed to proceed.[2] The ending of this effort was, needless to say, accompanied by much negative publicity for all concerned.

So it was with a sense of some relief and anticipation that I looked forward to representing the Holy See in September of 2001 at a Jewish–Lutheran International Consultation in Budapest. I figured that I could get some needed rest, having lost my summer vacation to death and dialogical disaster. True, it would overlap my birthday on September 10, but I would not have to give a paper or try to respond to expressions of outrage by either Jews angry with the Catholic Church or Catholics angry that I was not doing enough to defend the Church. I could follow the sage advice of keeping my mouth shut, smiling benignly, and speaking only when I had something useful to contribute. In short, a restful respite from my usual job of overseeing Catholic–Jewish relations in the United States, which I often described, with only slight exaggeration as "the Crisis of the Month Club."

And so it was, for the first two days. The Lutherans and Jews, interestingly, had picked a Jesuit retreat house, Manresa, halfway up a mountain outside, as I recall, Pest, for their meeting, and I was just beginning a wise

---

Second Guerre mondial (*ADSS*).

2. The Preliminary Report of the Historical Committee, along with four of the six papers produced by the scholars, and the correspondence between them and the Holy See, can be found in the journal *Catholic International: The Documentary Window on the World* 12/2 (May 2002) 50–99.

and useful comment in an entirely relaxed mode when one of the young Hungarian staffers of the facility burst in, shouting and with tears in her eyes. We could not make out much of what she said, but her urgency impelled us to follow her. We arrived at the lobby to see a rerun of the attack on the first tower on the large-screen TV they had there. Then, horrified, we watched live the explosions of the second tower and at the Pentagon. All the while the commentators were speaking about another plane, which, they felt, was aimed for the White House.

This is what differentiates New York, New Jersey, and Washington residents from the rest of the country in our memories of 9/11. I knew my daughter, out at her school in the suburbs, was alive and safe. I did not know about my wife. At nine o'clock in the morning, I knew, she would be on Constitution Avenue, in front of the White House, a potential victim for that airplane, still out there. A slight miscalculation and she could be included among the victims. In fact, she was there in front of the White House, as I feared.

The day wore on, I remained in a combined state of fear and rage, an indescribable state of helplessness. There was a reception scheduled that evening for the participants and the Catholic and Lutheran bishops of Budapest. I was speaking with the Catholic archbishop, through an interpreter, when another staffer burst into the room and cried out: "There is a call for Dr. Fisher from Washington!" My heart plunged. Was I about to be informed of the death of my wife? In absolute dread I ran from the room to the phone. And there was my wife assuring me that both she and my daughter were well, that she had taken other children home from school because their parents could not get to them. She had spent two hours in front of the White House, watching the smoke curling up from the Pentagon and wincing whenever a plane (and there were many) flew overhead. The most traumatic day of my life was over. I will forever be grateful to the heroes of the Pennsylvania flight who took down their plane rather than let it fly on to, most probably, the White House, where it could have crashed down on Constitution Avenue and my wife.

My story, of course, is not unique. But it was such that if one mentions 9/11 to me, I cannot not repeat it. And those who went through similar experiences understand fully this compulsion, which we share.

One who went through that horrible day with me, and the days after (I was not able to get a flight home to Washington until September 17), was Rabbi Leon Klenicki, of blessed memory. We spent our time together, watching what was happening in the wake of the attack, and praying together. Together we went to the Jewish center in Budapest and to Sunday mass at the Cathedral. Even though the mass was in Hungarian, I was able to tell Leon what was happening by the gestures and motions of the archbishop, who was the celebrant. And even though we could not understand a word of Hungarian, we knew what the sermon was about, because the words "Washington" and "New York" came through.

Leon and I, who had worked together for years writing and editing articles and books,[3] came to a new and deeper understanding of each other during this time of shared anguish, pain and, curiously, hope. In short, one result of 9/11, ironically, was a deepening of Jewish–Christian dialogue and understanding, certainly in New York and Washington where we were, together and equally, victims of a hatred and a murderous intent that wished nothing more than to kill us both.

Leon was able to leave a day earlier than I, but my time was filled with another encounter with a New York Jew whom I had known since even before coming to the U.S. bishops' conference in 1977. This was Judith Banki, whom I had met originally when researching my dissertation on the treatment (and mistreatment) of Jews and Judaism in Catholic teaching materials on the primary and secondary levels,[4] and with whom I have also worked and published.[5] Judy was not trapped in Budapest, as Leon and I were, however. She had arrived by train, with her husband, Paul, of blessed memory, who was of Hungarian descent. They were visiting his relatives, and would be going on by train to Paris. As an aside, the fact that Paul had relatives to visit in Hungary can be ascribed in large part to the heroic efforts of the papal nuncio in Budapest, Archbishop Angelo Rotta, who was the first to realize the likely fate of Hungarian Jews, and who convened a secret meeting of the ambassadors of neutral nations to convince them to coordinate their efforts to save Jews, regardless of religious background.

3. E.g., Pope John Paul II. *Spiritual Pilgrimage, Texts on Jews and Judaism, 1979–1995*, with commentary and introduction by Eugene J. Fisher and Leon Klenicki (New York: Crossroad, 1995), which won a 1995 National Jewish Book Award; this was the first time, we were sure, that a collection of papal texts had ever won a Jewish book award. The third and final edition of the collection, with extensive commentary, was completed before Rabbi Klenicki's death and is at the publisher.

4. A summary of my research can be found in Eugene Fisher, *Faith without Prejudice: Rebuilding Christian Attitudes toward Jews and Judaism*, rev. and exp. ed., Shared Ground among Jews and Christians 4 (New York: Crossroad, 1993) 109–20.

5. Judith Banki and Eugene J. Fisher, eds., *A Prophet for Our Time: An Anthology of the Writings of Rabbi Marc H. Tanenbaum* (New York: Fordham University Press, 2002). Obviously, we finished this book together in the tumultuous year 2001.

It was the result of this meeting that the Swedish government sent Raoul Wallenberg to Budapest to assist in the efforts initiated by Rotta. Rotta declared as many properties as he could to be official Vatican property, thus immune to searches by the Nazis. Here, of course, Pope Pius XII's often criticized policy of neutrality during World War II became instrumental in the saving of lives, since Jews were sequestered on those properties while the nunciature was cranking out false baptismal documents that they could use to obtain valid passports to leave the country, usually for Istanbul, where the other "Angel of the Holocaust," then Archbishop Angelo Roncalli (later Pope John XXIII) would provide them with visas for what was then called Palestine. This was of course done with the complete knowledge and encouragement of the Holy See, i.e., Pope Pius XII. At one point Rotta sent a message to the Vatican secretary of state, Cardinal Maglione, noting that he had just given out the forty thousandth such document to Jews. Maglione sent back a two-word message to Rotta: "Bravo, Monsignore!"[6]

Sadly, such active involvement by the Holy See in saving European Jews occurred only toward the end of the war, when many of the six million had already been killed. But it did happen and should be part of the debate, once again energized as I write by the unwise action of the Holy See in moving forward the case of beatification of Pope Pius XII before releasing the archives of the period 1939–1946. It is, as the scholars involved in the International Catholic–Jewish Historical Committee noted, a complex picture, a mixture of shades of gray, not the totally black (Hitler's pope) or totally white (Pius did everything right) portraits that the attackers and defenders of Pius most often fall into. Hopefully, by the time this essay is published, the Vatican will have released the archival documents for scholarly study and this paragraph will be out of date.

The point of raising this, along with the not entirely unrelated digression, is that as with the deepening of my relationship with Leon, the fact that Judy Banki, albeit experiencing 9/11 from afar in Budapest as had Leon and I, had spent much of the day worrying about whether relatives and friends had survived the onslaught, moved our relationship to a new level of bonding. As I and Leon did, so Judy and I shared a mutual victimhood, an enemy who wished to murder both of us, precisely because we were Jews and Christians. I believe that this deepening of understanding between Jews and Christians as sharing not only a troubling past, which

---

6. This and other materials indicating direct knowledge and encouragement of activities to save Jews are to be found in the aforementioned *ADSS*.

drives us apart, but a present in which we are both, equally and together, potential victims of a hatred that wishes to do violence to both of us, is one of the results of 9/11. An unintended consequence, if you will, of al-Qaeda's potentially genocidal mania.

Catholic–Jewish Dialogue

I do not think it coincidental, therefore, that, for example, the summer of 2002 saw the issuance by the representatives of the United States Conference of Catholic Bishops (USCCB) and the National Council of Synagogues of the document *Covenant and Mission*, which became the focus of (in my opinion) so much unnecessary controversy in the summer of 2009. Lest anyone make again an old mistake, this was not an official statement of the USCCB or of the Bishops' Committee for Ecumenical and Interreligious Affairs (BCEIA), as the statement itself said very clearly and unequivocally. It was the statement of a group of trained Catholic scholars well experienced in the field, who had long been involved in the dialogue with the Jewish people in this country. What the Catholics involved in the statement, myself among them, wanted to do was to take the next step in the careful building of renewed Catholic teaching about Jews and Judaism as embodied in the long list of official statements by the popes, the Holy See's Commission for Religious Relations with the Jews, and bishops' conferences around the world, including in the United States. That step, we Catholics agreed, was to make explicit what was implicit in Pope John Paul II's assertion of God's enduring covenant with the Jewish people ("a covenant never revoked by God," strengthening the Second Vatican Council's citation of St. Paul's statement of God's "irrevocable covenant" with the Jews, and removing any ambiguities from it): that God's enduring covenant with Jews must have, in the words of Cardinal Walter Kasper, the head of the Holy See's Commission for Religious Relations with the Jews, a "salvific significance" of some meaningful sort for them. If this is so, the Catholics appointed by the BCEIA agreed, then the question of God's relationship with the Jews should, for solid theological reasons, be left to God, and not interfered with by the Church.

This was not at all to diminish in any way the universal significance of the Christ event. All humans who are saved are saved through the grace of Christ's incarnation, sacrifice, and resurrection. But, as has long been Church teaching, this does not mean that an individual has to be baptized to be saved. If one lives as best as one can in the light of one's conscience,

Christ's grace will be available. If this is true of humanity in general, our reasoning went, how much more so would it be true of the Jewish people, God's first love, his permanently chosen people?

It was the notion of a theological caveat, even though presented by a pope and by the head of the Vatican's Commission for Religious Relations with Jews, that seems to have gotten the statement into trouble, at least with those who attacked it seven years after it came out. There has been since October 28, 1965, the date of the issuance by the Second Vatican Council of the Declaration *Nostra Aetate*, an understanding that no organizations would be established under Church auspices to proselytize Jews. This was because of the awareness by the Church that any such organizations would inevitably raise in Jewish hearts and minds the remembrance of the fact that virtually all such attempts over the course of two millennia of Jewish–Christian history had ended in tragedy for Jews, thus impeding and destroying the freedom of faith relationship between God and the Jews. Hence, for pastoral and historical reasons, the Church has not, and I think will not for the foreseeable future, sanction any such organizations aimed at the conversion of Jews. *Covenant and Mission*, however, took the next step beyond official statements up to that time and stated that not only for pastoral but for theological reasons there should not be any organized attempts by the Church to convert Jews. September 11, I think for all of us, certainly for me, was part of the reason we wanted to push forward the agenda on the Catholic side of the dialogue.

Cardinal Walter Kasper, the recently retired head of the Pontifical Commission for Religious Relations with the Jews, did not object to this line of reasoning, since it clearly reflected his own. His immediate predecessor, Cardinal Edward Idris Cassidy, praised the statement in his book on ecumenical, Catholic–Jewish, and interreligious relations, saying, among other things,

> The document stresses that evangelization, or mission, in the church's work cannot be separated from its faith in Jesus Christ in whom Christians find the kingdom present and fulfilled. But it points out that this evangelizing mission goes far beyond the invitation to a commitment to faith in Jesus Christ and to entry through baptism into the community of believers that is the church. It includes the church's activities of presence and witness; commitment to social development and human liberation; Christian worship, prayer, and contemplation; interreligious dialogue; and proclamation and catechesis.[7]

---

7. Edward Idris Cassidy, *Ecumenism and Interreligious Dialogue*, Rediscovering

But given the "utterly unique relationship of Christianity with Judaism," and the many aspects of this spiritual linkage, "the Catholic Church has come to recognize that its mission of preparing for the coming of the kingdom is one that is shared with the Jewish people, even if Jews do not conceive of this task christologically as the Church does." In view of this, the 2002 document "Reflections on Covenant and Mission" quotes Professor Tommaso Federici and Cardinal Walter Kasper to state that there should not be in the church any organization dedicated to the conversion of the Jews. From the Catholic point of view, Judaism is a religion that springs from divine revelation. The quotation from Cardinal Kasper runs as follows: "God's grace, which is the grace of Jesus Christ according to our faith, is available to all. Therefore, the church believes that Judaism, i.e., the faithful response of the Jewish people to God's irrevocable covenant, is salvific for them, because God is faithful to his promises."[8]

> Since, in Catholic teaching, both the church and the Jewish people abide in covenant with God, they both therefore have missions before God to undertake in the world. The church believes that the mission of the Jewish people is not restricted to their historical role as the people of whom Jesus was born "according to the flesh" (Rom 9:5) and from whom the church's apostles came. It quotes the following statement from Cardinal Ratzinger: "God's providence . . . has obviously given Israel a particular mission in this *time of the Gentiles.*" Only the Jewish people themselves can articulate their mission, "in the light of their own religious experience."[9]

The Catholic section of the document concludes with this profound statement: "With the Jewish people, the Catholic Church, in the words of *Nostra Aetate,* 'awaits the day, known to God alone, when all peoples will call on God with one voice and serve him shoulder to shoulder.'"[10]

Vatican II (New York: Paulist, 2005) 252–56.

8. "Reflections on Covenant and Mission" is available online: http://www.ccjr.us/dialogika-resources/documents-and-statements/interreligious/bceia-ncs/1056-ncs-bceia02aug12. Cf. Walter Kasper, "Dominus Iesus," Address at the 17th Meeting of the International Catholic–Jewish Liaison Committee, New York, May 1, 2001.

9. Ibid. Cf. Joseph Ratzinger, *One Covenant, Many Religions: Israel, the Church, and the World* (San Francisco: Ignatius, 1999) 104.

10. "Reflections on Covenant and Mission" (online: http://www.ccjr.us/dialogika-resources/documents-and-statements/interreligious/bceia-ncs/1056-ncs-bceia02aug12). See also Pope Paul VI, *Nostra Aetate*, October 28, 1965. Online: http://www.vatican.va/archive/hist_councils/ii_vatican_council/documents/vat-ii_decl_19651028_nostra-aetate_en.html/.

Unlike Cardinals Kasper, Cassidy, and Keeler (who had authorized it with a clarification, making even more explicit than the statement, as Cardinal Kasper had also done, the fact that all who are saved are saved through the grace of Christ), staff members of the Secretariats for Doctrine and Ecumenism and Interreligious Affairs felt that the statement needed to be clarified even further. In the summer of 2009, seven years after its release, they convinced the two bishops' committees, and through them the USCCB as a whole, to issue a statement that they had prepared without consultation with anyone in the field of Catholic–Jewish relations.[11] The statement reflected the lack of experience and training in the field of its authors. It did not refer to a single statement of the Holy See or the USCCB, a number of which were pertinent to the issues it raised. It stated, for example, that Catholics in the dialogue with Jews come to the table with an implicit intent to convert the Jews. Theologically, it took a pre-*Nostra Aetate* position that God's covenant with the Jewish people was not simply fulfilled but abrogated by the coming of Christ and the advent of the New Covenant, "historically and theologically." It ignored completely the eschatological caveat, which is that while in one sense the coming of Christ fulfilled the biblical promises, we still await their "perfect fulfillment" with his coming at the end of time. This was stated quite clearly and unambiguously by the Holy See's Commission on Religious Relations with the Jews in its first major statement in 1974: "When commenting on biblical texts, emphasis will be laid on the continuity of our faith with that of the earlier Covenant, in the perspective of the promises, without minimizing those elements of Christianity which are original. We believe that those promises were fulfilled with the first coming of Christ. But it is nonetheless true that we still await their perfect fulfillment in this glorious return at the end of time."[12]

The 1985 *Notes on the Correct Way to Present the Jews and Judaism in Catholic Preaching and Teaching*[13] place the fulfilled/not-yet-perfectly-

---

11. "A Note on Ambiguities Contained in 'Reflections on Covenant and Mission.'" This and related documents can be found on the website, http://www.ccjr.us/dialogika-resources/documents-and-statements/roman-catholic/us-conference-of-catholic-bishops. The final version of the "Note on Ambiguities" can also be found on the website of the USCCB: http://www.usccb.org/doctrine/covenant09.pdf.

12. Pontifical Commission for Religious Relations with the Jews, *Guidelines and Suggestions for Implementing the Conciliear Declaration "Nostra Aetate,"* no. 4 (December 1, 1974) II.

13. The papers, minutes, and other related materials of the Kennedy Institute Trialogue are housed in the files of the USCCB, Secretariat for Ecumenical and Interreligious Affairs, and the Shriver Institute.

fulfilled teaching, which is of course basic to the teaching of the Church, in a positive light with respect to Catholic understanding of God's enduring covenant with the Jewish people:

> 10. Furthermore, in underlining the eschatological dimension of Christianity we shall reach a greater awareness that the people of God of the Old and the New Testament are tending towards a like end in the future: the coming or return of the Messiah—even if they start from two different points of view. It is more clearly understood that the person of the Messiah is not only a point of division for the people of God but also a point of convergence (cf. *Sussidi per l'ecumenismo* of the diocese of Rome, n. 140). Thus is can be said that Jews and Christians meet in a comparable hope, founded on the same promise made to Abraham (cf. Gen 12:1–3; Heb 6:13–18).
>
> 11. Attentive to the same God who has spoken, hanging on the same word, we have to witness to one same memory and one common hope in Him who is the master of history. We must also accept our responsibility to prepare the world for the coming of the Messiah by working together for social justice, respect for the rights of persons and nations and for social and international reconciliation. To this we are driven, Jews and Christians, by the command to love our neighbor, by a common hope for the kingdom of God and by the great heritage of the Prophets. Transmitted soon enough by catechesis, such a conception would teach young Christians in a practical way to cooperate with Jews, going beyond simple dialogue (cf. *Guidelines and Suggestions for the Implementation of Nostra Aetate, No. 4*, IV).

It was a long summer and early fall, the first time that a crisis in Catholic–Jewish relations had ever been precipitated by the action of the U.S. Conference of Catholic Bishops and the first time that all five of the Jewish groups involved in dialogue with the bishops had joined together to address them with one voice. Finally, on October 13, 2009, the BCEIA issued a response to the Jewish letter, which dropped the idea of using the dialogue as a covert means of converting Jews to Christianity and spoke simply about the New Covenant fulfilling the Old (though it did not go into the careful distinctions and affirmations put forth by the Holy See, as above).

Jewish–Christian–Muslim Trialogue

If 9/11 deepened the already well-developed Jewish–Christian and more specific Catholic–Jewish dialogue, it not only deepened but spread widely Muslim–Christian and Jewish–Christian–Muslim trialogue. Those of us involved in Jewish–Christian relations reached out to Muslims in America to reassure them that the entire religion was not to be blamed for the terrorism of the few, to learn to understand them and their traditions, and to work to ensure that they understood and respected our traditions too. While I was not deeply involved in this positive surge in the number of dialogues and trialogues involving Muslims after 9/11, I had a lot of experience in the latter, especially, in the first decade of my tenure with the US Conference of Catholic Bishops.

Before I get into the discussion of my experience with the Abrahamic trialogue, as it is often called (since all three traditions regard Abraham as the father of their faith), I should doubtlessly defend my use of the term. As its critics have noted, *dialogue* does not mean words spoken between two people, but words spoken and received in such a way that the two involved are able to see into each other, and to understand how the other sees the one and the world from, as it were, the inside. The word *dialogue*, the understanding of which we owe to the Jewish philosopher Martin Buber, represents an "I–Thou" relationship as opposed to an instrumental "I–It" relationship, such as one might have with a grocery store vendor or with neighbors far down the street whom one recognizes and greets but whose life one does not really know. It is *di* as in *diaphanous*. The critics of *trialogue*, therefore, have a point of real substance in their urging that we use *trilateral dialogue* rather than *trialogue* in speaking of Jewish–Christian–Muslim relations.

In my experience, however, the realities of a two-way (say, Jewish–Christian) and a three-way dialogue are also substantive, even with religious traditions as closely intertwined as Judaism, Christianity, and Islam; so that a different word, which, while evoking the Buberian understanding, can also acknowledge that it is not the same sort of reality when the third tradition (chronologically, Islam) enters the room and sits down at the table of dialogue. True, the goals are the same and the methodology is the same. But three-way dialogue is not the same as two-way.

For one thing, the dialogue between Jews and Christians is not the same as that between Jews and Muslims or Christians and Muslims. The Jewish–Muslim dialogue can be quite close because of the similarity of their sacred tongues and the fact that *shariah* (Muslim religious law) and *halakah* (Jewish religious law) therefore share many legal terms and concepts in common. But Islam does not share sacred texts with either Jews or Christians in the way that Jews and Christians share (to wrangle over and debate for their significance for our religious lives) the Hebrew Scriptures. Indeed, it is not accurate to call Jewish–Christian dialogue an interfaith dialogue at all. We claim as our own the faith of Abraham and a share in God's enduring covenant with the Jews (however we wrangle within our Christian community over how to articulate that sense of sharing in God's one covenant with the Jews). Jesus was a Jew, and a faithful, pious Jew all his life. He was killed by the Romans as a Jew. Christianity claims to be (and is) a renewed form of Judaism, not an entirely separate religion. As the 2002 statement of the Pontifical Biblical Commission stated, Christians can and should learn from Jewish biblical interpretations how better to understand and interpret those sections of Scripture that it calls "their [the Jews'] Sacred Scriptures in the Christian Bible."[14] Likewise, Jewish biblical scholars do read and learn from and use in their own writings insights gained from Christian studies of the Hebrew Scriptures. (One cannot say "the Jewish Scriptures," of course, because the New Testament is by and large the product of Jewish authors.) Jewish–Christian relations can be called an interreligious dialogue—since we are bound (*religio*) to God by differing interpretations of the same Scriptures—but not an interfaith dialogue.

Neither Jews nor Christians can say the same thing in the same way regarding Muslim readings of the Scriptures we share in common with each other. The claim of Islam is that the original revelations to Jews and to Christians were God's word to us. But in writing down what we heard from God, we Jews and Christians made mistakes. Only the Quran, according to Islam, is accurate to God's revelation. So Muslims do not regard either the Hebrew Scriptures or the New Testament as sacred and binding upon themselves in the sense that both Jews and Christians regard and revere the Hebrew Scriptures. Thus, while the interrelatedness of the three Abrahamic traditions renders dialogue among the three necessary and holds the promise of great insight and hope, the dialogical atmosphere is different when Jews and Christians sit down from when all three are present. There are also historical differences in the relationships, of course, but these are conceivably manageable while the theological differences strike to the core of our respective faith traditions.

14. Pontifical Biblical Commission, *The Jewish People and Their Sacred Scriptures in the Christian Bible* (Vatican City: Libreria Editrice Vaticana, 2002) no. 22.

9/11: Dialogue and Trialogue

The dialogical experience that I referred to at the outset of this section of my paper, and that gave me the above reflections on dialogue and trialogue, took place over a five-year period in the late 1970s and early 1980s. For the first ten years of the thirty I spent at the USCCB, I was *de facto* in charge of Catholic–Muslim as well as Catholic–Jewish relations, since the Secretariat for Interreligious Relations, which the bishops had voted to create after the Council, had not received from the bishops any funding. Fr. Hotchkin figured, rightly or wrongly (and he usually figured right), that if I could handle two of the three Abrahamic traditions, I could probably muddle through with the third, derived as it is from its earlier faith communities. So when Sargent Shriver (then directing the Kennedy Institute in Washington) was approached by the great pioneer of Abrahamic trialogue in this country, Professor Leonard Swidler of Temple University, with the idea of the Institute sponsoring such a dialogue, Shriver asked Msgr. George Higgins if anyone at the Conference might be able to direct such a thing for the Institute and keep it, from a Catholic perspective, *kosher*, and Msgr. Higgins recommended me. It was for me and I think for all concerned a great five years.

The Kennedy Institute Trialogue went into virtually all of the areas needing mutual exploration that were, after 9/11, the staples of their early efforts. Topics ranged from creation and revelation to our understandings of the one God to our various historical memories of relations with one another. The trialogue produced papers that would have become a published book, were it not for the group's untimely demise due to incompatible responses to events in the Middle East at the crucial point when the papers, collected and edited, would have gone to the publishers.[15]

There were many great moments, however: moments of true "I–Thou" dialogical insight, which had moved us beyond many previous blocks to ever-deeper bonding and understanding. The group issued two public statements urging greater understanding, and reacting to issues of the moment. And it provided President Jimmy Carter with references from Jewish, Christian, and Muslim Scriptures and traditions, which he used in the famous meeting of Anwar Sadat and Menahem Begin.

One moment I shall never forget. The Muslims were berating us Christians for the Crusades when one of our members, a Syrian Orthodox, broke out in Arabic to remind them that the Crusades, in fact, were

---

15. The papers, minutes, and other related materials of the Kennedy Institute Trialogue are housed in the files of the U.S. Conference of Catholic Bishops, Secretariat for Ecumenical and Interreligious Affairs, and the Shriver Institute.

fought as a war of self-defense on the part of Christianity, since much of the spread of Islam had been at the expense of the traditionally Christian territories of the Middle East, North Africa, Spain, and up to the gates of Vienna. He also reminded them, in Arabic, that it was Orthodox Christians who translated the Greek philosophers into Arabic for them, thus giving them the basis for the great surge of intellectual energy that created the Golden Age of Spain and ultimately the Renaissance in Italy.

The conclusion of my reflections is stated already above. September 11 may have inaugurated a world of fear and terrorism on the one hand, but it also prompted innumerable people of goodwill—Jews, Christians, and Muslims—to turn toward one another in dialogue and deepen and intensify efforts at outreach across the permeable boundaries of our three faiths. Sometimes, good can be wrung out of evil.

It might be noted, with regard to both Christian–Muslim and Jewish–Muslim dialogue today, that whereas Jews and Christians have in their separate but very much interrelated ways come to grips with the Enlightenment (in so doing forging new understandings for themselves of the relationship between faith and reason), Islam did not have to face this profound challenge to its understanding and tradition. Judaism and Protestant Christianity, it may be said, encountered and reacted to the Enlightenment earlier than the Catholic tradition, which began to make peace with, for example, modern biblical scholarship only with Pope Pius XII's 1943 encyclical *Divino Afflante Spiritu*, and did not fully embrace it until the Second Vatican Council (1962–1965). The Council, however, not only embraced but made its own the Church's "return to history": to scientific methodology and reasoning and to an ecumenical vision of relations with other Christians, as well as a mandate to dialogue—which emerged from Judaism and Christianity—and with other major world religions. Error, the Catholic Church had come to understand, has rights. And those who disagree with Catholic theology may, and indeed will, have profound things to teach us spiritually and theologically.

Islam, however, has never had anything like a Second Vatican Council—an opportunity to encounter, take into account, and respond internally to the challenges of the modern, post-Enlightened world. This imbalance between the Jewish and Christian traditions on the one hand, and the Islamic tradition on the other, means that the three are not on the same page, or even in the same chapter, in their respective histories of development. A whole set of issues, understandings, ideas, and resolutions, which Jews and Christians in their differing yet interrelated ways share, are simply not recognized by many Muslims as applicable to them. The result can diminish the effectiveness of even the most sincere dialogue attempts.

On the other hand, as American Muslims come to grips with living within a pluralist society at the heart of which is the separation of church/synagogue/mosque and state, they will perforce be undergoing such an encounter with the Enlightenment and its many implications for how faith traditions can and must recast themselves in the light of scientific and dialogical reasoning. I have seen such happen in this country in trialogues in which I have been involved. My fervent hope and prayerful expectation is that American Muslims can communicate these new insights to the Muslim communities within the countries of their origin, thus setting the groundwork for more productive and profound dialogue among the Abrahamic traditions globally.

American Muslims, unlike their European counterparts, have no realistic hope of becoming a sizeable minority within this country, much less a majority; so they do not have the option of living in large, self-imposed, self-contained ghettoes as do most European Muslims. Thus, for them, coming to grips with pluralism as a positive value is a necessity, not a luxury. In this fact, as I noted above, I see hope for the future for all of us, Christians and Jews no less than Muslims.

seven

Defining Catholic Identity against the Jews

Pope Benedict XVI and the Question of Mission to the Jewish

JOHN T. PAWLIKOWSKI

From the second century of the Common Era until the time of the Second Vatican Council the Catholic Church has largely defined its basic identity over against Jews and Judaism. It termed itself the "New Israel"; it announced that it had replaced the Jewish people in the ongoing covenant with the Creator God. It described Jesus as fulfilling the original covenant with the Jewish people, basically leaving Judaism denuded as a valid religious tradition. Sometimes the self-definition over against Judaism was articulated in extremely vitriolic language, particularly among the church fathers, language that persisted well into the mid-twentieth century as various studies on Catholic textbooks clearly revealed. At other times the tone was somewhat softer, praising Judaism for its original covenantal understanding and its prophetic tradition but insisting that, in the end with the coming of Christ, everything good in Judaism had been absorbed by Christianity.

The legacy of Christian self-definition over against the Jews came to an abrupt halt, at least so we thought for some forty years, with chapter four of Vatican II's *Nostra Aetate*. With good reason in light of the history of the Catholic Church's "against the Jews" stance, the Canadian theologian Gregory Baum (who contributed to the original framing of the text of the conciliar document) termed this chapter the most radical change in the ordinary magisterium of the church to emerge from Vatican II.[1] *Nostra Aetate* certainly did not settle every theological issue regarding the Christian–Jewish relationship. But it set the discussion on a fundamentally new course. Jews were now to be seen as continuing in the ongoing covenantal relationship with God. They were not displaced with the coming of Christ. Jesus's positive links with the Judaism of his time were highlighted. And the historic charge of "deicide" against the Jewish community, the basis for so much theological anti-Judaism in Christianity, was declared null and void because it was a spurious charge in the first place. Jews were not exonerated by Vatican II as some newspaper headlines proclaimed at the time. Rather the Catholic Church acknowledged that they were victims of a false accusation that wreaked havoc on the Jewish community for centuries in Christian-dominated societies. *Nostra Aetate* redefined the relationship with Jews and Judaism from a perspective which viewed Christianity as standing over against Judaism, in contrast to one which saw the Jewish community in a basic partnership with the Church in the process of bringing about the final eschatological reign of God. They had truly moved, as the late Pope John Paul II put it, to a point in their mutual relationship were they had become a "blessing to one another."

But this new perspective has experienced a severe challenge in recent years. Some have begun to argue that *Nostra Aetate* was merely a "pastoral" document intended to improve social relations between Jews and Catholics but without any theological significance. In short, Vatican II did not officially change the classical theological vision of the Church's relationship with the Jewish people. The Jewish covenant is still to be viewed as coming to fulfillment in Christ and the missionizing of Jews, albeit with a special catechetics that shows respect for their initial contribution to the dynamics of human salvation, remains an imperative for Christians. The late Cardinal Avery Dulles, SJ, in his response to the study document *Reflections on Covenant and Mission*, which emerged (along with a Jewish document on the same themes) from an ongoing dialogue between the U.S. Conference of Catholic Bishops (USCCB) and the Synagogue Council of America, strongly argued that Vatican II did not settle the questions of whether the covenant with Israel remained valid and insisted that we must once again take seriously the two statements in the Letter to the Hebrews

---

1. Gregory Baum, "The Social Context of American Catholic Theology," *Proceedings of the Catholic Theological Society of America* 41 (1986) 87.

that seem to render the Jewish covenant obsolete after the Christ event.[2] He repeated this argument in a 2006 address at a conference in Washington commemorating the fortieth anniversary of *Nostra Aetate* and later published in the American conservative magazine *First Things*.[3]

More recently Cardinal Albert Vanhoye, a biblical scholar who has specialized in the study of the letter to the Hebrews for some thirty years has entered the discussion about the continued validity of the Jewish covenant. Cardinal Vanhoye is close to the present Pope as his selection to conduct an annual retreat for the papal household (including Pope Benedict himself) and to deliver the opening address at the 2008 Bishops' Synod on the Bible clearly shows. Following the same line of thought as Cardinal Dulles, Cardinal Vanhoye has insisted that Hebrews must be taken seriously in its claim about the abrogation of the Jewish covenant. While Jews may still enjoy a more generic covenant relationship their specific covenant has been supplanted by the new covenant in Christ.[4]

In addition, in the current discussion in the United States about the statement from the US Bishops' Committee on Doctrine in collaboration with the Secretariat for Ecumenical and Interreligious Affairs criticizing certain "ambiguities" in the statement *Reflections on Covenant and Mission* as well as the change introduced into the Adult Catechism which has changed the statement about the Jewish covenant from the present tense (still intact) to the past tense (fulfilled in Christ), a very disturbing attitude has surfaced.[5] This perspective coming from some people within the USCCB is saying that neither the many statements made by Pope John Paul II during his long pontificate nor the statements from the Holy See's

---

2. Avery Dulles, "Covenant and Mission," *America* (October 21, 2002, 8–11. (The article includes responses by Mary Boys, Philip Cunningham, and John T. Pawlikowski.)

3. Avery Dulles, "The Covenant with Israel," *First Things* (November 2005) 16–21. Online: http://www.firstthings.com/article/2008/08/the-covenant-with-israel/.

4. Albert Vanhoye, "The Plan of God Is a Union of Love with His People," Rome: Zenit News Service, October 2008. Online: http://www.zenit.org/article-23841?l=english/.

5. USCCB Committees on Doctrine and Interreligious Affairs, "A Note on Ambiguities Contained in 'Reflections on Covenant and MIssion,'" *Origins* 39:8 (July 2, 2009) 113–16. For a revision of this statement by US bishops, cf. Cardinal Francis George and four other bishops, "Clarification on Dialogue with Jewish Groups," *Origins* 39/19 (October 15, 2009) 308–10. On the issue of mission, cf. John T. Pawlikowski, "Maintaining Momentum in a Global Village," in *Jews and Christians in Conversation: Crossing Cultures and Generations*, ed. Edward Kessler et al. (Cambridge: Orchard Academic, 2002) 75–91. Also cf. John T Pawlikowski, "Mission and Dialogue in Contemporary Catholicism," *Modern Believing* 51/3 (July 2010) 47–55.

Commission for Religious Relations with the Jews have any magisterial authority behind them.

Recently I learned from a German colleague who serves on the Holy See's Commission for Religious Relations with the Jews that there is a certain history to such an attitude and it very much related to Cardinal Vanhoye. Immediately after Pope John Paul II's groundbreaking statement to the Jewish community in Mainz, Germany, in 1980 where he clearly rejected the notion of supersession in the Christian–Jewish relationship, Vanhoye organized a small-scale conference to reassert the primacy of Hebrews' invalidation of the Jewish covenant and undercut the vision put forth by John Paul II. This effort never achieved much success during the papacy of John Paul II and no publication ever emerged from this meeting. But clearly the seeds spread at the meeting may have finally found some fertile soil. Given the cardinal's close relationship with Benedict XVI, this effort will have to be closely monitored. It has become a major argument in the discussion about how to respond to the challenge from Orthodox, Conservative, and Reform Jewish leaders together with the Anti-Defamation League and the American Jewish Committee presented in a letter to the US bishops raising serious questions as to whether the bishops are now promoting evangelization of the Jews and have declared the Jewish covenant to be null and void. If this is the case, the Jewish leaders have asserted, the continuation of the Catholic–Jewish dialogue is in serious jeopardy. Let me add that the International Council of Christians and Jews as well as some members of the US Bishops' Advisory Committee on Catholic–Jewish Relations, myself included, have raised similar questions as the Jewish leaders in separate letters to the USCCB. I would also make the point that this should not be regarded as only an American matter. For we know that pressure for these recent statements came from Cardinal William Levada, the head of the Congregation for the Doctrine of the Faith, and the change in the Adult Catechism was recently granted a *recognitio* by the Vatican.

Finally, let me also make reference to the situation in Germany where an important statement from the Central Committee of German Catholics and Jews which has undertaken serious and constructive work in the theological implementation of *Nostra Aetate* has received considerable criticisms from members of the German Episcopal Conference for unambiguously rejecting any missionizing of Jews.[6] In an address at the Uni-

---

6. An English version of the German statement can be found online: http://www.jcrelations.net/.

versity of Cambridge in 2002, I asserted that "mission" remained a central unresolved issue in the Christian–Jewish relationship and that we had simply pushed it under the table. Some of my colleagues in the dialogue at the conference criticized me for this assertion insisting that the Catholic Church at least had given up any mission to the Jews. But regrettably I have been proven at least somewhat correct as the issue of mission now surfaces quite strongly in key countries for the Christian–Jewish dialogue such as Germany and the United States.

The above narrative can certainly engender considerable discouragement. But fortunately it is not the whole picture in terms of contemporary Catholic–Jewish relations. There are members of the Catholic hierarchy who still share a profound commitment to the vision of *Nostra Aetate* and of Pope John Paul II. One such bishop is Richard Sklba who chaired the U.S. Bishops' Secretariat for Ecumenical and Interreligious Affairs until recently and who is a biblical scholar in his own right. Bishop Sklba has written perceptively on the Christian–Jewish relationship. In the initial stages of the development of the document from the U.S. Bishops' Committee on Doctrine Bishop Sklba stood up and refused to sign off on the first version of the present statement relative to *Reflections on Covenant and Mission* which had even harsher language than the revised text. Unfortunately Bishop Sklba's leadership of the committee expired just after he took this action. And we have also seen important episcopal support within the German hierarchy on these questions in recent months. Regrettably, and I say that with continuing respect for his contributions to the Christian–Jewish dialogue over several years, Cardinal Walter Kasper had decided to stay on the sidelines during the current conflicts arguing that these are matters for the local church. Yet we know that pressure has come from CDF on the core issues of mission and fulfillment in Christ. And certainly the American and German churches have been in the forefront of the efforts to implement Vatican II on the Jewish question. Hence an attack on their efforts clearly has implications beyond their national boundaries.

How, we must ask, does Pope Benedict XVI fit into what appears to many as a deteriorating situation in terms of the Catholic–Jewish relationship? This picture is rather complex, Pope Benedict entered the papacy with some track record with respect to Catholic–Jewish relations. This is especially true in terms of the theological understanding of Christianity's relationship with Judaism. Benedict XVI made a number of brief addresses in the context of the Christian–Jewish relationship in the early

Defining Catholic Identity against the Jews

part of his papacy. The first was in connection with a June 9, 2005, visit to the Vatican by representatives of the International Jewish Committee for Interreligious Consultations.[7] This is the global body established by the major organizations within the world Jewish community for official dialogue with the Vatican, the World Council of Churches, and other international religious institutions. The second statement was delivered by the pope during his visit to the synagogue in Cologne as part of his participation in World Youth Day 2005.[8] The third was a letter sent to Cardinal Walter Kasper on October 26, 2005, the day prior to the Vatican's official commemoration of the fortieth anniversary of Vatican II's *Nostra Aetate*.[9] In all these statements Pope Benedict expresses his firm determination to follow in the footsteps of Pope John Paul II whose papacy is credited with providing chapter four of *Nostra Aetate* a solid footing in Catholicism. *"It is my intention to continue on this path"*—these words, italicized in the official text released by the Vatican from the June 2005 meeting with the international Jewish leadership, constitute the most important statement in these initial addresses.

In these early statements as a whole, but especially in the more substantive Cologne declaration, Pope Benedict clearly rejects anti-Semitism in any form. On this point he has been firm and consistent through his papacy. While he has refrained from applying the adjective "sinful" to anti-Semitism, something that John Paul II did on several occasions, there is little doubt that Benedict XVI shares with his predecessor a fundamental intolerance for anti-Semitism in any guise. He was quite forceful in this regard in his address in Cologne: "Today, sadly, we are witnessing the rise of anti-Semitism and various forms of general hostility toward foreigners. How can we fail to see in this a reason for concern and vigilance? The Catholic Church is committed—and I reaffirm this again today—to tolerance, respect, friendship and peace between all people, cultures and religion."[10] He repeated this condemnation of anti-Semitism in an address

---

7. Pope Benedict XVI, "First Major Meeting with World Jewish Leaders," *Origins* 35/6 (June 2005) 88–89.

8. Pope Benedict XVI, "Visit to the Cologne Synagogue," *Origins* 35/12 (September 2005) 205–7.

9. Pope Benedict XVI, "Letter of His Holiness Benedict XVI to the President of the Commission for Religious Relations with the Jews . . ." Online: http://www.vatican.va/holy_father/benedict_xvi/letters/2005/documents/hf_ben-xvi_let_20051026_nostra-aetate_en.html/.

10. Pope Benedict XVI, "Visit to the Cologne Synagogue," *Origins* 35/12 (September 2005) 205–7.

to Jewish leaders on his visit to France where he insisted that anti-Semitism "can never be theologically justified."[11]

Pope Benedict's remarks regarding the Holocaust during his papacy, particularly in his Cologne address and his statement at the Birkenau extermination camp where I was present, remain somewhat more questionable. And his lifting of the ban of excommunication from Bishop Richard Williamson of the breakaway Society of St. Pius X put into serious question his position on the Holocaust. While he immediately followed this regrettable incident with strong condemnations of the Holocaust, including one in the presence of American Jewish leaders where, as Rabbi David Rosen, who was present in the room told me, the pope spoke with considerable emotional intensity, questions still linger about this episode. But, while Benedict XVI clearly had not one iota of sympathy for Holocaust denial, he continues to exhibit a profound reluctance to confront Christian complicity in the Holocaust. He tends to characterize the Holocaust as an attack on all religion by fundamentally pagan forces. In this regard he has been far less forthright than John Paul II or, for example, the French Bishops. There is little question in my mind that this reluctance to deal with the dark side of Catholicism during the period of the Holocaust is rooted in his general reluctance to acknowledge that ecclesiology can be affected directly by how the church acts in historical time. For Benedict XVI the church is fundamentally ahistorical and is in no way impacted at its core by the moral failures of its members.

Some positive development on the question of Christian complicity is finally to be seen in Benedict XVI's most recent speech on Catholic–Jewish relations given during his visit to the synagogue in Rome on January 17, 2010.[12] In this address Pope Benedict does make his own the well-known words of Pope John Paul II acknowledging Christian complicity in the Holocaust, which in written form John Paul had placed in the Western Wall during his visit to Jerusalem.[13] While this gesture certainly is a welcome advance in Pope Benedict's perspective, it would have been good if, as a German Christian, he would have added some words of his own regarding the issue. Prior to entering the synagogue the pope stopped at the memorial site for the Jews of Rome who were rounded up by the

11. Pope Benedict XVI, "French Visit: Meeting with Jewish Leaders." *Origins* 38/16 (September 2008) 248.

12. Pope Benedict XVI, "Visit to the Rome Synagogue, January 17, 2010." Online: http://www.vatican.va/holy_father/benedict_xvi/speeches/2010/january/documents/hf_ben-xvi_spe_20100117_sinagoga_en.html/.

13. http://www.ccjr.us/dialogika-resources/...john-paul-ll/338-jp2-oomar26/.

Defining Catholic Identity against the Jews

Nazis. Though he spoke movingly of their suffering, he never tied it in any way to the lack of Catholic response, including that of Pope Pius XII. In fact, in offering a rather weak defense of Pius XII during his remarks in the synagogue in response to Jewish and Christian criticisms of Pius XII, he undercut to a degree his first embrace of the notion of Catholic complicity in the opening part of his synagogue address.

The most important aspect of Pope Benedict's statements on Jews and Judaism for our discussion relates to his theological perspective on the Christian–Jewish relationship, something that can have practical import as the language he chose for his Good Friday prayer in the Tridentine rite clearly shows. To understand his present outlook we need to go back as far as October 1987. In an interview in the Italian Catholic publication *Il Sabato* on October 24th then-Cardinal Ratzinger, speaking to the interviewer in German as head of CDF, argued that church teaching must always reflect the "theological line" that Judaism finds its fulfillment in Christianity. The aim of the dialogue is to arrive at truth rather than to exchange opinions. For Cardinal Ratzinger in that interview, Christianity must see itself as united with the faith of Abraham, but also emphasize the reality of Jesus Christ in which the faith of Abraham finds its fulfillment.[14] This interview caused widespread negative reaction in Jewish circles and led to the postponement of a scheduled session of the official Vatican–Jewish dialogue. Subsequently the cardinal claimed that his German was not accurately translated by the Italian interviewer. He wanted to emphasize that this was the Catholic perspective, which he recognized Jews would not likely accept. This interview I judge important because it began a line of thinking on the part of Cardinal Ratzinger/Pope Benedict that has remained fairly consistent. Hence Cardinal Ratzinger has always maintained the position that we can only speak of a single covenant linking Jews and Christians. Any talk of dual covenants is tantamount to heresy.

For a rather brief moment some years ago it looked as though Ratzinger might be open to some adjustments in his earlier perspective. There is no question that Cardinal Ratzinger regarded the Christian–Jewish relationship as *sui generis* theologically, something clearly acknowledged in an endnote in the official CDF notification on the writings of the late Fr. Jacques Dupuis, SJ, in particular his volume *Towards a Christian Theology of Religious Pluralism* where Cardinal Ratzinger insists that the

---

14. Cf. Ari L. Goldman, "Cardinal's Remarks on Jews Questioned," *New York Times*, November 18, 1987, 10; "Dialogue with Jews must reflect Catholic theology, says official," *National Catholic Reporter*, October 30, 1987.

relationship between Christianity and Judaism requires "an altogether singular explanation."[15]

At the end of the nineties and in early 2000 Cardinal Ratzinger did offer some succinct perspectives that appeared to make him somewhat more open in terms of theological issues in the Christian–Jewish relationship than was evident in his controversial remarks made in 1987. These perspectives came in two articles, one book, and in the laudatory introduction he wrote for the 2001 Pontifical Biblical Commission's (PBC's) two hundred plus page monograph on *The Jewish People and Their Sacred Scriptures in the Christian Bible*.[16] The articles were "The Heritage of Abraham: The Gift of Christmas," which was published in the December 29, 2000, edition of *L'Osservatore Romano*[17] and a Spring 1998 essay in *Communio* entitled "Interreligious Dialogue and Jewish–Christian Relations." The latter piece was eventually incorporated into a full-length book (though in a somewhat different translation), *Many Religions, One Covenant: Israel, the Church, and the World*.[18]

In the two major articles Ratzinger seemed to propose an understanding of the Christian–Jewish relationship as one in which the two faith communities move along distinctive, but not separated paths. Ratzinger clearly affirms that the Jewish community advances to final salvation through continuing obedience to its revealed covenantal tradition. In the end Christ will confirm that Jewish covenant. Thus Christ remains central to ultimate Jewish salvation, though it is not fully clear whether Ratzinger believes Jews must explicitly acknowledge Christ to attain full salvation. What does seem to be present in these two is an acknowledgement that there is no need for Christians to proselytize Jews in the preeschatological era. Here Ratzinger seems to be close to Cardinal Kasper's explicit assertion that the church has no need to proselytize Jews since they are already part of the one covenantal relationship with God, though, unlike Kasper, he does not make his position as clear cut. This viewpoint on the

---

15. Jacques Dupuis, *Towards a Christian Theology of Religious Pluralism* (Maryknoll, NY: Orbis, 1997). The Note from the Congregation of Sacred Doctrine was issued on January 24, 2001.

16. Pontifical Biblical Commission, *The Jewish People and Their Scriptures in the Christian Bible* (Vatican City: Libreria Edifice Vaticana, 2002).

17. Joseph Ratzinger, "The Heritage of Abraham: The Gift of Christmas," *L'Osservatore Romano*, December 29, 2001, 1.

18. Joseph Ratzinger, "Interreligious Dialogue and Jewish-Christian Relations," *Communio* 25 (Spring 1998) 29–41; Ratzinger, *Many Religions, One Covenant: Israel, the Church and the World* (San Francisco: Ignatius, 1999).

two distinctive paths may account for Pope Benedict's claimed willingness to endorse an exclusively eschatological interpretation of his Tridentine Good Friday prayer put forth by Cardinal Kasper, though we have no evidence for such an endorsement save for Cardinal Kasper's claim.

The 2001 Pontifical Biblical Commission's document, despite some significant limitations in the way it portrays postbiblical Judaism, makes an important contribution to the development of a new constructive understanding of the Christian–Jewish relationship. Picking up on *Nostra Aetate*'s central assertion that Jews remain in the ongoing covenant after the Christ Event, the document includes two statements that are particularly relevant for any discussion of such a theological understanding.

In the first of these assertions, which Cardinal Ratzinger explicitly supported in his introduction to the Pontifical Biblical Commission's document, one finds the statement that Jewish messianic hopes are not in vain. In other words, there exists an authentic, parallel interpretation of the texts of the Hebrew Scriptures on the part of the Jews which stands side by side with the interpretation of such texts within the New Testament. Though this is rather oblique language and likely will not inspire loud cheers from the Jewish side, it seems to move in a direction similar to the distinctive paths notion advocated by Cardinal Kasper when he wrote, "if they [i.e., the Jews] follow their own conscience and believe in God's promises as they understand them in their religious tradition they are in line with God's plan."[19] But since Kasper has also insisted that we must retain a universal significance for Christ in any interreligious dialogue, including with Jews, he would seem to be close to Ratzinger's idea of eschatological confirmation of the Jewish path to salvation through Christ. At a conference at Cambridge University in December 2004, in response to a question I put to him, Kasper strongly insisted that there exists only one salvific path in the end, not two parallel ones. But Jews on that singular path advance in ways that are distinctive from the ways of Christians. Obviously considerable ambiguity remains in the perspectives both of Ratzinger/Benedict and Kasper.

The second affirmative statement with the Pontifical Biblical Commission's document, a statement not explicitly mentioned in Cardinal Ratzinger's introduction, is the claim that when the Jewish Messiah comes

---

19. Walter Kasper, "The Commission for Religious Relations with the Jews: A Crucial Endeavor of the Catholic Church." Address at Boston College on November 6, 2002. Online: http://www.bc.edu/dam/files/research_sites/cjl/texts/cjrelations/resources/articles/Kasper_6Novo2.htm/. See also Kasper, "Christians, Jews and the Thorny Question of Mission," *Origins* 32:28 (2002).

he will have the same traits already recognized by Christians in Christ. While this assertion is also quite oblique, perhaps deliberately so, I have argued that it may provide some additional opening for Jewish distinctiveness within a single covenantal framework. For the document seems to leave open the question whether Jews must name these messianic traits also revealed in and through Jesus in explicitly Christological language. Can Jews authentically express such messianic traits in theological language and symbols more in keeping with their tradition? I have explored this question at further length in an essay in the *Irish Theological Quarterly*. The PBC document does not clearly say they can; but neither does it seem automatically to rule out a distinctive set of terms in Judaism. And it appears to put the two messianic revelations on more or less equal footing. One has to assume that Cardinal Ratzinger had at least some openness to such an idea since he did not object to the inclusion of this language in the document which ultimately depended on his approval as head of CDF.

In any discussion of Pope Benedict's views on a theology of the Christian–Jewish relationship one must also go to the pope's book (written in the name of Joseph Ratzinger theologian) titled *Jesus of Nazareth: From the Baptism in the Jordan to the Transfiguration*.[20] In chapter 4 of this volume Ratzinger enters into a dialogue with a book by the Jewish scholar Jacob Neusner in which Neusner has created a mythical dialogue between himself and Jesus involving the Sermon on the Mount. In this dialogue Neusner strongly objects to Jesus referring to himself as embodying Israel's Torah. Ratzinger jumps in to say that Neusner has hit the nail on the head in terms of the basic difference between Judaism and Christianity. Jesus, in the eyes of Ratzinger, has become both Torah and Temple, something that Neusner strongly rejects. The problem with this exchange is that the mythical dialogue presents a rather stereotypical view both of Judaism and Christianity in which neither Neusner nor Ratzinger really introduce more complicated perspectives on the Jewish–Christian relationship emerging from recent biblical scholarship. A Jewish biblical scholar such as Mark Nanos sees some positive possibilities in the "Jesus as Torah" language as does the Catholic German theologian Hans Hermann Henrix, a member of the Holy See's Commission for Religious Relations with the Jews. But both insist that such language requires a far

---

20. Pope Benedict XVI, *Jesus of Nazareth: From Baptism in the Jordan to the Transfiguration* (New York: Doubleday, 2007). Recently a sequel was published: Part 1: *Jesus of Nazareth, Part 2: Holy Week: From the Entrance into Jerusalem to the Resurrection* (New York: Doubleday, 2011). In this volume Pope Benedict affirms the continuity of the Jewish covenant and appears to reject organized efforts to convert Jews.

more developed understanding of *nomos* than Ratzinger or Neusner offer us in this exchange.

In considering Pope Benedict's theological outlook relative to the Church's relationship with Judaism we also need to factor into the mix the controversial declaration *Dominus Iesus* released by the CDF in 2000, which most commentators see as coming directly from the hand of the then Cardinal Ratzinger. *Dominus Iesus* raised serious concerns within the Jewish community, though not as severe as in certain sectors of the non-Catholic Christian community. Cardinal Edward Idris Cassidy and then Archbishop Kasper along with Archbishops William Keeler and Michael Fitzgerald did everything possible to calm the waters. Cassidy and Kasper insisted immediately that the document did not pertain to the Jews. That viewpoint seemed to have prevailed though it would have been much easier to argue that if *Dominus Iesus* had itself explicitly excluded Jews from its framework. For the logic of its argumentation would seem to apply to all non-Christian religions, including Judaism. The entire ethos of the document is such that it places Catholicism above every other religious tradition. Hence Judaism by implication is relegated to a fundamentally inferior position along with all other faiths.

Overall Pope Benedict XVI's theology of the Christian–Jewish relationship remains ambiguous at best, sometimes clearly leaning in a pre-*Nostra Aetate* direction. He has never developed the theological kernels, if I may call them that, which he put forth a decade ago nor has he ever repeated even the kernels as pope. While he likely endorses the words of the last Synod of Bishops on Christianity's deep connection with the Jewish tradition and that Jesus did not come to abolish the law, his perspective is tilted towards an understanding of the fulfillment of the Jewish covenant in Christ that borders on supersessionism. For example, in a March 15, 2006, speech during a Wednesday General Audience at the Vatican in which he launched a new cycle of catechesis on the relationship between Christ and the Church the pope spoke of the arrival of the definitive eschatological time in Jesus: "the time for rebuilding God's people, the people of the twelve tribes, which is now converted into a universal people, the Church." The twelve tribes, Benedict added, are "reunited in a new covenant, the full and perfect accomplishment of the old."[21] And in a widely publicized letter to an Italian senator for inclusion in a book by

---

21. Pope Benedict XVI, Speech at Wednesday General Audience, March 15, 2006. Cf. Center for Christian-Jewish Learning at Boston College, 2006: http://www.vatican.va/holy_father/benedict_xvi/audiences/2006/documents/hf_ben-xvi_aud_20060315_en.html.

the senator on interreligious dialogue Pope Benedict basically returns to the perspective of *Dominus Iesus*: that Catholicism possesses the full truth so that it ultimately has nothing to learn theologically from interreligious dialogue, including by implication the dialogue with Judaism. Such dialogue may enhance collaboration on issues of justice and positively impact culture but it offers no possibility of exposing new truth from the Catholic perspective. So all the talk about "learning from Judaism" in some of the pope's more popular statements to the Jewish community seems to ring hollow and takes on a very superficial flavor. In an address for the annual celebration of Mission Sunday in global Catholicism in October 2009, the pope called for a renewed commitment to the *missio ad gentes* on the part of all Catholics, to establishing the salvific sovereignty of Christ over all peoples, a statement that brought a strong rebuttal from Jewish and Hindu leaders in India.

Once more the recent synagogue address in Rome seems to return us to the possibility of a more positive development of the theology of the Christian–Jewish relationship. The potential is definitely there as Pope Benedict spoke of the Jewish covenant in the present tense, not the past, and turned to the 2001 Pontifical Biblical Commission document as well as classical Jewish sources in mounting his argument. A letter to the pope from the leadership of the International Jewish Committee for Interreligious Consultations (IJCIC) following his address praised the words of the pope and interpreted them as a papal endorsement of the continuing validity of the Jewish covenant. But the letter also correctly acknowledged that there is need for further clarification because certain developments within Catholicism such as the change in the Adult Catechism in the United States seem to move the language regarding the Jewish covenant back to the pre–Vatican II past tense. So there is need for further clarification about the matter. Should the Adult Catechism, for example, be returned to its original present tense description of the Jewish covenant in light of Pope Benedict's statements at the Rome synagogue? Only time will tell the full impact of this statement on a theology of the Christian–Jewish relationship within official Catholicism.

The above narrative can lead to considerable pessimism about the future prospects for advancement in the Catholic–Jewish dialogue. But let me insist at this point that it is not the complete picture by any means. Very positive developments continue in the scholarly world and in classroom teaching. Too many people, particularly within the Jewish leadership, tend to ignore these positive developments, giving the impression

Defining Catholic Identity against the Jews

that the institutional relationship is the only one worth considering. Yet this "theological magisterium," as the late Cardinal Avery Dulles once termed it while he was still in his creative rather than his later critical mode, I would maintain is having a stronger impact on many people in the Catholic Church, particularly at the university level, than the more official magisterial pronouncements. There is no doubt that we are seeing a widening gap between the two levels of teaching, one that may not be overcome for the foreseeable future.

Let me now offer a brief sketch of some of the new developments in understanding the Christian–Jewish relationship, particularly in the time of its origins. Most of this new scholarship associated with the so-called parting-of-the-ways discussion and the new perspectives on Paul and Judaism (especially his views on Torah) has been undertaken by biblical scholars, both Christian and Jewish. Regrettably it has not in the main significantly impacted systematic or liturgical theology as yet, though some breakthroughs are beginning to occur. Reconsideration of the controversial passages in Hebrews that have been interpreted by scholars such as Dulles as seemingly abrogating the specific covenant with the Jewish people after Christ is also part of this new enterprise.

The scholarship continuing to emerge from the "parting of the ways" research is doing much to reintegrate Jesus and the early church within the wide tent that constituted the Jewish community in the first and second centuries of the Common Era. It has clearly tended to push back the date for significant separation between church and synagogue well beyond the end of the first century and even later as we move to the Christian East. And even when the separation did occur this scholarship has brought forth evidence of some continuing constructive interaction. To emphasize this point one important collection of essays looking at this question has been titled *The Ways That Never Parted*.[22]

Early on in the "parting of the ways" research my former colleague in the cluster of theological schools at the University of Chicago, Dr. Robin Scroggs, offered a concise summary of the directions in which this research was taking us.[23] His analysis was favorably quoted by the late Joseph Cardinal Bernardin of Chicago, an episcopal leader in the Christian–Jewish dialogue, in his own writings on the relationship between the Church and

---

22. Adam H. Becker and Annette Yoshiro Reed, *The Ways That Never Parted: Jews and Christians in Late Antiquity and the Middle Ages*, Texte und Studien zum antiken Judentum 95 (Tübingen: Mohr/Siebeck, 2003).

23. Robin Scroggs, "The Judaizing of the New Testament," *Chicago Theological Seminary Register* (Winter 1986) 1.

the Jewish People. Scroggs made the following affirmations in his distillation of the new scholarship on Jesus's relationship with Judaism and on the Jewish setting of early Christianity. (1) The movement begun by Jesus and continued after his death in Palestine can best be described as a reform movement within Judaism. There is little extant evidence during this period that Christians had a separate identity from the Jews. (2) The Pauline missionary movement, as Paul understood it, was a Jewish mission that focused on the Gentiles as the proper object of God's call to his people. (3) Prior to the end of the Jewish war with the Romans which ended in 70 CE, there was no such reality as Christianity. Followers of Jesus did not have a self-understanding of themselves as a religion over against Judaism. A distinctive Christian identity only began to emerge after the Jewish–Roman war. And (4) the later sections of the New Testament all show some signs of a movement towards separation, but they also generally retain some contact with their Jewish matrix.

Another pioneering scholar in the initial phase of the "parting of the ways" discussion was the late Anthony Saldarini. In various essays he underlined the continuing presence of the "followers of the Way" in the wide tent of Judaism over the first few centuries. Saldarini especially underscored the ongoing nexus between Christian communities and their Jewish neighbors in Eastern Christianity, whose theological outlook is most often ignored in presentations about the early church within Western Christian theology.[24]

As the profound reevaluation of the church's origins begun by scholars such as Scroggs and Saldarini has continued we see further development of the initial themes. The biblical scholar John Meier in the third volume of his comprehensive study of the New Testament understandings of Jesus argues that from a careful examination of the New Testament evidence Jesus must be seen as presenting himself to the Jewish community of his time as an eschatological prophet and miracle worker in the likeness of Elijah. He was not interested in creating a separatist sect or holy remnant along the lines of the Qumran community. But he did envision the development of a special religious community within Israel. The idea that this community "within Israel would slowly undergo a process

---

24. Anthony J. Saldarini, "Jews and Christians in the First Two Centuries: The Changing Paradigm," *Shofar* 10 (1992) 32–43; Saldarini, "Christian Anti-Judaism: The First Century Speaks to the Twenty-First Century," The Joseph Cardinal Bernadin Jerusalem Lecture 1999 (Chicago: Archdiocese of Chicago, The American Jewish Committee, Spertus Institute of Jewish Studies and the Jewish United Fund/Jewish Community Relations Council, 1999)..

Defining Catholic Identity against the Jews

of separation from Israel as it pursued a mission to the Gentiles in the present world—the long-term result being that his community would become predominantly Gentile itself—finds no place in Jesus' message or practice."[25]

In a more recent study David Frankfurter adds further to the notion of significant intertwining between Christians and Jews for a period well after Jesus' lifetime. He has insisted that within the various "clusters'" of groups that included Jews and Christians there existed a "mutual influence persisting through late antiquity." There is evidence for a degree of overlap that, all things considered, threatens every construction of an historically distinct Christianity before at least the mid-second century."[26]

The growing number of biblical scholars who have become engaged in this "parting of the ways" discussion all stress the great difficulty in locating Jesus with any precision within the ever-changing context in the first century. Some speak of "Judaisms" and "Christianities" in this volatile period, almost all involving some mixture of continued Jewish practice with new insights drawn from the ministry and preaching of Jesus. For scholars such as Paula Fredriksen even speaking of the "parting of the ways" is unhelpful because it implies two solid blocks of believers. The various groups in fact were entangled for at least a couple of centuries. So, as Daniel Boyarin has rightly insisted, we cannot speak of Judaism as "the mother" or "the elder brother" of Christianity in a simplistic way. These are essentially linear images that this new scholarship has discredited as misleading in terms of the actual reality. Rather, what eventually came to be known as Judaism and Christianity in the Common Era resulted from a complicated, parallel "co-emergence" process over an extended period of time during which various themes became associated with one or two major focal points. Many factors contributed to this eventual differentiation including Roman retaliation against "the Jews" for the late first century revolt against the occupation of Palestine and the development of a strong "against the Jews" teaching during the patristic era. The "conversion" of Emperor Constantine also proved decisive for the eventual split into two distinctive religious communities.

25. John P. Meier, *A Marginal Jew: Rethinking the Historical Jesus*, vol. 3, *Companions and Competitors* (New York: Doubleday, 2001).

26. David Frankfurter, "Beyond Jewish Christianity: Continuing Religious Subcultures of the Second and Third Centuries and Their Documents," in *The Ways that Never Parted: Jews and Christians in Late Antiquity and the Middle Ages*, ed. Adam H. Becker and Annette Yashiro Reed, Texte und Studien zum antiken Judentum 95 (Tübingen: Mohr/Siebeck, 2003) 131–43.

Within the overall "parting of the ways" scholarship one of the most important results has been the significant reevaluation of Paul's outlook on Judaism. Traditionally Paul has been viewed both in popular and scholarly circles in Christianity as in many ways its founder. He has been credited with bringing about the decisive break with Judaism, largely based on the increasingly discredited master narrative in Acts, through his rejection of any Torah obligations for Gentile converts in the first century at the so-called Council of Jerusalem. Paul has often been portrayed as espousing a view in which Christianity clearly holds a position of theological superiority over Judaism. This view of Paul continued to prevail in most Christian circles during the recent Pauline Jubilee year, including in many speeches by Pope Benedict XVI, despite its increasing abandonment by a growing number of Pauline scholars.

Increasingly Paul is now being viewed as an integral member of the complicated Jewish–Christian scene brought to the surface through the "parting of the ways" scholarship rather than someone who stood totally apart from this scene and repudiated its basic orientation. Shortly before his death the prominent New Testament scholar Raymond Brown said in a public speech in Chicago that he had now become convinced that Paul had a very high regard for Torah, including its ritual dimensions, and that, if he had a son, would likely have had him circumcised. Even Paul's "Christological" reflections are now seen as having links to parts of the Jewish mystical tradition of the time. The Jewish mystical approach to Paul has been further developed in recent years, including in a new volume by Benjamin D. Sommer of the Jewish Theological Seminary in New York titled *The Bodies of God and the World of Ancient Israel*.[27]

The new scholarship on Paul and Judaism, now moving into a second phase that is bringing Paul into even greater continuing relationship with Judaism and respect for its Torah, is clearly undercutting how the Pauline materials have been used classically in Christian systematic theology and ethics. Major projects such as the multi-year effort on Paul and Judaism at the Catholic University of Leuven in Belgium are definitely moving in this direction and re-uniting Paul in a profound way with the Judaism of his time. In all the papers presented at a September 2009 conference at Leuven under the sponsorship of this project there was considerable emphasis on Paul's emphasis on the church's continued linkage with Judaism despite his desire to find a way to include Gentiles in the covenantal relationship

---

27. Benjamin D. Sommer, *The Bodies of God and the World of Ancient Israel* (Cambridge: Cambridge University Press, 2009).

renewed in Christ without forcing observance of all ritual obligations upon them.

One final point in terms of positive developments that have occurred in recent scholarship: It concerns the Letter to the Hebrews and its controversial passages about the abolition of the Jewish covenant being promoted anew by the likes of Cardinals Vanhoye and Dulles. While there is limited scholarship interest in Hebrews a number of key voices such as Alan Mitchell[28] and Luke Timothy Johnson[29] do exist. In major recent volumes on Hebrews they have both argued that the letter is directed exclusively to Christians to sustain their faith and does little to settle the issue of the ongoing validity of the Jewish covenant. This new biblical scholarship substantially undercuts the attempt by Dulles and Vanhoye to interject Hebrews back into the discussion of the theology of the Christian–Jewish relationship over against Vatican II's reliance on Romans 9–11.

Overall then we discern a growing movement away from the historic model of Catholic identity being stated over against the Jews towards an embrace of one that centers on Christian–Jewish partnership within key elements of the scholarly community. This is continuing to challenge the growing movement in certain Catholic circles to return at least in part to the classical "over against." I see no real resolution of this tension anytime soon. But I can say that the scholarly community is very unlikely to cease continuing on its recent road simply because the institutional church tries to reassert dominance of the older model.

The pursuit of a new model certainly faces continuing problems and challenges, and that includes challenges for the Jewish side. The historic commitment to mission and evangelization in Christianity cannot be simplistically discarded. Freedom of religious expression, including the right to engage in mission, needs to be protected within limits. But we cannot glibly continue to maintain that mission and dialogue are easily compatible. They are not without major refinement in the approach to mission. The new "parting of the ways" scholarship represents one major challenge to traditional notions of mission that requires ongoing profound reflection. Perhaps my major source of consolation in the midst of the growing tension in terms of Catholic–Jewish relations is that major, constructive change never comes easily. It is that awareness that sustains myself and

---

28. Alan Mitchell, *Hebrews*, Sacra Pagina 13 (Collegeville, MN: Liturgical, 2007).

29. Luke Timothy Johnson, *Hebrews: A Commentary*, New Testament Library (Louisville: Westminster John Knox, 2006).

many of my colleagues as we continue to pursue a new model of partnership despite the odds against us.

A brief word, in conclusion, on how the dialogical model emerging in the Christian–Jewish relationship as a replacement for the traditional confrontational model impacts the developing relationship between Christianity and Islam. The dynamic in this regard is somewhat different but there are parallels as well. Christianity did not see itself as the fulfillment of Islam in the way it did with regard to Judaism. But in arguing for the total fulfillment of the biblical tradition in the Christian church it rejected any possible learning from Islamic interpretations of the Hebrew Scriptures and the New Testament. So there certainly exist similarities with the church's classical outlook on Judaism. The major difference is that the church regarded Judaism as having authentic revelation even though Christianity was seen to have absorbed that authentic revelation after Christ. Christianity has never acknowledged any authentic revelation within Islam.

The emergence of the dialogical model in the Christian–Jewish relationship along with a far more critical and nuanced perspective on "fulfillment" in Christianity as part of this model will necessitate some issues such as "authentic revelation" and "fulfillment" relative to Islam. While Christianity will certainly never accept any notion of Islamic "fulfillment" of Judaism and Christianity, it will need to become far more open to possible new authentic understandings of biblical revelation through the lens of Islam. In some ways such a development represents a far greater challenge to Christian identity than even the emerging understanding of profound Jewish–Christian theological bonding.

eight

This I Believe

MARY C. BOYS

Readers who listen to National Public Radio (NPR) may be attuned to a brief segment, "This I Believe." The NPR website describes "This I Believe" as a "national media project engaging millions of people in writing, sharing, and discussing the core values and beliefs that guide their daily lives." It instructs potential contributors to frame their essay in a concrete belief or conviction. "Then tell us a compelling story about how you came to hold that belief, or a time that belief was challenged, or how that belief shapes your daily activities."[1]

This I believe: interreligious dialogue is holy work. It summons us to the sacred terrain of the divine where we must take off our shoes, lest we tread carelessly or unsympathetically on another's belief or practice. It strips us of superficial presuppositions and calls us to extend the horizons of our knowledge. It invites us to view our own tradition in the mirror of the Other's eyes. It requires us to develop empathy as we engage with persons who, though different from us in profound ways, also bear the image of the divine.

This I believe: the holy work of dialogue with Jews and study of Judaism are imperative for Christian theology. NPR's contributors must adhere to a three-minute limit. I can most succinctly express what I believe about being a Christian theologian in three sentences: "We believe that revising Christian teaching about Judaism and the Jewish people is a central and indispensable obligation of theology in our time. It is essential that Christianity both understand and represent Judaism accurately, not only

---

1. Online: http://www.thisibelieve.org/about/.

as a matter of justice for the Jewish people, but also for the integrity of Christian faith, which we cannot proclaim without reference to Judaism. Moreover, since there is a unique bond between Christianity and Judaism, revitalizing our appreciation of Jewish religious life will deepen our Christian faith."

The use of first-person plural suggests that these sentences represent more than a personal belief—and they are. They appear in "A Sacred Obligation," a statement issued in 2002 by the Christian Scholars Group on Christian–Jewish Relations and which I had a hand in writing as a member of that group.[2]

For much of its history, Christianity has understood itself as superseding Judaism. Consequently, its theology has typically represented Judaism as legalistic and tribal, as the mere promise to the fulfillment Christianity represents. Beginning in the late 1940s, however, with the formation of the International Conference of Christians and Jews, and given a critical stimulus by the Roman Catholic Church's *Nostra Aetate* in 1965, many Christian denominations have been engaged in rethinking their stance toward Jews and Judaism. "A Sacred Obligation" articulates the conviction of our study group that the work of revising Christian teaching in light of a more adequate understanding of Jews and Judaism belongs not on the periphery of the church's theological agenda but at its center. Uprooting inadequate conceptions of Judaism that too often accompanied Christian truth claims is a way of doing justice to a people that has suffered greatly at the hands of those who used the charge of "Christ killers" to rationalize vilification and violence. Revising Christian teaching is also a way of revitalizing it, discovering previously unrecognized layers in the Scriptures, engaging with the insights of Jewish scholars, and breathing new life into central doctrines.

Because from its origins Christianity had to justify itself vis-à-vis Judaism, much Christian self-understanding was by nature "over against" Judaism. Seeing Jesus as the fulfillment of God's promises to Israel and itself as *verus Israel*, Christians typically understood Judaism to have no further reason for existence, as the light of Christ thereby extinguished the

---

2. Issued on September 5, 2002, and signed by the then twenty-one members of the ecumenical Christian Scholars Group on Christian–Jewish Relations. For the history of this group, see online, http://www.bc.edu/research/cjl/meta-elements/sites/partners/csg/history.htm. "A Sacred Obligation" is a brief statement available in full online: http://www.jcrelations.net/en/?item=986; the jcrelations.net website also has it available in translation into eight languages. An anthology of essays by the Christian Scholars Group develops the statement; see Mary C. Boys, ed., *Seeing Judaism Anew: Christianity's Sacred Obligation* (Lanham, MD: Rowman & Littlefield, 2005)

"light of the nations."[3] For centuries the church premised its superiority on what it regarded as an outmoded, lesser religious tradition. *It therefore never developed a theology adequate to explain itself in light of the enduring character of Judaism.*

The challenge of our time—one my colleagues and I hold to be a "sacred obligation"—is to offer a compelling narrative of Christianity grounded in a faithful portrait of Judaism. This entails asking how we might teach, preach, and worship so as to encourage knowledge of the Christ and a profound commitment as "followers of the Way" without disparaging the tradition from which we came and with which we are still in relationship. It also involves facing the history of our relationship with Jews so that we deepen awareness that theological claims have consequences in the realm of everyday life. How we speak of the religious Other shapes attitudes that play out in deeds.

In recent years major sectors of the Christian tradition have explicitly and officially acknowledged that Judaism's covenant with God is eternal. For example, Pope John Paul II inaugurated a critical turn for the Catholic Church when he referred to Jews in 1980 as "the people of God of the Old Covenant, never revoked by God, the present-day people of the covenant concluded with Moses."[4] He made a similar reference to Jews as "partners in a covenant of eternal love which was never revoked," in 1987.[5] Both references continue to be widely cited. Other denominations have taught this recognition in various ways. The second of the *Talking Points* of the Department for Ecumenical Affairs of the Evangelical Lutheran Church in America begins with the affirmation, "Living in the new covenant given by God in Jesus Christ, we also affirm God's continuing faithfulness to the covenant with the Jewish people." In the final paragraph, the document speaks of Christians "joined in continuity to those who have already

---

3. "The fathers [of the Church, e.g., Melito, Augustine, John Chrysostom] thought Judaism was dying, that the victory of the Church signified the demise of Judaism. They created a caricature to meet their expectations and refused to look at Judaism for what it really was. But the problem of Judaism arose as a theological issue because Judaism had not died. It had not come to an end in Jesus, and it was still a force to be reckoned with in the Roman empire" (Robert Wilken, *Judaism and the Early Christian Mind* [1971; reprinted, Eugene, OR: Wipf & Stock, 2004] 229).

4. Pope John Paul II, "Address to the Jewish Community in Mainz, West Germany," November 17, 1980; online: http://www.ccjr.us/dialogika-resources/documents-and-statements/roman-catholic/pope-john-paul-ii/297-jp2-80nov17.

5. John Paul II, "Address to Jewish Leaders in Miami," September 11, 1987; online: http://www.ccjr.us/dialogika-resources/documents-and-statements/roman-catholic/pope-john-paul-ii/308-87sep11/.

been made God's people in the covenant of Sinai, and rejoicing with them that God's covenant, new and old, is a gift that is "irrevocable" (Rom 9:4; 11:29).[6] The 2001 document of the Leuenberg Church Fellowship (an alliance of Reformation Churches in Europe) claims: "From the point of view of the Christian faith, it must be said that the continuing place which belongs to Israel is the result of the divine act of election. Israel itself defines itself as the context of the life of a people. Christians are aware that the community of the people of Israel is based on God's act of election which relates to a life context with both social and religious dimensions."[7]

In my judgment, these acknowledgments of the enduring character of Israel's covenantal relationship—and many more might have been cited—mean that everything premised on the previous argument that Judaism has been superseded must be rethought. Christology must (re)situate Jesus in the matrix of Second Temple Judaism, and New Testament texts in the context of the Roman Empire as well as in the milieu of a developing rivalry between the followers of Jesus and (Other) Jewish groups. Terms such as *salvation*, *redemption*, and *resurrection* need to be viewed both through the lens of their origin in Judaism, and then through the lenses of their journey over time in both Judaism and Christianity. Particular attention must be paid to the ways Judaism developed over time, lest it be reduced to the religion of the "Old" Testament.

This rethinking, which I have sketched only in general terms, is the subject of an extensive and ever expanding library of books, articles, statements, and research projects.[8] It is most fruitful when done in conversation with Jewish scholars. As Clark Williamson has rightly remarked, "Conversation with Jews is indispensable to understanding Christian faith . . . the historical evidence massively attests to the fact that apart from listening and talking with Jews, we will misunderstand the Christian faith and act on our misunderstandings."[9]

---

6. These "Talking Points" may be accessed at http://www.elca.org/ecumenical/interreligious/jewish/talkingpoints/index.html. See also *Covenantal Conversations: Christians in Dialogue with Jews and Judaism*, ed. Darrell Jodock (Minneapolis: Fortress, 2008), which develops each talking point.

7. "The Church and Israel: A Contribution of the Reformation Churches in Europe to the Relation between Christians and Jews, 3.1.1. Full text online: http://www.jcrelations.net/en/?item=1009.

8. I have sought explain this rethinking in my book, *Has God Only One Blessing?: Judaism as a Source of Christian Self-Understanding* (New York: Paulist, 2000).

9. Clark Williamson, *A Guest in the House of Israel* (Louisville: Westminster John Knox, 1993) 9.

Of course, Jews and Christians come to dialogue with different needs, agendas, and responsibilities. For Jews, a major task is moving beyond an identity as victims, especially vis-à-vis Christianity, to a fuller identity based on involvement in Jewish life and knowledge of Jewish texts.[10] An even greater, more controversial challenge would be to understand Christians as partners in the covenants of redemption, as does Irving (Yitz) Greenberg:

> Jews today need to look at the issue, not just from the internal community vantage point, but from the perspective of the hypothetical divine plan. Assume there is a divine strategy for redeeming the world using human agents; assume it is the divine will that Judaism and Christianity are together in the world; assume that both are ways of affirming "yet" and "not yet" with regard to redemption. Assume both are true but that each needs each other to embody the fullest statement of the covenantal goal and process. What one individual cannot say without being hypocritical or confused, two communities can state as a balance and corrective toward each other.[11]

There is, however, another dimension to the "central and indispensable obligation" of revising Christian theology: making it widely accessible so that the conversation extends beyond the circle of scholars. This too I believe: attention to spirituality and education is vital to the dialogue with Jews that is so vital to doing Christian theology today.

Interreligious Dialogue and Spirituality

What is the purpose of interreligious dialogue? I suggest the following:

- Gives entrée into another tradition's beliefs and practices
- Heightens awareness of ways in which 'the Other' has been represented and misrepresented in one's own religious tradition. This may heighten realization of one's parochialism; it may also reveal some of the long lasting effects of racism and xenophobia.

---

10. I thank my colleague in many Jewish–Christian involvements, Professor Sara S. Lee of Hebrew Union College–Jewish Institute of Religion in Los Angeles for this insight. See also our jointly authored Boys and Lee, *Christians & Jews in Dialogue: Learning in the Presence of the Other* (Woodstock, VT: Skylight Paths, 2006).

11. Irving Greenberg, *For the Sake of Heaven and Earth: The New Encounter between Judaism and Christianity* (Philadelphia: Jewish Publication Society, 2004) 176.

- Intensifies desire to broaden and deepen understanding of one's own tradition
- Offers another angle of vision on one's own tradition
- Draws one into elements of a way of life that may give rise to "holy envy"

Dialogue, according to the philosopher Nicholas Burbules, is a "continuous, developmental communicative interchange through which we stand to gain a fuller apprehension of the world, ourselves, and one another."[12] The phrase, "a fuller apprehension of the world, ourselves, and one another," implies that without dialogue we are emptier. This is not so easy to admit, most especially if we hold to the truthfulness of our own religious tradition. Hence, the importance of spirituality—that is, a "lived experience," a "conscious involvement in the project of life integration through self-transcendence toward the ultimate value one perceives."[13] Although Burbules does not use the term *spirituality*, he places what he calls the "communicative virtues" at the heart of dialogue. They are general dispositions and practices that help support successful communicative relations with a variety of people over time: tolerance, patience, an openness to give and receive criticism, a readiness to admit that one may be mistaken, the desire to reinterpret or translate one's own concerns so that they will be comprehensible to others, the self-imposition of restraint in order that others may speak, and the willingness to listen thoughtfully and attentively.[14]

Dialogue is at heart the admission that the way we see the world is not the way it is. Someone asks a question we've never thought of before. We try to explain in our best, if stumbling way—and realize our own understanding is not so profound. Someone recognizes the hypocrisy or corruption that is part of our religious tradition; most likely, this is not news to us, but it is difficult to feel so exposed. Someone questions a belief or a practice dear to our heart; we know that everyone doesn't believe or practice as our tradition does, but still—how can they not? And they seem so

---

12. Nicholas C. Burbules, *Dialogue in Teaching: Theory and Practice* (New York: Teachers College Press, 1993) 8. See also Burbules and Bruce Bertram, "Theory and Research on Teaching as Dialogue"; online: http://faculty.ed.uiuc.edu/burbules/papers/dialogue.html.

13. Sandra M. Schneiders, "Christian Spirituality: Definition, Methods, Types," in *The New Westminster Dictionary of Christian Spirituality*, ed. Philip Sheldrake (Louisville: Westminster John Knox, 2005) 1.

14. Burbules, *Dialogue in Teaching*, 42.

sincere, so good, so religiously knowledgeable. In short, dialogue involves disequilibrium.

If dialogue does not grow out of true humility, it certainly contributes to it. Dialogue is founded on the recognition that 'the Other' has views, convictions, and commitments that complement or challenge or contradict mine. As the late Brazilian activist, lawyer, and educator Paulo Freire said:

> How can I dialogue if I always project ignorance onto others and never perceive my own? How can I dialogue if I regard myself as a case apart from others—mere "its" in whom I cannot recognize other "I's"? How can I dialogue if I consider myself a member of the in-group of "pure" men and women, the owners of truth and knowledge, for whom all non-members are "these people" or the "great unwashed"? How can I dialogue if I start from the premise that naming the world is the task of an elite and that the presence of the people in history is a sign of deterioration, and thus to be avoided? How can I dialogue if I am closed to—and even offended by—the contribution of others? How can I dialogue if I am afraid of being displaced, the mere possibility causing me torment and weakness? Self-sufficiency is incompatible with dialogue.[15]

Humility—experiencing one's limitations, true self-knowledge, the realization we are more a part of the earth (L., *humus*) than the heavens—should lead to prayer. Perhaps it is for that reason that English Jesuit and scholar of India's religions Michael Barnes describes interreligious dialogue as "first and foremost a practice of faith."[16]

A contemplative attitude lies at the heart of dialogue. Raimundo Panikkar calls this *intrapersonal dialogue*: "an inner dialogue within myself, an encounter in the depth of my personal religiousness, having met another religious experience on that very intimate level."[17] As a meeting of persons who share a common humanity, dialogue is not primarily an intellectual activity but a religious one that demands rigorous listening and attentive observation.

Likewise, Barnes emphasizes the necessity of "interior dialogue": a process of letting the imagery, symbols, and basic concepts of another

---

15. Paulo Freire, *Pedagogy of the Oppressed*, trans. Myra Bergman Ramos (New York: Continuum, 1970) 78–79.

16. Michael Barnes, *Theology and the Dialogue of Religions*, Cambridge Studies in Christian Doctrine (Cambridge: Cambridge University Press, 2002) 16.

17. Raimundo Panikkar, *The Intrareligious Dialogue* (New York: Paulist, 1978) 40.

tradition penetrate into one's being. Dialogue, says Barnes in his earlier work, *Christian Identity and Religious Pluralism*, is about "learning who the other is in order to find out who I am." It requires spiritual preparation: "Dialogue forces us—myself and the other—to find the ground of our common search in the Divine." Such dialogue demands commitment, honesty and openness to learn—qualities he says are as hard to sustain as the "single-minded zeal that characterized the greatest of the old missionaries."[18]

All these speak to the importance of our own spiritual practices. In entering the realm of another religious tradition, profound differences emerge. These differences can indeed be destabilizing, revealing the parochialism of our own perspectives or causing us to question long-held beliefs. In a world that seems to grow ever more frightening, and in which entrepreneurs of fear manipulate our emotions (often for political gain), we may be tempted to hang on to what seem to be religious certitudes, perhaps confusing them with faith. Yet interior dialogue is a spiritual practice that sustains us in pondering our own faith tradition more intensely and enables us to live with a heightened sense of mystery and paradox—what Martin Buber termed "holy insecurity."[19]

The experience of disequilibrium in crossing religious borders can lead to another temptation, one that I think Christians are especially prone to: fitting the Other into some sort of theological scheme or overarching narrative. Yet, as Barnes says, dialogue entails "encounter with the irreducible mystery of otherness," and the dislocation and vulnerability one experiences in the face of the Other have "something to do with God."[20] There is a dying to self that enlarges and revivifies:

> Transformative dialogue can be simultaneously destabilizing and strengthening. To be thrown "off center" can be strengthening when the ego is marginalized and the ultimate returned to centrality, or when the "stability" that is revoked had been conservative, unresponsive, and narrow. If by "strengthened" we mean "made more alive," then the person who in dialogue becomes more open, sensitive, and aware is indeed strengthened.

---

18. Michael Barnes, *Christian Identity and Religious Pluralism: Religions in Conversation* (Nashville: Abingdon, 1989) 115.

19. See Sandra B. Lubarsky, "Dialogue: Holy Insecurity," *Religious Education* 91/4 (1996) 545 [540–46]; she draws the phrase "holy insecurity" from Buber's biographer, Maurice Friedman, *Martin Buber: The Life of Dialogue*, 3rd ed. (Chicago: University of Chicago Press, 1976).

20. Barnes, *Theology and the Dialogue of Religions*, 22; 182–83

Yet at the same time, that person is made more fragile. If the goal of religious traditions is not impenetrability or indestructibility, but receptivity to truth and beauty, then it is the tender strength of the butterfly, not the stone, that is to be valued.[21]

Two virtues, in particular, give depth to interreligious dialogue. The first, "holy envy," is a term I learned from the late Krister Stendahl, the New Testament scholar, former dean of Harvard Divinity School, and Lutheran bishop. At least as I infer it from him, holy envy names the experience of something so profound in the beliefs, rituals, polity, or practices of another religious tradition that one wishes it were part of one's own tradition yet refrains from adopting it out of respect for the Other. Holy envy requires respecting boundaries of the Other.

Scholar of religions Lee Yearley coined the term *spiritual regret*. He defines it as "one of those virtues that concerns the appropriate response to the recognition that extremely varied, legitimate religious ideals exist and that no person can possibly manifest all of them."[22] More simply put, people in other religious tradition have experiences of the holy that we will not be able to have for ourselves. As Edward Kaplan, the biographer of Abraham Joshua Heschel, succinctly notes, "Spiritual regret is the recognition of a 'religious good' in the other person's tradition that we cannot share; 'holy envy' is realizing some deficiencies of one's own tradition."[23]

When dialogue between religious persons is sustained over time and is done with understanding and care, it beckons us to move deeper in our own self-understanding. It calls us to draw upon the spiritual practices and discipline of our traditions so that what we talk about is also what we walk.

Dialogue and Education

While I am immersed in the theological issues that both grow out of and contribute to Jewish–Christian exchange, I realize that my grounding in

---

21. Lubarsky, "Dialogue: Holy Insecurity," 543.

22. Lee H. Yearley, *New Religious Virtues and the Study of Religion*, University Lecture in Religious Studies (Tempe: Arizona State University Department of Religious Studies, 1994) 12.

23. Edward K. Kaplan, "Spiritual Regret and Holy Envy," *Spiritus* 5 (2005) 103–6. See also Kaplan and Samuel H. Dresner, *Abraham Joshua Heschel: Prophetic Witness* (New Haven: Yale University Press, 1998); and Kaplan, *Spiritual Radical: Abraham Joshua Heschel in America* (New Haven: Yale University Press, 2007).

educational studies and many years of teaching profoundly shape my approach to dialogue.

The educational task lies in how best to honor the "irreducible otherness" that is fundamental to moving across religious boundaries, how to structure and facilitate situations so that differences need no longer be a source of division, and how to create an environment in which participants will feel safe enough to engage difficult issues and to risk exploring new perspectives.

When the educational dimension of interreligious dialogue is given short shrift, its potential for transformation is lessened. And when it is ignored, it can be disastrous. I still have vivid memories of a gathering about fifteen years ago, "Women of Faith"; the conference brought together forty-five Muslim, Christian, and Jewish women for two days. The conveners asked us to participate in an exercise in which we were to gather in our "faith alike" group and generate a list of five stereotypes of each of the other two traditions. This seemed like a very bad idea—and it was. When the groups returned for the plenary session and began to read out their lists, fury broke out. As should have been anticipated, each stereotype elicited a vigorous defense as old (and not-so-old) wounds were opened up. This session poisoned the rest of the conference; I was not the only one for whom its conclusion brought relief. This incident was a prime example of failing to think educationally about interreligious exchange. In emphasizing confrontation instead of learning, conference planners did not establish an atmosphere in which conversation could take place.

In contrast, my own work, especially that done in collaboration with Sara S. Lee, emphasizes what we have come to call "interreligious learning," that is, "a form of interreligious dialogue emphasizing study in the presence of the religious other and encounter with the tradition the other embodies."[24] It involves fostering relationships *among* participants and *with* key practices, texts, and beliefs of the Other's tradition. Those who facilitate interreligious learning are responsible for establishing the environment, experiences, and resources that enable participants to risk engaging the religious Other and then to integrate that learning into their own religious identity.

Interreligious encounter is an emotional experience. It necessitates careful leadership in designing processes that enable persons to engage intensely with the religious Other. Participants (and leaders) arrive with their own insecurities, stereotypes, and agendas. History looms in the

---

24. Boys and Lee, *Christians & Jews in Dialogue*, 95.

background, and frequently in the front of the room as well. Unanticipated questions arise, more complex understandings do not feel as comfortable as earlier ones, and the grasp of one's own faith may suddenly seem tenuous. Acknowledging the emotional dimension is crucial, but so too is addressing the intellectual aspects.

For example, in the early 1990s Sara Lee and I directed a three-year project: the Catholic-Jewish Colloquium, sponsored by the Lilly Endowment. The twenty-two participants, educational leaders (or potential leaders) in their own traditions, met in six intensive, two-day seminars. Each seminar focused on a particular aspect of Jewish–Christian relations over the centuries and probed its educational and pastoral implications. This Colloquium gave rise to our understanding of the dynamics of interreligious learning.[25]

When our Colloquium participants studied the history of Catholic-Jewish relations over the centuries, all were struck by the complexity, intensity, and duration of the process by which the Christians and Jews separated. As the rivalry of the early relationship hardened into disputation and enmity, Catholic participants were humbled and distressed as they learned a shadow side of their tradition that their own education (graduate degrees in theology or religious education) had not revealed. The Jewish participants were moved by the anguish and vulnerability they witnessed among the Catholics with whom they were studying. Having confronted this history, one woman said, "Now we can get off the medieval battlefield."

One realization that became especially important to us about interreligious learning is the need for participants to have opportunity to share their deep connection to their own traditions. In the Colloquium, we initiated sessions that gave opportunity for participants to take a specific aspect of a personally meaningful text, ritual, or holy season and explain its significance to others in a small group. We witnessed powerful sharing. Similarly, in 2007 one of the Jewish members of my course at Union Theological Seminary, "Studies in Jewish–Christian Relations," invited the class to his family's home for the Seder. Only a few of the Christian students had previously been to one, and the care, creativity, and religious depth with which our hosts celebrated the Seder made it a memorable experience. As I looked around the room as we were singing the wonderful children's

---

25. For a detailed analysis of this Colloquium, see *Religious Education* 91/4 (1996); the entire issue is devoted to the Colloquium. The issue is also available online: http://www.bc.edu/dam/files/research_sites/cjl/sites/partners/erpp/CJC_Contents.htm.

songs that conclude the Seder, I saw understandings of Judaism among the Christian guests that no amount of time in a classroom or library could have provided in the same way.

Experiences such as these enable participants to enter empathically into the Other's tradition. Yet for all the very real emotional and affective elements in educating for dialogue, interreligious learning certainly requires intellectual engagement. It might appear that differences are best dealt with through argumentation, that seemingly more rigorous exercise of logic and rationality. Argument does have its uses in interreligious encounter, but it is a far less valuable resource than conversation. Dialogue doesn't preclude argument, but is better thought of as a *conversation*. So often, schools teach us how to argue—and the ability to frame solidly substantiated arguments is indeed an educational desideratum. But debate has one especially fatal weakness when it comes to dialogue. Debate means that much of our listening focuses on refuting the Other.

Argument can all too easily focus on winning rather than on understanding. Argument, as philosopher of education Margret Buchmann points out, involves contestants, whereas conversation involves partners. She continues: "What makes conversation attractive is its reciprocal quality, breadth of subject matter, the room it gives to different voices, and the delightful turns it may take. Conversations have flexible rules of relevance and evidence. All manner of impressions, ideas, and experience can enter." As she notes, in conversation "ideals of perfection in clarity and coherence" are not as important as in argument. Thus, "one may get answers to questions one never thought of asking (but ought to have asked) or have one's answers answered. Yet conversation is not mere talk; it can include argument and has its own logical postulates."[26] Moreover, dialogue in many respects is countercultural; what seems to be the increasing lack of civility, and polarization, in the public square suggest that skills and sensibilities for dialogue need to be taught. We cannot assume participants come prepared for it.[27]

As Buchmann reminds us, conversation is educative only when the conversation partners already know something—knowledge of self, as well as the subject at hand. Hence, the importance of stimulating the conversation with excellent resources and questions that demand thought. It

---

26. Margret Buchmann, "Improving Educating by Talking: Argument or Conversation?" *Teachers College Record* 86/3 (1985) 451 [441–53].

27. An especially useful text for leading dialogue is Stephen Brookfield and Stephen Preskill, *Discussion as a Way of Teaching: Tools and Techniques for Democratic Classrooms* (San Francisco: Jossey-Bass, 1999).

is not the educator's job to control the conversation but to provide ample stimuli so discussants can speak with curiosity and candor, empathy and desire to know the Other. Thereby, the "goal is changed from conquering to growing, from silencing to knowing, from telling to asking. Questions are employed as tools for probing, not weapons for stabbing. New possibilities are considered."[28]

Dialogue happens in various ways. A Vatican publication identifies four forms of dialogue: of *life*, of *action*, of *theological exchange*, and of *religious experience*.[29] In whatever form, however, it is not a mere method, but a way of life. It is hard work—a commitment to persevere when understanding seems elusive, a desire to see a relationship preserved and deepened even when conflict arises, and a conviction that differences need not be a source of division but can be a source of mutuality.

This I believe: The holy work of interreligious dialogue, especially that between Jews and Christians, demands theological grounding, spiritual practice, and sensitive educational strategies. Is it not a "sacred obligation" of our time?

---

28. Phelps, *More Light, Less Heat*, 20.

29. Pontifical Council for Interreligious Dialogue, *Dialogue and Proclamation*, 1991: #42; cf. *Dialogue and Mission*, 1984: #s28–35). See Pontifical Council on Interreligious Dialogue, "Dialogue and Proclamation: Reflections and Orientations on Interreligious Dialogue and the Proclamation of the Gospel of Jesus Christ," in *Redemption and Dialogue: Reading "Redemptoris Missio" and "Dialogue and Proclamation,"* ed. William R. Burrows (Maryknoll, NY: Orbis, 1993) 3–55.

nine

Globalization, Human Rights, and the Catholic Response

DONALD J. DIETRICH

1.

In a controversial article appearing in *Foreign Affairs* (1993), Samuel Huntington explored what he perceived as the new world order. His thesis was that post-cold war world politics would be structured along fault lines that separated civilizations and cultures rather than around principles of ideology or of economics. Civilizations are distinguished from one another by "history, language, culture, tradition, and, most importantly, religion." From one perspective, 9/11 helped validate his thesis. Such a diagnosis has raised the possibility of religious conflict on a global scale and seems to make religion a public danger. In Huntington's view, religious communities would probably not be the actors delineating the common good in pluralistic societies or in an interdependent global order, since they seem only able to draw sharp boundaries between the faithful and others. Along these lines, a common good would only be a common good of some specific subgroup. Thus, the pursuit of a "common good" would merely become the threat to peace and to the freedom of the "others" outside specific religious communities. Such a view has been opposed by John Paul II, who said that the precondition of a humane market economy and of a just democracy is a culture of the common good (i.e., of objective morality). Such a culture can only be effectively secured by a theism—a widespread, stable commitment to a greater-than-human source for meaning and value, which would be the foundation for the common good.[1]

Huntington's thesis is particularly frightening and confusing when seen in a context of globalization. The term *globalization* can have both negative and positive meanings. Ralph Nader has identified it with the dominating control of transnational corporations. K. N. Panikhar observes that globalization ensures the necessary climate for domination and hegemonization of developing countries by the consortium of world capitalist countries. Others such as Martha Nussbaum assert that global interconnections can open up positive forms of cross-cultural understanding. Nussbaum has written that the imagination can cross cultural boundaries and can lead to the acknowledgement of certain common needs and goals among the many local differences that divide persons. Which opinion is correct? To answer this question and to respond to Huntington's reductionistic thesis, the connections among people must be put back at the center of social and moral inquiry. A form of moral inquiry that explores how human interconnections are essential to obtaining or failing to attain the good life seems crucial. If the differences between negative and positive aspects of globalization are to be discerned, then a more discriminating vision opposed to an autonomy-based normative framework is needed.[2]

In essence, a social vision that does not see human connections as central to the attainment of well-being would lack the conceptual framework needed to reflect on the issues of globalization. Humans have become increasingly embedded in a transnational and complex web of interdependence. Their well-being is increasingly connected on levels including environmental, economic, cultural, and political dimensions. A value system that postulates nonintervention or noninterference would seem to lack the criteria required to address concerns in a critical fashion. Such a critical approach seems to need a starting point that mandates a framework that can assess the relational merits of different modes of *living*

---

1. Samuel P. Huntington, "The Clash of Civilizations?" *Foreign Affairs* 72 (Summer 1993) 22–49; David Hollenbach, *The Common Good and Christian Ethics*, New Studies in Christian Ethics (Cambridge: Cambridge University Press, 2002) 90–91; Robert P. George and Gerard Bradley, "Pope John Paul II (1920–2005)," in *The Teachings of Modern Christianity: On Law, Politics, and Human Nature*, vol. 1, ed. John Witte, Jr., and Frank Alexander (New York: Columbia University Press, 2006) 250.

2. Hollenbach, *The Common Good*, 43–44; Ralph Nader, "In the Public Interest"; K.N. Panikhar, "Globalization and Culture," *Voices from the Third World* 20 (1997) 50; Martha C. Nussbaum, *Cultivating Humanity; A Classical Defense of Reform in Liberal Education* (Cambridge: Harvard University Press, 1997) 83; see also chaps. 2 and 4, and the conclusion.

together. Linking the vision of Catholic social thought to the practice of key Christian virtues (solidarity, compassion, hospitality) may offer a way to facilitate the concrete realization of the common good. It necessitates a new cognitive stance about how the common good might play a more central role in world affairs.[3]

Globalization requires that we think again about universalistic ethical principles, and whether they are possible as well as real, and whether they inhibit or enhance the prospects of a genuine and principled pluralism. To speak of human rights in this context is to conceptualize irrespective of social and cultural differences. Human rights need to be embedded in a broader view of ethics, a deeper view of social history, and a higher view of meaning if they are to be actualized in a more embracing web of duties, virtues, commitments to justice, and concerns for the common good. Perhaps a theological view of globalization especially one grounded in concrete experiences, would offer a more universal and inclusivistic account than a secular view that could be perceived as more particularistic or narrow.[4]

Thus, the task is to identify where in the depths of the varied religious traditions there resides the capacity to recognize and further refine the truth and justice of human rights, which is necessary in order to overcome what could be a "clash of civilizations." Uncovering the human rights religious traditions provides a model for a just reconstruction of a global civil society. Human well-being from this vantage point is intrinsic to what is morally good and right. One feature of much of philosophical and religious ethics has been the belief that what is morally good and right is bound to the flourishing of humans and their communities. In essence, the end of freedom (the good) is the integrity of life; and the resources can be discerned for considering the connections between power and value, as well as claims about the worth of finite life and even how to respond to the other. The moral diversity of multicultural communities need not yield to an easy relativism. Rather, admission of fallibility means that any claim to truth about common life, any belief about how we can and ought

---

3. Hollenbach, *The Common Good*, 56; Christopher Vogt, "Fostering a Catholic Commitment to the Common Good: An Approach Rooted in Virtue Ethics," *Theological Studies* 68 (2007) 394 [394–417].

4. Max Stackhouse, "Why Human Rights Needs God: A Christian Perspective," in *Does Human Rights Need God?*, ed. Elizabeth Bucar and Barbra Barnett (Grand Rapids: Eerdmans, 2005) 30–32; see also Max Stackhouse and Peter Paris, eds., *God and Globalization*, vol. 1, *Religion and the Power of the Common Life* (Harrisburg: Trinity, 2000); Max Stackhouse and Diane Obenchain, eds., *God and Globalization*, vol. 3, *Christ and the Dominions of Civilization* (Harrisburg, PA: Trinity, 2002).

to organize our political existence, must be incarnated by open or public debate. Social density and global reflexivity highlight memories of suffering and hatred even as they open new possibilities for understanding and forgiveness. In the wake of the attacks on the World Trade Center this has become abundantly clear.[5]

In the Catholic tradition "rights talk" has a long and tenacious history, but the most modern segment of this tradition is rooted in Vatican II (1962-1965) and in subsequent encyclicals. In theological research some Catholic moral scholars have also grappled with the issues of how to uncover the "common good" in a pluralistic cultural environment and thereby how to root human rights in the religious resources of every faith tradition.[6] This decades-long discernment process was only amplified and made more urgent in light of 9/11. The Catholic model that has emerged is the path that one religious tradition has followed and may help open a perspective on how the globalization of the human rights discussion can be anchored in the pluralistic communities that embody the world's great religious traditions.

2.

The early encyclicals (Leo XIII, *Rerum Novarum*, 1891; Pius XI, *Quadragesimo Anno*, 1931) were clearly written within the framework of a natural law conceptual ethic.[7] In these cases the popes utilized the language of rights to defend workers against economic exploitation. Their use of the rights argument, however, was neither comprehensive nor systematic. Economically, Leo XIII and Pius XI wanted the state to intervene to assist workers. Politically and culturally, these popes supported the system of subsidiarity to restrain the intervention and reach of the nation-state. When the logic of this position on the state was followed consistently, it

---

5. Stackhouse, "Why Human Rights Need God," 40; William Schweiker, *Theological Ethics and Global Dynamics: In the Time of Many Worlds* (Malden, MA: Blackwell, 2004) 13-14, 16, 114, 199, 213; Philippa Foot, *Natural Goodness* (Oxford: Clarendon, 2001); Jürgen Habermas, *Postmetaphysical Thinking: Philosophical Essay*, trans. W. M. Hohengarten, Studies in Contemporary German Social Thought (Cambridge: MIT Press, 1992).

6. Donald J. Dietrich, *Human Rights in the Catholic Tradition* (New Brunswick, NJ: Transaction, 2007).

7. J. Bryan Hehir, "Religious Activism from Human Rights," in *Religious Human Rights in Global Perspective*, ed. John Witte and Johan D. van der Vyver (The Hague: Nijhoff, 1996) 100-101.

inevitably raised questions about the rights of citizens as well as about the role that the state and church should be playing in an increasingly complex world.

In the development of Catholic human rights teaching, Pius XII is a transitional figure. He did not change the framework that held the teaching, but rather opened the door for further development by his successors. The major contribution of Pius XII involved both the substance and the scope of Catholic rights teaching. He moved beyond economic rights to address political-civil rights and the Church's traditional adversity toward democracy. He began to elaborate a philosophy of modern citizenship by insisting that the Church had to confront the totalitarian/authoritarian state in all its multiple forms. This concern drove him to acknowledge the value of democratic politics in a way unlike his predecessors. He recognized the benefits of modern democracy as a viable system supported by such political liberties as freedom of speech, press, and association. Pius XII's second contribution to the Church's teaching on human rights was his expansion of papal teaching beyond the modern focus on the nation to address the legal ordering of the international community.[8] He did not push to reconceptualize totally the antidemocratic teaching of the Church. He merely opened and extended the conversation. In brief, all three of Pius XII's contributions—the inclusion of political-civil rights into moral theology, the limits on the role of the state, and the international dimension of human rights—set the stage for John XXIII and Vatican II.

Pacem in terris established John XXIII as the pivotal figure in the inception of the modern development of the Catholic human rights theory manifested in *Nostra Aetate* and *Dignitatis humanae*. For John XXIII, the foundation for and the purpose of all rights rest on the dignity of the human person. *Pacem in terris* provided an authoritative and theological framework for an understanding of human rights within the theology of the Catholic Church. The encyclical maintained a natural law framework and incorporated as much as seemed feasible from the natural rights tradition. In doing so John XXIII managed to construct an overarching framework that relied on the classic theme of social solidarity. This theme itself

---

8. John Courtney Murray, "Leo XIII: Two Concepts of Government," *Theological Studies* 14 (1953) 551–60; John Courtney Murray, "The Problem of Religious Freedom," *Theological Studies* 25 (1964) 503–47; David Hollenbach, *Claims in Conflict: Retrieving and Renewing the Catholic Human Rights Tradition*, Woodstock Studies 4 (New York: Paulist, 1979) 59–64.

was crucial to the debate among theologians and clerical leaders, which today is swirling around the meaning of the "common good."[9]

Human dignity in *Pacem in terris* became the foundation for the developing theology of human rights. One aspect of the common good, therefore, was to consist in the maintenance and protection of personal rights and obligations. While historically the Catholic Church has tended to subordinate the individual to the community, with Vatican II it sought a balance between the rights of the individual and the rights of society. The connection between individual and community would be achieved through the link of philosophical personalism. In contrast to the liberal tradition stemming from the Enlightenment, Catholic personalism maintained that human dignity was based on both duties and rights, and its starting point was that men and women are social beings. *Pacem in terris* leaves unresolved the issue of how the "common good is to be recovered, especially as we interact with those outside the western tradition."[10]

By affirming the right to religious freedom in principle, which was a crucial step; by endorsing constitutional limits on the power and intrusiveness of the state (subsidiarity); and by joining religious freedom with other human rights, the Second Vatican Council substantively moved beyond Pius XII. The Catholic Church now could support the full panoply of the freedoms needed in the political order to defend human dignity. Natural law was not abandoned, but was now viewed as joining constitutive ideas previously barely tolerated but not fully embraced by the Church. Two conciliar documents, *Nostra Aetate* and *Gaudium et spes*, provided the doctrinal foundation and theological legitimization for an aggressive Catholic involvement in furthering human rights. Theologically, the reason to highlight personal dignity was as an invitation to communion with God. The Council itself went beyond the pronouncements of Pius XII and John XXIII.[11] The Church became engaged in the struggle to delineate human rights as a moral and political task.

---

9. See Hollenbach, *The Common Good*.

10. John XXIII, *Pacem in Terris* (Boston: Daughters of St. Paul, 1963) par. 23, 40–48, 60, 145; Alf Tergel, *Human Rights in Cultural and Religious Traditions*, Uppsala Studies in Faiths and Ideologies 8 (Uppsala: Academiae Ubsaliensis, 1998) 147; John Paul II, "Address to the United Nations, 1979," in *The Political Papacy: John Paul II, Benedict XVI, and Their Influence*, ed. Chester Gillis (Boulder, CO: Paradigm, 2006) 106.

11. Hehir, "Religious Activism from Human Rights," in Witte and van der Vyver, *Religious Human Rights in Global Perspective*, 102, 106; Hollenbach, *Claims in Conflict*, 64.

Trialogue and Terror

At Vatican II, ecclesial leaders from the United States and European nations sought to open up issues of religious freedom and pluralism. To be theologically consistent meant that they had to acknowledge that all men and women deserved religious freedom. This very central affirmation contained the nutritional essence that propelled the ensuing lengthy conversation on human rights. Every human person was thought to have a right to religious freedom, which meant that coercion is forbidden from intruding into this area of human activity. "The Synod [Vatican II] further declares that the right to religious freedom has its foundations in the very dignity of the human person as this dignity is known through the revealed word of God and by reason itself."[12] This right was also to be considered a civil right.

This "Declaration on Religious Freedom" (*Dignitatis Humanae*) had a decisive impact on the subsequent history of the Church's political initiatives. It confirmed that Catholicism should enter the debate over the right ordering of society and be seen as the defender of the human person, made in the image and likeness of God with intelligence and free will. This person was the bearer of rights and obligations that were his or hers by nature, prior to any status as a citizen in a state. Thus, the Church's primacy in the realm of society and politics would be to defend human dignity through the defense of the human conscience against all who would abuse it for the ends of power.[13] Such a principled disentanglement of the Church from the partisanship of ecclesial and political factions gave it a moral stake at the most basic level of politics, i.e., the definition of a social and political order commensurate with human dignity.

The continuing theological case for human rights was reinforced by John Paul II. Both a theologian and a philosopher, this pope was convinced that only a theological analysis could help uncover the depth of the evil that had to be addressed in this combustible world. It could be maintained that the Church's role was to exist as a sign of and safeguard for the transcendence of the human person. The fulfillment of such a mission necessarily posited a robust ministry of human rights. The conciliar teaching was reinforced by John Paul II and tied to the entire social teaching

---

12. *Dignitatis Humanae*, 2, in *The Final Revolution: The Resistance Church and the Collapse of Communism*, ed. George Weigel (New York: Oxford University Press, 1992) 72.

13. Weigel, *The Final Revolution*, 73–74; for a critique of the traditional Catholic institutional approach to political issues, see Reinhold Niebuhr, "Germany," *Worldview* 16 (June 1973) 17; John Courtney Murray, "The Issue of Church and State at Vatican II," *Theological Studies* 27 (1966) 580–606.

tradition with its stress on social justice and human rights, and so to the very essence of the Church through defining its ministry as the defense of every person. International perspectives on human rights required concrete institutions to address them.[14] The Vatican II documents, especially such crucial statements as those in *Nostra Aetate*, as well as the interests of John Paul II, propelled the Catholic Church into human rights struggles throughout the international system during the past few decades, and gradually moved the conversation on rights back into a search for the "common good."

3.

It is astonishing that it took Catholic theologians so long both to give a proper and substantive interpretation to the meaning of modern human rights and to inquire into the sense in which the concept of such rights has been influenced by a biblical understanding of the human condition. According to *Nostra Aetate*, an expansive understanding of the Catholic tradition and its place among other religious communities, and a renewed interest in the Bible, enabled a discussion of human rights to assume a heightened priority. Two interests pushed the project forward. First, there was an interest to clarify the motives for Catholics and their Church in promoting human rights, and a need to practice solidarity with the victims of oppression and alienation. Second, there began to blossom a still ongoing debate whether modern human rights truly can be called universal, when such rights have somehow to be related to the specific cultural tradition of the Western Enlightenment nurtured by Judaism and Christianity, as well as to the array of religious traditions at the root of non-Western civilizations. Both questions were of great theoretical and practical interest, because a consistent understanding of the universality of human rights was necessary to motivate individuals and associations to work for an explicit attention to specific rights in different cultures. In recent years, another perspective has added a further dimension to the issue of the religious roots of modern human rights and to a methodology that can help us discover the common good, from which can emerge a substantive global

14. Hehir, "Religious Activism from Human Rights," in Witte and van der Vyver, *Religious Human Rights in Global Perspective*, 106-7, 110-12; John Paul II, *Redemptor Hominis = The Redeemer of Man* (Boston: St. Paul, 1979); Ivan Vallier, "The Roman Catholic Church: A Transnational Actor," in *Transnational Relations and World Politics*, ed. Robert Kephan and Joseph Nye (Cambridge: Harvard University Press, 1970) 129-52.

system of rights. Crises frequently are global and demand common ethical convictions with respect to rights to support humanity. These global or communitarian rights include the right to development, to peace, and to the protection of the environment.[15]

Nostra Aetate offered some positive insights into the construction of the methodology needed to help explore the relationship between the common good and human rights, as well as to help design an approach that facilitates faith engaging culture. This document reminds Catholics that the task of the Church is to foster unity and love among all persons and nations. To do this, it is necessary to uncover what humans have in common. The document treats, for example, the relation of the Church toward Hindus, Buddhists, Muslims, and Jews. To set the stage, the Council Fathers recommended that dialogue and collaboration be used with the "followers of other religions, and in witness of Christian faith and life, acknowledge, preserve, and promote the spiritual and moral goods found among men as well as the values in their society and culture." Toward the end of the document, the authors insisted that the ground was to be removed from every theory and practice that distinguishes, i.e., marginalizes, persons in the matter of human dignity and the rights that flow from it.[16]

One could affirm from one perspective of the Christian tradition that universal moral standards are "in principle" knowable by all persons, but that in practice revelation is needed because of the weakness of the human mind and its continued distortion through sin.[17] In the concreteness of existence, for most people revelation and grace are useful in order to know and live by the natural law. Augustine, Thomas Aquinas, and Calvin, among others, would be comfortable in this tradition. One problem, of course, is that those rooted in this dimension of the tradition frequently ignore the presence of sin in the Christian community itself. One could also argue, as has John Paul II, that the authoritative teaching of the Church guarantees that the magisterium is capable of finding and teaching the universally normative natural law in ways that are preserved by the

---

15. Wolfgang Huber, "Human Rights and Biblical Legal Thought," in Witte and van der Vyver, *Religious Human Rights in Global Perspective*, 47, 61; Ronald Traer, *Faith in Human Rights: Support in Religious Traditions for a Global Struggle* (Washington, DC: Georgetown University Press, 1991).

16. Walter M. Abbot, ed., *The Documents of Vatican II* (New York: Herder & Herder, 1966) 660, 662–63, 667.

17. Walter Kasper, "Human Rights and the Church," in Tergel, *Human Rights in Cultural and Religious Traditions*, 168.

Holy Spirit. How can such a stance, however, provide a common morality in a pluralistic world?

Dialogic pluralism seems to offer a promising possibility. Its conception of reason is more historical and less abstract than that propagated by the Enlightenment or by systematic theology. Reason is seen to be embedded in history. Rational argument, therefore, has to be shaped by the tradition in which the inquirer has been educated. Neither the questions addressed by rational discourse nor the thought patterns available to address these questions are the products of a philosophically and historically pure reason. Urgent questions, for example, arise from the anomalies that become apparent within an ongoing and historically concrete tradition of inquiry.[18] The response to historical events shapes reason as a cognitive tool.

4.

An array of Catholic theologians have tried to combine fidelity to the particularistic, Catholic-based social thought with a commitment to the common morality needed in a pluralistic, historical, and interdependent world.[19] The awareness of historical, cultural, and religious pluralism has been reintroduced into Catholic thought with force since Vatican II. This sensitivity has raised new questions about the possibility of the transcultural, universal ethic sought by natural law theory, based on the so-called transhistorical human reasoning. Doubts about such powerful claims for pure reason led the Council to reemphasize the distinctively religious basis of Catholic social thought. The same historical consciousness that led to this recognition of pluralism, however, simultaneously led to a heightened awareness of the need for a transcultural ethic for an interdependent world.

---

18. Paul Gordon Lauren, *The Evolution of International Human Rights: Visions Seen*, Pennsylvania Studies in Human Rights (Philadelphia: University of Pennsylvania Press, 1998); Hans Küng, *Global Responsibility: In Search of a New World Ethic*, trans. John Bowden (New York: Crossroad, 1991); Robert J. Schreiter, *The New Catholicity: Theology between the Global and the Local* (Maryknoll, NY: Orbis, 1997).

19. James Keenan, "Moral Theology and History," *Theological Studies* 62 (2001) 86–104; James Keenan, "Notes on Moral Theology: Fundamental Moral Theology at the Beginning of the Twenty-First Century," *Theological Studies* 67 (2006) 99–119; Jean Porter, "The Search for a Global Ethics," *Theological Studies* 62 (2001) 105–21; Dietrich, *Human Rights*, chaps. 7 and 8.

Trialogue and Terror

The Council began to respond to the paradox or anomaly of the new situation by stressing dialogue and mutual inquiry across the boundaries of diverse communities. For the Catholic Church this seems to mean starting the pursuit of a common morality from the vantage point of its own theological convictions. It also has to mean bringing these convictions into an active encounter with other religious communities, with other traditions, and with non-Western histories. This method of dialogue does not necessarily mean relativism. The commitment to dialogue and mutual inquiry suggests just the opposite—that there is a truth about the human good that must be pursued and that makes a claim on the minds and hearts of all persons.[20]

The Council documents and the decades-long conversation they have evoked also stress the unity of humanity and encourage dialogue among religious traditions to assist in discerning the culturally pluralistic meaning of revelation. All religious traditions can be seen, according to this model, as instantiating values connecting humans with God. Thus, a presumptive commitment to dialogue seems to be both a demand of Christian faith and a requirement of reasonableness. From this viewpoint, Christian faith entails care and respect for all persons, and respect for their dignity means listening to their interpretations of the common good. Likewise, Christians themselves have called for the construction of the bonds of solidarity among all persons. Such solidarity would seem to require efforts to understand those who are different, to learn from them, and to contribute in light of the Catholic tradition to their understanding of the good life as well. Similarly a reasonableness that avoids the rational dismissal of historical traditions and communal particularities will take the diversity of the traditions and cultures of the world seriously enough both to listen carefully to them and to respond with respect. It is reasonableness that expects all parties to learn from one another and to teach through the give-and-take of dialogue. For Christians, such dialogue embodies the dynamic interaction between the biblical faith handed on to them through the centuries and the attribute of reason that is manifested in the *imago Dei* (image of God) in all human beings.[21]

---

20. Makau Mutua, "A Novel Cause Wrapped in Arrogance", *Boston Sunday Globe*, April 19, 2001, 08; John Shattuck, "Dignity and Freedom Are for Everyone," *Boston Sunday Globe*, April 19, 2001, D8; Alasdair MacIntyre, *Three Rival Versions of Moral Enquiry: Encyclopedia, Genealogy and Traditions* (Notre Dame: University of Notre Dame Press, 1990) chap. 10.

21. See Abbott, *Documents of Vatican II*, 662–63.

The dialogue between and the dynamic linkage of faith and reason has implications for such substantive questions of social morality today as the delineation of an ethic of human rights in both its political and economic dimensions. The location of this commitment to human rights, based on dignity and solidarity, in the context of an ethic of dialogue has ramifications for the way these rights are perceived. A dialogical ethic means that any engagement has to be constructed with a deep respect for those who hold differing beliefs. Thus, the faithful should "at all times refrain from any manner of action which might seem to carry a hint of coercion."[22] Persuasion through reasonable discourse is the proper mode of public participation by religious believers, especially when they seek to influence law or public policy.

More broadly, such a dialogical understanding has implications for how to address the full range of human rights. The West, for example, has generally been inclined to conceive of human rights in individualistic terms and to give priority to the civil and political rights intrinsic to free speech, due process of law, and political participation. Those nations more inspired by Marxist ideology, as well as Third World nations, have stressed such social and economic rights as adequate food, work, and housing. A dialogical ethic suggests not only that these two traditions ought to learn from the strengths of each other, but also that the opposition between individual freedoms and natural solidarity in society is a false dichotomy. Persons can live in dignity only when they live in a community of freedom, in which both personal initiative (i.e., diversity) and social solidarity are valued and embodied. This linkage of personal initiative and social solidarity has material dimensions and can emerge only when persons have both economic and political space for action, and the institutional as well as the material prerequisites of a communal life that makes such actions possible. Despite the challenging nature of such an agenda, it can give substantive guidance for social, political, and economic institutions that a one-sided emphasis on the pluralistic interpretation of human rights in our world fails to provide.[23]

22. See ibid. for *Dignitatis Humanae* nos. 2–4; *Gaudium et spes*, nos. 25, 41.

23. See David Hollenbach, "A Communitarian Reconstruction of Human Rights," in *Catholicism and Liberalism: Contributions to American Public Philosophy*, ed. R. Bruce Douglass and David Hollenbach (Cambridge: Cambridge University Press, 1999) 127–50; and Hollenbach, "Afterword: A Community of Freedom," 323–43 in ibid.; Paul F. Knitter and Chandra Muzaffar, eds., *Subverting Greed: Religious Perspectives on the Global Economy*, Faith Meets Faith (Maryknoll, NY: Orbis, 2002); Ira Rifkin, *Spiritual Perspectives on Globalization: Making Sense of Economic and Cultural Upheaval*, Spiritual Perspectives (Woodstock, VT: Skylight Paths, 2003).

The same need for a dialogical or solidaristic approach to the interpretation of human rights is evident in the context of religious diversity in the world today. Human rights, of course, are moral norms proposed as protections for the sacredness of persons independent of their religious and cultural traditions. They apply universally to all persons. Western Enlightenment thought interpreted this claim to universality to mean that human rights are moral standards independent of all traditions, cultures, and religions. The contemporary awareness of the embeddedness of rationality, however, has raised serious doubts about the claim and need to transcend history and communal traditions.[24] Mainstream Catholic thought continues to affirm the reality and universality of human rights. Any such defense of human rights must take into account the ways the justification of normativity and the interpretation of their concrete implications vary in notable ways from one philosophical, ideological, or religious tradition to another.

For example, Judaism, Christianity, and Islam as religious traditions each have a powerful influence on the way human rights are understood by their respective adherents. The central place of communal identity and of the land of Israel in Judaism leads to a reading of human rights that emphasizes the right to national self-determination and to the possession of Israel by the Jewish people. Western Christians understand rights in a way that gives greater emphasis to the rights of individual persons, since the universal mission of Christianity relativizes the importance of national identity. The radical monotheism of Islam leads many Muslims to argue that universal human rights will only be secured in a society submissive to Allah—an Islamic state. The religious beliefs of each of these communities shape the intellectual and affective horizons, against which human rights are viewed. Thus, both the theoretical and practical defense of human rights must take into account the influence of these religious traditions and must try to find common core values.[25]

Pursuit of respect for human rights requires an ongoing dialogue about how the universal standards sought by discourse can relate to the distinctive, particularistic self-understanding of the religious communities

---

24. Alasdair MacIntrye, *After Virtue: A Study in Moral Theory* (Notre Dame: University of Notre Dame Press, 1981) 67; Richard Rorty, "Postmodernist Bourgeois Liberalism," in *Hermeneutics and Praxis*, ed. Robert Hollinger, Revisions (Notre Dame: University of Notre Dame Press, 1985) 219–20.

25. Brian D. Lepard, *Rethinking Humanitarian Intervention: A Fresh Legal Approach Based on Fundamental Ethical Principles in International Law and World Religions* (University Park: Pennsylvania State University Press, 2002) 39–146.

of the world. Such a perspective means that the commitment to ecumenical and interreligious dialogue is at least one prerequisite for uncovering a global human rights ethic in the post-9/11 era. David Hollenbach, for example, has argued that the current Catholic ideal of human rights has reinterpreted the individualist presuppositions of liberalism in light of a more communitarian take on the social order. Hollenbach has also forcefully proposed a "'dialogical universalism,' in which reason is embedded in history and shaped by traditions, yet also committed to seeking something appropriating a 'transcultural ethic for an interdependent world.' Respect for human rights requires an ongoing dynamic between universal standards of justice in an inclusive community and the particularist self-understanding of diverse local communities. 'Dialogue'—the active engagement of listening and speaking with others whose beliefs and traditions are different—is the key to such dynamism."[26]

5.

History has led Catholic intellectuals to understand that moral theology is not immutable, since norms have to be consonant with human motivations and experiences. Historical investigations into the world of marching soldiers has served as a corrective to the merely theoretical insights that support abstract moral norms. Christianity has developed through its practices, and these activities continuously identify Christianity's moral concerns. The very success of pragmatic political negotiations over the last few decades seems to suggest at the very least that there are significant commonalities in human existence that make cross-cultural consensus a real possibility. We cannot, of course, take such a consensus as a given, bestowed on us by universal morality, but that does not mean that we have to despair of developing it through authentic dialogue that is sensitive to the concrete realities impacting on men and women.[27]

26. David Hollenbach, "A Communitarian Reconstruction of Human Rights," 127–50; Hollenbach, "Spécificité de la pensée sociale catholique et bien commun de l'humanité," in *Église et société: un dialogue orthodox russe–catholique romain*, ed. Jean-Yves Calweg and Anatoli Krasikov (Paris: Cerf, 2001) 91–108; for an earlier treatment of dialogue and religious traditions, see Hans Küng and Karl-Josef Kuschel, eds., *A Global Ethic: The Declaration of the Parliament of the World's Religions*, trans. John Bowden, (New York: Continuum, 1993).

27. Keenan, "Moral Theology and History," 99, 109; Porter, "The Search for a Global Ethics," 120; Bradford Hinze, "Ecclesial Repentance and the Demands of Dialogue," *Theological Studies* (2000) 219; Calvin Schrag, *The Self after Postmodernity* (New Haven: Yale University Press, 1997) 128–38.

Whether Catholicism can actually meet the practical moral test of creating real communities, in which these ideals begin to be realized, and so can make a significant moral impact both locally and globally, remains to be seen. A dialogical model is risky, of course, because it may not produce an "objective" truth that will comfort all the participants, but it at least remains true to the origins of Christianity, which offered a "way" to God, but did not spell out the landmarks in that process. Increasingly, many Catholics have come to the realization that the landmarks have to be found in all the religious traditions constructed by men and women and not just in a privileged Christianity.

To develop a theory that addresses the importance of solidarity with victims the first step is to show, as the above indicates, that Catholic social thought can facilitate an understanding of the global common good. Current realities in the world of terrorists have confronted all religious communities with a fundamental challenge: how to relate their distinctive visions of the good life with the growing awareness that all persons are linked together in a web of global awareness. In this interdependent world, the need for a clear vision of the common good for the whole human race is becoming more evident. Religious and cultural pluralism are becoming more a part of our environment. Pluralism means that there may be a limited agreement about the meaning of the "good life," and engaging in the process toward that meaning may be the best that we can do. Also, the complexity of emerging world realities seems to be leading many communities to seek reaffirmation of the distinctive traditions that have historically set them apart from others. Thus, we face an apparent paradox: attaining a vision of the global common good is increasingly problematic at the very historical moment when the need for such a vision is growing.[28] John Witte has stated that the challenge of the twenty-first century will be to transform religious communities from agents that assist in the birth of rights' norms conceived elsewhere to associations that create their own unique contributions to the delineation of rights' norms and practices in an ongoing conversation.[29]

---

28. Lynn H. Miller, *Global Order: Values and Power in International Politics*, 4th ed. (Boulder, CO: Westview, 1998); Jonathan Moore, ed., *Hard Choices: Moral Dilemmas in Humanitarian Intervention* (Lanham, MD: Rowman & Littlefield, 1998); Matthew L. Lamb, *Solidarity with Victims: Toward a Theology of Social Transformation* (New York: Crossroad, 1982).

29. John Witte, Jr., "The Spirit of the Laws, The Laws of the Spirit: Religion and Human Rights in a New Global Era," in *God and Globalization*, vol. 2, *The Spirit and the Modern Authorities*, ed. Max Stackhouse and Don Browning (Harrisburg, PA: Trinity, 2001) 87.

Roman Catholic social thought has sought to address this paradox. Since Vatican II, one tradition of Catholic social thought has been more deeply rooted in the distinctive biblical and religious faith of the Church, while it has sought to contribute to the common moral vision needed in an interdependent world. The Catholic community has been only partially successful in these efforts to be faithful to its own beliefs, while making a contribution to comprehending the global common good in this period of reflection from Vatican II into the third millennium with its complex new world ordering. But at least it has recognized the need for the enterprise.

ten

"Blow on the Coal of the Heart"

September 11 and the Book of Job

THERESA SANDERS

I did not know anyone who died in the Twin Towers. I did not know anyone who died in the plane that smashed into the Pentagon or the one that went down in the field in Pennsylvania. My reflections on religion after 9/11, then, cannot hope to convey the pain of those who lost family or friends that day.

Neither can I speak with the authority of those who, through luck or determination or the courage of others, managed to survive the carnage. A year after the attacks, the PBS news show *Frontline* produced a series of programs titled Faith and Doubt at Ground Zero, which included interviews with several of the people who had fled from the World Trade Center shortly before its collapse. In one interview, a loan officer named Stanley Praimnath describes how he watched a plane heading straight towards him from his desk on the eighty-second floor. Within seconds after the impact, his office started to collapse around him, and Praimnath screamed out for help. Then, he says, "I felt like this strange force came over me. This power that I've never felt before." He punched his fist through one of the walls and was pulled into the next room by a man whom he did not know; both were able to escape. Praimnath was understandably grateful for his life, and he credited God with saving him. But he also questioned why others were not as fortunate: "And here I am, got delivered, and I'm angry. Angry because all of these good people who were there, the firefighters, the cops, the EMS workers, all of these good people who were left in this building, which I am sure they were, that couldn't come down from the 81st or 82nd floor because of all of this debris. They perished. So I'm angry."[1]

Praimnath can ask questions about God with an urgency that I, from the safety of my living room, cannot feel or even fully understand.

As is true for most people, my own experience of the events of September 11 came through the medium of television. The fact that I live and work in Washington DC, however, lent a heightened sense of tension to what I was seeing on CNN. On that day a colleague and I climbed to the rooftop of a dormitory on campus and were able to see the smoke rising from the Pentagon. My apartment is less than a mile from the vice president's residence, and so for many nights following September 11, I fell asleep to the buzz of surveillance helicopters circling overhead. Even now, signs on subways and near bridges in DC urge citizens to report "suspicious" behavior. And in the back of my closet is a box with flashlights and batteries and water and peanut butter. I call it my September 11 box.

In thinking about trialogue and terror after 9/11, neither do I have any particular insight into the mindsets of the men who hijacked the planes. I cannot give an analysis of the sociological implications of religious belief or of the relation between religion and politics in the contemporary world. I do not know very much about the various theological and exegetical trends that influenced those who ordered the attacks. My own questions are much more personal. As philosopher Philippe Nemo observes, "Those who have died in collective catastrophes are first of all private souls, each of whom saw death approaching for himself or herself alone."[2] My question, then, is how the private soul makes sense of the knowledge that someone wills to destroy it. How can I comprehend not just the inevitability of my own death but the knowledge that there are people in the world who actively will my death? How can I, how can any of us, live in the face of what Nemo calls "the excess of evil," an evil "that unhinges all human know-how and hurls it into the abyss, precipitating the appearance—a veritable apparition—of the abyss in which the whole world sinks"?[3] How do we continue to go to work, board airplanes and trains, gather at arenas and shopping malls—in short, live life, knowing that someone intends us mortal harm? How do we reconcile the mundane with the excess of evil?

---

1. Online: http://www.pbs.org/wgbh/pages/frontline/shows/faith/questions/911.html/.

2. Philippe Nemo, *Job and the Excess of Evil*, trans. Michael Kigel (Pittsburgh: Duquesne University Press, 1998) 1.

3. Ibid, 85–86.

Nemo's reflections arise in the context of his examination of the biblical book of Job. Job's story is one that I have taught many times in my sections of a course called "The Problem of God," a course that nearly all first-year students at my university take. After all these years, I am no closer to a definitive interpretation of that book than I was when I began. The text is so complex that perhaps no single interpretation can do justice to all its twists and turns. And yet it does offer some insights into how we might live after 9/11.

First, the book of Job muddies any effort to discern a correspondence between being righteous and being rewarded. When disasters strike, pundits and religious leaders are often quick to describe the events as God's hand meting out punishment. Job's story, however, calls for caution in assigning blame.

Second, we learn that it is permissible, and even required, for humans to contest with God. Job cries out against what appears to be God's judgment and defends his ways despite overwhelming evidence that God has found him guilty.

Third, the fact that humans are merely "dust and ashes" is not an excuse for us to abdicate moral responsibility. There is much that we do not understand about the workings of the universe. That does not absolve us, however, from recognizing injustice or from acting justly ourselves.

Finally, the book reminds us with pitiless clarity that the world is a frightening place and that we are at the mercy of forces over which we have no control. Reconciling ourselves to the fact that the world does not conform to our sense of right and wrong, however, allows space for us to love. As the protagonist's wife, Sarah, in Archibald MacLeish's play *J. B.* tells her husband, "I couldn't help you any more. You wanted justice and there was none—Only love." To this J. B. responds, "He [God] does not love. He Is." Sarah answers, "But we do. That's the wonder."[4] What we learn from the book of Job is that we are creatures who must take responsibility for our actions even when it is not clear to us that God is inclined to do the same.

"I Alone Escaped to Tell You" (1:15)

Two years after the terrorist attacks, children of the victims gathered at Ground Zero to read the names of the dead. The following year, parents did the same: "Many parents struggled to utter their child's name; when

---

4. Archibald MacLeish, *J. B., A Play in Verse* (Boston: Houghton Mifflin, 1958) 152.

her turn came, Maureen Santora—whose son Christopher, a twenty-three-year-old firefighter, rushed to the Trade Center on September 11 even though his shift was over—paused and choked back tears."[5]

∽

According to the Bible, Job was a man blameless and upright, a man who feared God and shunned evil. He was also the wealthiest man in the East and had been blessed with seven sons and three daughters (Job 1:1–3). Then one day catastrophe struck. In the course of a few short hours, Job lost his oxen, his sheep, his camels, and all ten of his children. *Lost* is not really the right word, though, since the story says that the oxen were stolen by the Sabeans, the camels were taken by the Chaldeans, and the children were killed when a mighty wind caused their eldest brother's house, where they had gathered, to collapse. To modern ears, it sounds strange that in all this misfortune Job never considers the possibility that he has simply had a run of bad luck or that he has been the victim of ordinary crimes. He does not blame the Sabeans or the Chaldeans, though they were the ones who took his herds, nor does he blame the architects who built his children's house. Instead, he concludes, "The Lord gave, and the Lord has taken away; blessed be the name of the Lord" (1:21). In Job's mind, the events of that horrible day did not happen by chance but were rather the will of God.

He is correct about this. The book's prologue tells us that a heavenly figure called the Accuser (Hebrew: *ha-satan*)[6] had goaded God into causing Job's misfortunes in order to test whether or not Job would blaspheme. When Job continued to praise God despite his misfortunes, God said to the Accuser, "He still persists in his integrity, although you incited me against him, to destroy him for no reason" (2:3). Clearly what happened to Job was the result of divine intent.

---

5. Lydia Polgreen, "Rituals of Grief, On a Day Eased Only by Time," *New York Times*, September 12, 2004, 1.

6. The NRSV renders *ha-satan* as "Satan" but adds a note with the term "the Accuser." See *The HarperCollins Study Bible* (New York: HarperCollins, 1989). The Jewish Publication Society uses the title "the Adversary" and does not equate *ha-satan* with one of the "divine beings" (Hebrew: *bene ha-elohim*, lit., "sons of God") who present themselves before God. See *JPS Hebrew-English Tanakh*, 2nd ed. (Philadelphia: Jewish Publication Society, 1999). Stephen Mitchell translates the word as "the Accusing Angel" and implies that he is one of the angels who came to testify before the Lord. See Mitchell, *The Book of Job*, rev. ed. (New York: Harper Perennial, 1987) 6.

Trialogue and Terror

When the first round of calamities did not bring the desired effect, the Accuser tried once again to show God that Job's piety was not "for nothing" (1:9) but was an indication that neither property nor children meant as much to Job as did saving his own skin: "But stretch out your hand now and touch his bone and his flesh, and he will curse you to your face" (2:5). God agreed to allow the Accuser to torment Job again, authorizing anything short of taking his life. Thus Job was struck by a severe inflammation that covered his body from the soles of his feet to the top of his head. And still he did not complain: "Shall we receive the good at the hand of God, and not receive the bad?" (2:10).

When Job's friends heard of his troubles, they came to comfort him. They tore their robes and sprinkled dust on their heads, and they threw themselves on the ground with him in grief. For seven days and seven nights they sat with him in silence. And then something shifted. The story does not tell us why, but at the end of those seven days, Job raised his voice in protest to God. He could no longer accept what God had chosen to do to him. Why did he change his mind? Perhaps during the long hours during which they sat together, the friends had been casting him accusing glances. Perhaps something in their sighs made Job feel that they blamed him for what had happened. We do not know. But at the end of the mourning period, Job had had enough, and he cried out: "God damn the day I was born and the night that forced me from the womb. On that day—let there be darkness; let it never have been created; let it sink back into the void" (3:3–5). He finished his outburst with these words: "My worst fears have happened; my nightmares have come to life. Silence and peace have abandoned me, and anguish camps in my heart" (3:25–26).[7]

There is much to consider in this opening volley from Job. Most intriguing is his statement that the things that have happened to him are *the very things that he feared most*; they are *the things that he dreaded the most*. One might ask why Job had been so beset by terror prior to these events. Why did he have nightmares? What did he have to worry about? After all, he was rich. He had not one son but seven, and three daughters as well. He had herds upon herds. God had always, as the Accuser put it, "put a fence around him and his house and all that he has, on every side" (1:10, NRSV). So why had Job not been sleeping the sleep of the just?

Job's worst fear, we can imagine, was not that one day he might lose all of his property. What he dreaded most was not the deaths of his children, terrible though those deaths were. What tormented Job as he lay awake

---

7. Mitchell, *The Book of Job*, 13.

in his bed was rather the possibility that, quite simply, the world does not make sense—that many times it eludes both prediction and explanation. There seems to be no cosmic balance sheet on which good and evil are recorded and compensated, no way of guaranteeing that being good or moral or pious will lead to being happy. Once one has recognized this, one cannot forget it. As Nemo puts the matter, "The impossibility of forgetting the truth is the first characteristic of anxiety."[8]

The Bible says that Job tried to forget the fact that inevitably, at some point, all of his efforts would end in the abyss of death. He tried to keep catastrophe at bay by doing everything correctly, even offering sacrifices on behalf of his sons and daughters, saying to himself, "It may be that my children have sinned, and cursed God in their hearts" (1:5). Job did everything that he could do to ensure a happy and prosperous life for himself and his family. And catastrophe struck anyway.

"Is Not Your Wickedness Great?" (22:5)

On September 14, three days after the terrorist attacks, the following item appeared in the newspaper: "Television evangelists Jerry Falwell and Pat Robertson, two of the most prominent voices of the religious right, said liberal civil liberties groups, feminists, homosexuals and abortion rights supporters bear partial responsibility for Tuesday's terrorist attacks because their actions have turned God's anger against America."[9]

The first thing that the Book of Job makes clear is that we can discern no clear correspondence between being righteous and being rewarded. Job's friends were quick to offer accounts of just exactly why events turned out as they did. Both Eliphaz and Zophar blamed Job for his misfortunes. Bildad the Shuhite gave the unkindest cut of all: "Your children must have been evil: he [God] punished them for their crimes" (8:4).[10] The friends,

---

8. Nemo, *Job and the Excess of Evil*, 23.

9. "God Gave U.S. 'What We Deserve,' Falwell Says," *Washington Post*, September 14, 2001, C3. Falwell later acknowledged that his remarks "seemed harsh and ill-timed," adding that he regrets that the timing and wording of the comments "have detracted from the spirit of this time of mourning." See the *Washington Post*, September 18, 2001, C4.

10. Mitchell, *The Book of Job*, 25.

Trialogue and Terror

in other words, refused to acknowledge what Job had already realized deep in his bones: that they could not explain why Job was suffering, and, worse, that they therefore could not predict what might happen next. As Job astutely pointed out, his wretchedness, and even more so the lack of rationale for it, filled them with fear (6:21).[11]

Job knew, and, as the prologue of the book tells us, God knew, that Job was blameless. But the friends could not, or would not, admit that there was no correlation between Job's actions and the calamities that befell him. The friends had to maintain order in their world, and so they ignored the evidence that stared them in the face. They accused him not only of hiding his own guilt but also of destroying the piety of others: "You are undermining religion and crippling faith in God" (15:4). Job, however, had already seen through them: "Will you lie to vindicate God? Will you perjure yourselves for him? Will you blindly stand on his side, pleading his case alone? What will you do when he questions you? Can you cheat him as you would a man? Won't he judge you severely if your testimony is false?" (13:7-10).[12]

Job's speech here is actually a bit of foreshadowing, because the fact is that at the end of the story God *does* judge the friends severely for their false testimony. God informs Eliphaz that God is actually *incensed* at him and his friends, "for you have not spoken of me what is right, as my servant Job has." God orders the friends to make a sacrifice in the presence of Job, warning that if they don't, and if Job doesn't agree to pray on their behalf, then God will treat them vilely in accordance with their folly (42:7-8).

At the beginning of the text, Job is a faithful servant of God and a wealthy man. Then his wealth is taken from him, though he is no less faithful a servant. At the end of the text, Job does what God tells him to do and is rewarded for it. Biblical scholar Edwin Good is correct that "this makes no unitary sense."[13] We cannot say on the basis of the Book of Job that God always rewards the faithful or that God always punishes the wicked. Nor, though, can we say that there is never a reason for the miseries that befall humans or the good things that come their way. All we can say is that neither disaster nor good fortune can be interpreted unambiguously as the plan of God.

---

11. Ibid., 22.

12. Ibid. 41, 34-35.

13. Edwin Good, *In Turns of Tempest: A Reading of Job, with a Translation* (Stanford: Stanford University Press, 1990) 396.

"Blow on the Coal of the Heart"

"I Will Speak the Bitterness of My Soul" (10:1)

In an essay written one day after the terrorist attacks, columnist Dan Savage echoed the sentiments of Job: "Who could be against prayer at a time like this? Or God? Well, I am. Does anyone doubt for a moment that the people on those four doomed planes were praying? Or that the people hanging out the windows at the World Trade Center were praying? . . . God listens. God cares. Does He really? If so, I'd really like to see Him get off His ass and prove it every once in a while."[14]

༄

The second thing that we learn from the Book of Job is that it is permissible, and perhaps even required, that we contend with God.[15] Often the Book of Job is interpreted as saying that Job should be ashamed of himself for questioning God's ways. When God finally answers Job's pleas and speaks to him from a whirlwind, God makes it clear that Job is nothing but a speck of dust when compared with the grandeur of the universe. In verse after verse, God recalls divine achievements and shows the impotence of Job. Finally, God finishes speaking, and Job is allowed one more opportunity to make his voice heard. What he says, however, is enigmatic. At first Job simply repeats a theme he has returned to again and again: divine power. He says to God, "I know that you can do all things, and that no purpose of yours can be thwarted." He then acknowledges his own limitations: "Therefore I have uttered what I did not understand, things too wonderful for me, which I did not know" (42:2-3). His final verse, though, is both difficult to translate and difficult to interpret. It is not surprising that renderings of Job 42:6 vary widely. However, how one interprets this small sentence affects how one understands the meaning of the entire book.

In Hebrew, the text of 42:6 reads *al-ken emas v-nihamti al-apar va-eper*. The first term, *al-ken*, simply means "therefore," or "upon such conditions." The second term, *emas*, is a verb that means to reject or to refuse or to despise. It is the term Job uses to describe how children react to his maggot-ridden body (19:18). The third term begins with the prefix that

---

14. Dan Savage, "Savage Love" (weekly column), *Washington City Paper*, September 21, 2001, 56.

15. The discussion of Job 42:6 that follows is adapted from my essay "Ash Wednesday after Auschwitz," which appeared in the *Journal of Ecumenical Studies* 41/1-2 (Winter 2004) 39-54, as well as in my book *Tenebrae: Holy Week after the Holocaust* (Maryknoll, NY: Orbis 2007).

means "and" and is a verb meaning to be sorry, to suffer grief, or to console oneself. The last two terms are preceded by a preposition and mean "dust and ashes." A literal translation thus might read, "Therefore I despise and I am sorry upon dust and ash."[16] Consider, though, how various translators have rendered the passage:

- Therefore I despise myself and repent in dust and ashes. (New Revised Standard Version)
- Therefore I recant and relent, being but dust and ashes. (Jewish Publication Society)
- Therefore I feel loathing contempt and revulsion (toward you, O God); and I am sorry for frail man. (John Briggs Curtis)[17]
- I shudder with sorrow for mortal clay. (Jack Miles)[18]

The first two translations assume that the target of Job's negative feelings is himself. The New Revised Standard Version (NRSV) makes this clear, inserting the object "myself" into the text even though the word does not appear in the Hebrew. Though the translation of the Jewish Publication Society (JPS) is not as explicit as that of the NRSV, it nonetheless portrays Job as dissatisfied with his words, if not with his very self, and thus as willing to "recant and relent."

The next translation, that offered by John Briggs Curtis, also hypothesizes that there is a missing object in the sentence. As Curtis reads the text, however, the implied object of Job's scorn is not himself but rather God. Curtis considers two other verses within the text (7:16 and 34:33) in which Job expresses revulsion, and he concludes that at least in 42:6, if not also in these other two, "there can be little doubt that the unexpressed object of the loathing is God."[19] Indeed, the JPS version of the Tanakh translates 34:33, in which Elihu reproaches Job, as, "Should He requite as you see fit? But you have despised (Him)!"[20] Here the translation apparently has no qualms about inserting the missing object, God, into the sentence. It is only later, when it comes to Job's final speech, that the JPS seems unwilling to make "God" the object of the sentence. Curtis speculates that in 42:6, if

---

16. Good, *In Turns of Tempest*, 25.
17. John Briggs Curtis, "On Job's Response to Yahweh," *Journal of Biblical Literature* 98 (1979) 505. In the original, the phrase "toward you, O God" is placed in brackets.
18. Jack Miles, *God: A Biography* (New York: Vintage, 1995) 325.
19. Curtis, "On Job's Response to Yahweh," 504.
20. In the original, brackets are used rather than parentheses.

not also in 7:16 and 34:33, an editor may have removed the name of God from the text in order to spare the sensibilities of more pious readers.

The translation of Jack Miles differs from that of Curtis in that Miles assumes that the object of both of the two verbs is not missing but is rather present in the sentence. Miles understands the pair of verbs to be two words expressing a single action. Hence, he renders the verbs as one movement; Job "shudders with sorrow." As Miles sees the passage, though, the cause of Job's shuddering is neither Job himself nor God, but rather humanity, humanity as the frail creature of God: as dust and ashes. According to Miles, when Job looks at the pathetic being whom God has created, he feels both disgust and pity. Job's encounter with the living God, in Miles's view, does nothing to change his mind about the wretched state of humanity. Rather, upon hearing the divine voice Job comes to know even more clearly that he is in the right and that God is in the wrong. God really has acted unjustly, and Job is correct to call him to account.

All of these interpretations are complicated by the fact that after Job finishes his speech, God has one last scene. In the last few verses of the book, God tells one of Job's companions, "I am incensed at you and your two friends, for you have not spoken the truth about Me as did My servant Job" (42:7). God then commands Job's three friends to sacrifice bulls and rams in the presence of Job, and God indicates that things will go very badly with them unless Job prays on their behalf. When Job does pray, God increases his holdings twofold. God gives him twice what had before as well as ten new children.

We must wonder, though, what exactly Job said that gained him such favor from God. The friends, we are told, did not speak the truth about God *as Job did*. What truth did Job speak? And where did the friends go wrong?

"I Will Defend My Ways to His Face" (13:15)

Twelve days after the World Trade Center was destroyed, a British reporter described his experience at Ground Zero:

> I looked around and all I could see was a smouldering mountain of wreckage. Every building was damaged. They were all coated with a thick layer of dirt and dust. And there was a horrible stench. It was a ghastly smell of death, a sickening smell that I'd experienced before in Africa and Rwanda and here it was again. The dust was getting into my eyes, down my throat and going

down into my lungs. All around me were mountains of mangled steel and rubble and I thought: how could this have happened?[21]

◦

The third thing that we learn from Job is that we are not absolved of moral responsibility simply because we are but "dust and ashes."

The first two translations of 42:6, those that see the passage as expressing repentance on Job's part, seem unable to provide satisfactory answers to the questions of what truth Job spoke and where the friends went wrong. For if we assume that Job spoke rightly during his long complaints against God, then why should Job despise himself, recant or relent in 42:6? If he had been telling the truth in his tirades against God, then recanting would be duplicitous. Alternatively, if we assume that Job spoke the truth in repenting in 42:6, then why are the friends taken to task by God? They, after all, were the ones who had urged Job to repent all along. Why should the friends be blamed by God for telling Job to repent if it was in his repentance that Job spoke the truth?

Of course, we might translate the text in line with the NRSV and the JPS but *interpret* it quite differently. Elie Wiesel, who so often identifies himself with Job in his own writings, does precisely this in an essay called "Job: Our Contemporary." In this essay, Wiesel at first expresses outrage at the cravenness of Job's final speech. He imagines Job as saying to God, "Yes, I am indeed small, insignificant; I had no right to speak, I am unworthy of Your words and thoughts. I didn't know, I didn't understand. I couldn't know. From now on I shall live with remorse, in dust and ashes."[22] Such cowardice on Job's part is a betrayal, as Wiesel sees it, of the millions who suffered unjustly, the millions who "could be seen on every road of Europe. Wounded, robbed, mutilated. Certainly not happy. Nor resigned."[23]

However, Wiesel also offers an alternative assessment of Job's words. Perhaps, he suggests, Job's quick abdication is really a gesture of defiance against and an indictment of God. Writes Wiesel, "He did not hesitate or procrastinate, nor did he point out the slightest contradiction. Therefore we know that in spite or perhaps because of appearances, Job continued to interrogate God. By repenting sins he did not commit, by justifying a

---

21. Mark Austin, "America at War," *Sunday Mirror*, September 23, 2001, 12.

22. Elie Wiesel, *Messengers of God: Biblical Portraits and Legends* (New York: Random House, 1976) 231–32.

23. Ibid., 233–34.

sorrow he did not deserve, he communicates to us that he did not believe in his own confessions; they were nothing but decoys."[24] In this reading of the text, Job does not surrender his dignity or his right to question God's justice, just as Wiesel himself continues to ask God about the murders of six million.

Wiesel's interpretation actually takes us closer to the translations of 42:6 offered by Curtis and Miles. Those renderings, it should be pointed out, seem better able than the first two translations to handle the Book of Job's conclusion. If in 42:6 Job expresses not repentance but rather contempt for God and/ or sorrow for human beings, then perhaps what follows is God's recognition of just how badly Job was treated. The fact that God gives back twice what Job had before his trials occurred might be read as evidence that in the text it is God who repents rather than Job. After all, the Torah stipulates, "In all charges of misappropriation . . . the case of both parties shall come before God: he whom God declares guilty shall pay double to the other" (Exodus 22:8, JPS).[25] By restoring the fortunes of Job, perhaps God is acknowledging divine wrongdoing and recognizing Job's uprightness. Moreover, God's anger at the friends would then be due to their willingness to speak well of God even when God does not deserve such praise. They would be told to offer sacrifices for acting as yes-men rather than as servants with the dignity and self-respect that Job exhibited.

If in 42:6 Job were to have repented for sins that both he and God knew he did not commit, then our very status as moral agents would have been undercut. The message of the book would have been something like, "Yes, God is arbitrary and capricious, but your job is to accede to divine whims at all costs." Human beings would then be relieved of any and all questions regarding justice or righteousness, and our role would simply be to cower in the face of divine command. The fact that this translation/ interpretation is less than persuasive indicates that craven obedience is not what the text seeks to endorse.

"And Job Died, Old and Full of Days" (42:17)

A survey taken in 2006 yielded the following information:

Among children who lost a parent on September 11, more than a third said they continue to have "intrusive thoughts" about the attacks,

---

24. Ibid., 235.
25. For this insight I am grateful to Tod Linafelt of Georgetown University.

42 percent underperformed at school and more than a third had post-traumatic stress or separation anxiety.[26]

~

The end of the Book of Job tells us that after his ordeal, Job lived to be 140 years old, and that he died "full of days" (42:17). Other translations render the phrase as "contented"[27] or "at a very great age."[28] In the end, it seems, in addition to being given new children, sheep, camels, oxen, and donkeys, Job was also given the blessing of a long life.

And yet we might speculate a little about those long years of Job, during which, the Bible says, Job was able to see his grandchildren and his great-grandchildren grow up. Having been the target of a divine whirlwind, could Job ever really breathe easily again? The text itself invites us to ask. The verb *saba* in the phrase "full of days" means "to be satisfied," or "to have one's fill of." Job lived a satisfying amount of time. Even in English, though, the idea of satiety can have a double-meaning. We say, "That's enough arguing!" or "I'm fed up with your complaining." In Hebrew the verb *saba* is likewise used at times to indicate a surfeit that is wearying.[29] In Isaiah 1:11, for example, God says to Israel, "I have had enough (*sabati*) of burnt offerings of rams and the fat of fed beasts; I do not delight in the blood of bulls, or of lambs, or of goats." Even in the Book of Job itself, the word is used to mean not just "enough" but "too much." In 7:4, Job describes his difficulty sleeping: "When I lie down, I say, 'When shall I rise?' But the night is long, and I am full (*ve-sabati*) of tossing until dawn."

It is true that the word "satisfied" is a standard way of describing the longevity of the biblical patriarchs. Abraham dies *sabea* in Genesis 25:8; his son Isaac dies "full of days" (*sba yamim*) in Genesis 35:29, as does King David in I Chronicles 29:28. It would be too much to claim that the primary meaning of the word in these cases is "fed up" or "weary of life." And yet, it is worth pointing out that Abraham, Isaac and David all suffered at the hands of God. Abraham was commanded to kill his son Isaac (though that death sentence was revoked before it was carried out), and God killed

26. Jennifer Harper, "9/11 Continues to Haunt Survivors," *Washington Times*, September 7, 2006, A3.

27. This translation comes from the *JPS Hebrew-English Tanakh*.

28. Mitchell, *The Book of Job*, 91.

29. For this insight I am indebted to Bible scholar Tod Linafelt, though he tells me that he was not the first to think of it.

David's unnamed first son after David had arranged for Uriah the Hittite to be killed. We might imagine that at the end of their lives, these three men, like Job, might be described not just as "satisfied" but as "having had enough" of life.

"Let Us Choose What Is Right; Let Us Determine among Ourselves What Is Good" (34:4)

Here is one of the many voice messages left on answering machines and cell phones by those on the planes:

"Honey. Something terrible is happening. I don't think I'm going to make it. I love you. Take care of the children."[30]

When Archibald MacLeish published his play *J.B.* in 1958, the world was still recovering from the devastations of two world wars. A retelling of the story of Job, *J.B.* recognizes that, as one of its characters observes, "There's always someone playing Job."[31] Unthinkable crimes are committed, and unspeakable acts are perpetrated, and the world keeps spinning despite it all.

MacLeish's version of the story is actually a play within a play. On stage, two characters named Zuss and Nickles put on the masks of God and Satan in order to act out Job's story. The object of their attention is a wealthy banker named J.B. who over the course of the play loses all of his possessions and all of his children. One daughter is raped and murdered, and another is killed in an explosion. A son is killed in a military fiasco; two more children die in an automobile accident caused by a drunken driver. Even his wife leaves him, frustrated as she is by J.B.'s insistence that if he tries hard enough, he will be able to make some sense of it all. Everything that J. B. holds dear is taken from him in a flash, and he cannot face the possibility that the world is nothing more than a tale told by an idiot signifying nothing. And so, like the original Job, J. B. searches for a meaning underlying his suffering: "What is my fault? What have I done?"[32] At

---

30. *Frontline: Faith and Doubt at Ground Zero*; online: http://www.pbs.org/wgbh/pages/frontline/shows/faith/questions/god.html.

31. MacLeish, *J. B.*, 12.

32. Ibid., 126.

stake is the rationality of the universe: "Unless guilt matters the whole world is meaningless. God too is nothing."[33]

When God finally speaks to J. B., however, a transformation takes place: J.B. becomes reconciled to the fact of injustice. He does not thereby lose his own sense of either justice or hope, though. Instead, he summons his integrity and finds a way to forgive God. It is, as Zuss says, "As though Job's suffering were justified not by the Will of God but Job's acceptance of God's Will . . . In spite of everything he'd suffered! In spite of all he'd lost and loved he understood and he forgave it!"[34] J. B. forgives God for the suffering that God has inflicted on him. He even has compassion for God, a fact that infuriates Zuss: "Then, he *calmed* me! Gentled me the way a farmhand gentles a bulging, bugling bull! Forgave me! . . . for the world! . . . for everything!"[35]

So much has been written about the topic of forgiveness that it would be impossible to summarize scholars' views here. For my part, I agree with Alan Berger who writes, "I may forgive one who has sinned against me. I may not forgive one who has taken the life of another."[36] J. B. cannot forgive God on behalf of his dead children. He is able, however, to forgive God for his own sorrow and pain. And recognizing that God either cannot or will not provide a just world, J.B. finds a way to live beyond that pain.

At the end of the play, J.B.'s wife Sarah comes to him holding a broken twig of forsythia, one of the first flowers to bloom in the springtime. She found the blossoms, she says, "growing in the ashes." She kisses J.B. and urges him,

> Blow on the coal of the heart.
> The candles in churches are out.
> The lights have gone out in the sky.
> Blow on the coal of the heart
> And we'll see by and by.[37]

MacLeish's answer to the question of how to live after catastrophe is simply that we "blow on the coals of our hearts," nurturing the small sprigs of hope that life presents to us and clinging to the people who know us

---

33. Ibid., 121.
34. Ibid., 139.
35. Ibid., 138 (ellipses original; italics original).
36. Alan L. Berger, in *The Sunflower: On the Possibilities and Limits of Forgiveness*, ed. Simon Wiesenthal, rev. ed. (New York: Schocken, 1998) 119.
37. MacLeish, *J. B.*, 150, 153.

and love us for who we are. The lights in the evening sky can be difficult to interpret, and the candles in the churches may have been snuffed out. But as J. B.'s wife Sarah reminds us, we can still love. And that's the wonder.

eleven

Dialogical Interaction or Post-Honor Confrontation?

KHALEEL MOHAMMED

For all the pain that disasters cause, they often have a side that allows us to appreciate the best in humankind. September 11 is a perfect example: while one of the worst manifestations of suffering caused by hate, it has propelled people of righteousness to work harder at promoting interreligious discussion in the noble quest for understanding and respect, with particular emphasis on the major three Abrahamic faiths. These attempts, however, are often marred by the urge to defend and be politically correct. Discussants are frequently only too happy to focus on issues of agreement or verses of Scripture, studiously ignoring the points of disagreement or difference that have, over the centuries, often resulted in bloody clashes. For many, personal faith is to be defended no matter what the cost; this often results in an impious paradox: while emphasizing that her religion stands for truth, an interfaith discussant often seeks to mask or overlook the truth in order to make her religion seem superior to others. It is for this reason that at the very beginning of this chapter I wish to draw attention to the vital fact that my concern is not only with Judaism, Christianity, and Islam at large, but specifically after 9/11. Nevertheless, it is necessary to deal with several pre-9/11 aspects of the interaction, as they do impact on the current state of affairs.

I have seen numerous Muslims after 9/11 seek to convince a skeptical public that the terrorists of that fateful day did not act in concordance with the Quranic teachings and that their actions should not be deemed representative of Islamic thought and religion. I certainly share this view, but I do not think that it is a valid response to the situation. Whether I like it or not, those terrorists were Muslim and, as later discovered, acted at the behest of a leader who is admired by more that just a few within Islam. To therefore cite the Quran and insinuate that it is the sole criterion by which to judge an action as Islamic or not would be disingenuous and downright misleading. As in any religion that has evolved, Islam has more than just its main Scripture as its source for creed and praxis. The hadith, Islam's oral tradition, and purportedly the extra-Quranic teachings of Muhammad have in fact supplanted the Quran. The rulings of the jurists throughout the centuries, as well as the development of sectarian and political biases, have all created an amorphous base for judgment of what is "true" Islam. To be sure, I will analyze what the Quran envisages as its message, but I cannot and will not seek to deny the fact that contemporary Islam is what it is, and that whether or not it agrees with the Quran, it must be addressed rather than explained away.

There is consensus among scholars of religion that as there is no one Judaism or Christianity, so too there is no one Islam. Even if one does not have access to history books, one simply has to read the daily newspapers to note the horrible internecine bloodbaths that today underline the sectarian divides in the religion. The Sunni–Shia clashes in Iraq and Pakistan, the outlawing of the Ahmadiyya sect in Pakistan all refute the concept of a single Islam. Al-Qaeda, the Taliban, Sipahi-i-Sahaba, and the army of the Mahdi—to name but a few groups—are not figments of the imagination, nor are they miniscule, isolated sects: they represent well-funded and established modern interpretations of Islam that do not subscribe to any idea of harmonious interaction with the perceived Other.

When seeking to foster clarity and understanding between the followers of Abrahamic religion therefore, I must take these facts into account if I wish to be honest. I must also realize that many Muslims, reeling from the pain of a largely alarmist and pejorative press in the United States may be pained by some of what I express. To them in particular—my beleaguered co-religionists—I declare with the firmest conviction: I am a Muslim and my Scripture commands me to tell the truth even if it is against my closest relatives (Q 4:135, 5:8). This personal conviction is buttressed by my professional ethic: as an academic, I adhere to the protocol that makes the admission of truth the highest ideal. I write with the hope that my co-authors and I have the same views about the essentiality of truth; I therefore eschew apologetic and empty rhetoric, in focusing on three themes: Theology of the Other; Concepts of salvation and Capacity for theological self-critique.

Trialogue and Terror

Theology of the Other

Despite possibly benign meanings for the word *Other*, as far as religious usage of the term is concerned, it almost always denotes that which is distinctly different from us—that which is not included. Othering is almost always negative: it applies to those who do not follow our religion, and since our religion must necessarily be true, then it follows that the Other must be false or somehow corrupt. The idea that this Other is to be extirpated, conquered, or converted has manifested itself in the most sanguinary fashion throughout our history. It has come to the point where for many of us there is an imagined geography, talking about a Christian West and a Muslim Middle East. The actions of 9/11 have brought home with the most stunning impact that while the concept of the Other may never totally divest itself of its negative connotation, its ubiquity demands that we reexamine our concepts of interaction or face the possibility of global warfare. Every single war, every single dispute in history has been based on some aspect of Othering, and it is obvious that this is the most important of the three themes and must necessarily be treated in the most detail.

Scholars of religion readily acknowledge that since Jews and Christians were part of the milieu to which Muhammad came, the Quran had to pay special attention to them. Indeed, such respect is paid to the Hebrew prophets and Jesus that early Western scholars of the academic study of religion argued whether it was Judaism or Christianity that had primacy of influence on Islam. Among the three major monotheistic faiths, Islam is the only one that has its name specially designated in its Scripture. The term, however, is so inclusive that, regarding verse 3:19 of the Quran, "Indeed the religion with God is Islam," Professor Wilfred Cantwell Smith remarked: "To many when it was first proclaimed and for some centuries after, this verse was saying what any man must say whose faith is vivid and whose orientation is moralist. Far from being primarily sectarian, it is, curiously, virtually identical even to the wording with the statement or definition given in the *Catholic Encyclopedia* 'Religion . . . means the voluntary subjection of oneself to God.'"[1]

In a similar vein, Professor Abdul Aziz Sachedina observes, "Islamic revelation presents a theology that resonates with the modern pluralistic belief that other faiths are not merely inferior manifestations of religiosity, but variant forms of individual and communal responses to the presence

---

1. Wilfred Cantwell Smith, *The Meaning and End of Religion: A New Approach to the Religious Traditions of Mankind* (New York: Macmillan, 1963) 112–13.

Dialogical Interaction or Post-Honor Confrontation?

of the transcendent in human life."[2] The Quran says that to each nation a messenger has been sent (Q 16:36) and further exhorts Muslims to believe in all the prophets without differentiating among them (Q 2:136). Otherness within the family of religions is acknowledged, with the idea of cultural and ritual differences being God-given. This idea is clearly put forth in the verse: "For each We have appointed a divine law and a traced out way. Had God so willed He could have made you one community. But (things are the way they are) that He may try you by that which He has given you. So vie one with another in good works. Unto God you will all return, and He will then inform you of that wherein you differ" (Q 5:48).

Yet, despite all these wonderful verses of recognition and acceptance of the Other, Islam had, within a few centuries of Muhammad's death, transformed this conceptualization. Almost every book of exegesis from the tenth century onwards seeks to explain away earlier verses of inclusivism, promoting the concept that the Quran had abrogated every previous Scripture, and Islam had supplanted every other religion. This universalist interpretation and the rapid Islamic conquests gave Muslims the idea that the world could be divided into two spheres: *Dar al-Islam* and the *Dar al-Harb*, translated respectively as the territory of Islam and the territory of War. Classical Muslim thinkers felt that the idea was to enforce the law of Islam by conquest, until there was no longer any territory of war.[3]

The inevitable clash with similar expansionist views of Christendom, and later European colonialism further exacerbated the mutual animosity that has prevailed ever since, despite periods of uneasy truce. The twentieth century saw the decline and fall of the Ottoman Empire as well as the establishment of the state of Israel, all events that were harsh blows to the self-image of majoritarian Islam. Towards the end of that century, there was a resurgence of Islamic consciousness that manifested itself in the appearance of several political parties that professed a desire to establish "true" Islam. In a most surprising development, Iran was changed into a theocracy, and the defeat of Soviet forces in Afghanistan revivified the use of Jihad rhetoric. Afghan-based Muslim fighters had used the term *Jihad* to describe their struggle, and had been recognized throughout the world as *mujahideen*—the term used to describe those who wage Jihad. Every single Muslim nation knew the rise of Islamic activism. The result is that today, even in Turkey, which had since the 1920s prided itself on its

---

2. Abdul Aziz Sachedina, *The Islamic Roots of Democratic Pluralism* (New York: Oxford University Press, 2001) 14.

3. Louay Safi, *Peace and the Limits of War: Transcending the Classical Conception of Jihad* (Herndon, VA: International Institute of Islamic Thought, 2001) 7.

secularism, Islamic activism has set the path for the de facto redefinition of that country's religious status. In Israel where the fight for Palestinian self-determination had long been conducted under a secular perspective, whether by the Popular Front for the Liberation of Palestine, the Palestinian Liberation Organization, or similar groups, extremist Hamas has been voted into power, proclaiming adherence to an extremely uncompromising Islam.

The rise of religious consciousness has not only been in the Muslim majority regions. In China, North America, and Asia, evangelism and missionary work have resulted in a new power wielded by televangelists and preachers. The power of religion has become so potent that in his book *The Dignity of Difference*, Jonathan Sacks, chief Rabbi of London, draws our attention to a fact that underlines the transformation from the twentieth to the twenty-first century. The twentieth century was dominated by the politics of ideology; the current century is dominated instead by the politics of identity.[4] Religion has become one of the great definers of identity, and in so doing, has created the "us" and "them" mentality—wherein the "them" are the people not like us. When the terrorists of 9/11 declared themselves Muslim warriors against America, the "us"-and-"them" paradigm manifested itself in its most extreme polarization. For most non-Muslim Americans, whose general view of Islam had historically been shaped by polemical depiction, Muslims became the hateful, barbaric, mysterious "them." Many Muslims were taken by surprise at the blanket condemnation of the entire religion, and the seeming cooperation of many Jewish and Christian figures to spew hateful rhetoric about Islam. To these Muslims, Jews and Christians became friends and protectors of one another, bent on demonizing and destroying Islam. This cooperation, accordingly makes Jews and Christians the hated Other.

Yet if we examine the theories of connection between Muslims and the Abrahamic Other, we can see that scholars have not always perceived a hostile relationship. To be sure, many popular writers have written books seeking to show that Islam was from the very start intent on world conquest and domination. The sad fact is that while these books are easily available, their authors are not scholars in the field and often write more from the point of view of religious polemic, revisionist hallucination, or pure Islamophobia. The scholars who write with some level of objectivity mostly do so within the ivory towers of academia. They address academics,

---

4. Jonathan Sacks, *The Dignity of Difference: How to Avoid the Clash of Civilizations* (London: Continuum, 2002) 10.

and even if the popular bookstores do carry their publications (which they generally don't), steep prices and specialist language almost always guarantee against significant sales numbers.

Even though most of the terminologies of early contact between the three Abrahamic religions focus on relations between one and a specific Other rather than concurrent consideration of the interaction between all three, I will still use the coinages as I find them functional. Shlomo Goitien, arguably the last century's most famous researcher on Judeo-Islamic relations, used the term "creative symbiosis" to indicate the mutually beneficial interaction between Judaism and Islam.[5] Indeed, he went so far as to state that it was the appearance of Islam that saved the Jewish people.[6] From the story of Mary and Jesus in the Quran and the imported Christian eschatological themes, one could easily argue for "creative symbiosis" as an equally applicable description of the relationship between Islam and Christianity. Muslim tradition remembers the actions of the Christian ruler of Abyssinia who granted asylum to the first Muslims, refusing to hand them over to the Arab pagans, in recognition that their beliefs in God and Jesus were no different than his.

Another term is "co-evolution," suggested by Steven Wasserstrom in his scholarly critique of Goitein's depiction.[7] *Co-evolution*, a natural science import, is defined as "a stochastic system of evolutionary change in which two or more species interact in such a way that changes in species A set the stage for the natural selection of changes in species B; later changes in species B, in turn, set the stage for the selecting of more similar changes in species A."[8] This term is more neutral in that it equally applies to the changes of interaction—positive and negative—and more clearly allows for the idea of interaction between Judaism, Christianity, and Islam.

Even if some scholars have criticized their peers' views of depictions of past relationships between Islam and the other two Abrahamic religions, one thing is clear: the "Other" in today's usage has not changed from its largely pejorative depiction. Goitein described the post-1900 relationship

---

5. Shlomo Dov Goitein, *Jews and Arabs: Their Contacts through the Ages*, Schocken Paperbacks (New York: Schocken, 1967) 11.

6. Shlomo Dov Goitein, "Muhammad's Inspiration by Judaism," *Journal of Jewish Studies* 9 (1958) 144–62.

7. Stephen M. Wasserstrom, *Between Muslim and Jew: The Problem of Symbiosis under Early Islam* (Princeton: Princeton University Press, 1995) 7.

8. Gregory Bateson and Mary Bateson, *Angels Fear: Steps toward an Epistemology of the Sacred* (New York: Macmillan, 1987) 207.

between Islam and Judaism as "the new confrontation."⁹ And, after 9/11, Professor Akbar Ahmed coined the phrase "post-honor" to describe the exaggerated expression of group loyalty and a perverted view of honor that manifests itself in violence against the Other in the most horrendous ways, including rape and the basest acts of violence.¹⁰ I think that a fusion of the two terms into "post-honor confrontation" best describes the current situation.

In response to what it deems as attacks on the honor of Islam, segments of the Muslim world have responded in making the "Other" such a malleable construct that it is now not only the non-Muslim that is the outsider, but indeed any Muslim that is perceived as having beliefs that are perceived as somehow different.¹¹ Never before in the history of human interaction, I think, has the Other, within or without the religion, been so pejoratively portrayed. In response to the Danish cartoons of Muhammad, there were parts of the Muslim world that arose in riots. Militant reactions to the Iraqi invasion as manifested in the filmed beheading of innocents, and the horrible suicide bombings against occupation forces and fellow Muslims have given rise to the perception that Muslims are a barbaric, bloodthirsty group of people. Since I write as a Muslim I shall not detail the actions committed by non-Muslims against the followers of Islam. The daily barrage of disparaging television depictions, Pope Benedict XVI's inflammatory statements about Islam that not so long ago made headlines, the pejorative portrayals of Muslims by Jewish right-wing activists are all not conducive to harmony.

Despite these setbacks, several of my coreligionists continue, as I do, to advocate for a Quranic inclusiveness of the Other, eschewing many of the constructs of later Islam. Such Muslims are often perceived by their coreligionists as being naïve or sometimes as having become stooges for "the American government"—a blanket term that has come to represent not only the country itself but also Jewish and Christian interests. Yet there are Muslim groups in this country that pride themselves on their inclusivist outlook. Outside Buffalo, in the West Valley Township, there is a small Muslim community in an area known as Jabal Arabia. The descendants of Black slaves who have made Jabal Arabia their home since the early

---

9. Goitein, *Jews and Arabs*, 12.

10. Akbar S. Ahmed, *Islam under Siege: Living Dangerously in a Post-Honor World*, Themes for the 21st Century (Cambridge: Polity, 2003) 7.

11. Hyder Mili "Jihad without Rules: The Evolution of al-Takfir wa'l Hijra," in *Terrorism Monitor* 4/13 (2006), Washington DC: The Jamestown Foundation. Online: http://www.jamestown.org/

Dialogical Interaction or Post-Honor Confrontation?

twentieth century are extremely proud of their American identity. In the communal graveyard, there are several American flags marking the resting spots of those whose relatives proudly identify them as having died for this country in war. I remember meeting Imam Obadiah Ramadan, leader of this community, shortly before his death in 2006. He recounted to me the story of a foreign Muslim who came to West Valley offering to teach them his interpretation of Islam and possibly providing financial help. Imam Obadiah detected some level of Islamic triumphalism in this would-be benefactor and rejected his proposal. I remember the passion in the imam's voice as he told me, "I said to him, 'Brother you and I ain't never going to be the same. You are where you are from and I am an American. I love this country. The only thing in common between us is Islam, but I have my way and you have yours.'"

At the beginning of this chapter, I pointed out the problems of many of the well-meaning interfaith conferences. It would seem that the passing of time has fortunately allowed some of us to put aside the veil of diplomatic platitudes and accept reality. I do not endorse many of the positions of the modern state of Iran, but I do feel that nation's leaders are rather candid about certain truths. On May 4, 2007, former Iranian president Muhammad Khatami met the pontiff in Rome at an intercultural conference. When asked if the tensions that arose after the pope's unfortunate remarks had been healed, Khatami responded, "Unfortunately, the wounds of this world are too deep and can't be closed easily, and maybe one meeting isn't enough.[12]

~

If the pope's faux pas—not acknowledged by many as an error—can take such a long time to heal, even after his visit to Turkey and several attempts at mollification, then one can only come to a single conclusion after reflecting on the fact that the encounter between Islam and the older Abrahamic religions has been marred by historical contentiousness rather than by tolerance: September 11 was not a single occurrence where differences manifested themselves in acts of violence; it was simply one of the most horrendous, and the hateful post-event rhetoric represented centuries of ill feeling. The president of the United States (George W. Bush at the

---

12. New York Times News Service, "Pope, Ex-Iran Leader Discuss Divisions," *San Diego Union Tribune*, May 5, 2007, A16; online: http://www.signonsandiego.com/uniontrib/20070505/news_7n5world.html/.

time of writing), an avowed Christian, created the term "axis of evil" that is, for many Muslims, a reference to all of Islam. For many Muslims, the post-9/11 wars, renewed pledges by the American president of support for Israel, and the invasion of Afghanistan and Iraq by the U.S.-led coalition only point to one thing: another Western crusade, except that this time, the Jews and Christians are clearly allies, both empowered, seeking to destroy "us." For the mullahs and demagogues, the scenario is either black or white: one cannot love those who want to destroy Islam, and any Muslim who supports the perceived enemy is to be counted as one of them.

Concepts of Salvation

"Truly, those who believe, the Jews and the Christians, the Sabeans, whomsoever believes in God and the Last Day and does righteous deeds, shall have their reward with their Lord. On them shall be no fear nor shall they grieve" (Q 2:62). This verse clearly indicates the Quran's inclusive salvific view as it pertains to Jews and Christians and some obscurely referenced monotheists. Even in its polemic, Islam's main document denies any sort of singularity of salvation, as shown in Q 111–112: "They say, "None shall enter Paradise unless he is a Jew or a Christian. These are their own desires. Say (to them): Produce your proof if you are telling the truth. Rather, whoever who turns his face to God and is a doer of good shall receive his reward with God; on such shall be no fear nor shall they grieve."

Rather than confronting the claimants to salvation with denial, the Quran challenges them to produce proof that only they are entitled—and sets the criteria for that right, in a manner that includes all those who are within the broadest definition of a God-centered spiritual path. Verses like these, as well as consideration of the evolution of religion, have led Professor Abdul Aziz Sachedina to ask, "How can Muslims conclude that the sole path to perfection, and hence, entitlement to salvation, is historical Islam with its beginnings in the seventh century?"[13]

His scholarly question however is rather simply answered. Quite early after the death of Muhammad, it seems that Muslim thinkers, in accordance with their universalist view, only paid lip service to any sort of recognition of the Other, and sought to refract the verses of the Quran through eisegesis. In the very first chapter of the Quran, where no reference is made to Jews or Christians, the last two verses read: "Guide us to the Straight Path, the path of those upon whom you have bestowed your

---

13. Sachedina, *The Islamic Roots of Democratic Pluralism*, 39.

bounty, not the way of those with whom you have warranted anger or those who have gone astray." One of the earliest extant works of exegesis, by Muqatil b. Sulayman (d. 767) explains that "those who have warranted anger" are the Jews and "those who have gone astray" are the Christians.[14] Throughout the centuries, this has become the standard interpretation of those verses. One of the latest editions of the translated Quran, published under the auspices of the King Fahd Complex in Saudi Arabia, provides footnotes to show likewise.[15] Considering that this is the first chapter that almost all Muslim children are taught, it is not difficult to understand how from a rather tender age, a Muslim might have the idea of salvation for his coreligionists only.

Even in the earlier reference where Cantwell Smith referred to the Q 3:19,[16] he had to acknowledge that later exegetes had limited the scope of the verse, as can be seen from the full citation:

> What in modern times has become: Verily *the* religion in the eyes of God is *Islam* originally meant (was taken to mean; for instance, by the most respected and authoritative of the early commentators, al Tabari) rather that to conduct oneself duly before God is to accept his commands; the proper way to worship him is to obey him—or simply true religion (*not* 'the true religion) is obeisance. To many when it was first proclaimed and for some centuries after, this verse was saying what any man must say whose faith is vivid and whose orientation is moralist. Far from being primarily sectarian, it is, curiously, virtually identical even to the wording with the statement or definition given in the Catholic encyclopedia, "Religion . . . means the voluntary subjection of oneself to God."[17]

Islam's supersession of Judaism, Christianity and all other religions is the normative idea in both classical and contemporary Quranic exegesis. Apart from the exegetical artifices provided above, the proponents of the doctrine generally rely on the verse that may be generally translated as "Whoever desires a religion other than Islam, it shall not be accepted of him; in the next world he will be among the losers" (Q 3:85).

14. Muqatil Ibn Sulayman, *Tafsir Muqatil Ibn Sulayman*, ed. Ahmad Fareed (Beirut: Dar al-Kutub al-Ilmiyya, 2003) 26.

15. Muhammad Taqi-ud-Din al-Hilali and Muhammad Muhsin Khan, trans. *The Noble Qur'an* (Madinah, Saudi Arabia: King Fahd Complex for the Printing of the Holy Quran, n.d.) 1, 2.

16. See note 1, above.

17. Wilfred Cantwell Smith, *The Meaning and End of Religion*, 112–13.

Since the use of the Internet has become popular among Muslims, it is interesting to note what Nuh HaMim Keller, an influential American Muslim, has written about the subject:[18] "As for today, only Islam is valid or acceptable now that Allah has sent it to all men, for the Prophet (Allah bless him and give him peace) has said, 'By Him in whose hand is the soul of Muhammad, any person of this Community, any Jew, or any Christian who hears of me and dies without believing in what I have been sent with will be an inhabitant of hell.'" Keller claims that this above hadith has been "rigorously authenticated" and that it clarifies Q3:85. [19]

Like most Muslim writers dealing with the explanation of Quranic verses or tradition, he cites classical scholars in support of his position: "'Someone who does not believe that whoever follows another religion besides Islam is an unbeliever (like Christians), or doubts that such a person is an unbeliever, or considers their sect to be valid, is himself an unbeliever (*kafir*) even if he manifests Islam and believes in it' (*Rawda al-talibin*, 10.70)."[20]

Keller continues, "This is not only the position of the Shafi'i school of jurisprudence represented by Nawawi, but is also the recorded position of all three other Sunni schools: Hanafi (Ibn 'Abidin: *Radd al-muhtar* 3.287), Maliki (al-Dardir: *al-Sharh al-saghir*, 4.435), and Hanbali (al-Bahuti: *Kashshaf al-qina'*, 6.170). Those who know *fiqh* literature will note that each of these works is the foremost *fatwa* resource in its school. The scholars of Sacred Law are unanimous about the abrogation of all other religions by Islam because it is the position of Islam itself."

His last claim about the scholars of Sacred law being unanimous about Islam having abrogated all other religions is problematic. The entire concept of abrogation in itself is a later construct that seeks to explain away apparently contradictory verses of the Quran. There certainly was no unanimity of the abrogation theory, which was one of the artifices used to override the Quranic verses of inclusiveness. This postulate was that a verse was abrogated by another verse or oral tradition. While this idea was indeed accepted by the majority of classical scholars, research on the

---

18. Nuh Ha Mim Keller, "On the Validity of All Religions in the Thought of Ibn Al 'Arabi and Emir 'Abd al Qadir." Online: http://www.masud.co.uk/ISLAM/nuh/amat.htm/.

19. Ibid.

20. Ibid.

subject has shown that all of the supposedly abrogated verses are still valid (al-Ghazali),[21] (al-Khui),[22] (al-Corentini).[23]

Throughout the centuries, in spite of all the polemic between the Abrahamic religions, it was generally accepted that even if non-Muslims disparaged Muhammad, they still did not deny that all three religions worshiped the same God. After 9/11, however, expressions of the God of Islam as being different or inferior to the God of Judeo-Christianity have become commonplace. General William G. "Jerry" Boykin, speaking of his Somalian experience, triumphantly exclaimed that the Muslim god was inferior to the God of Judeo-Christianity.[24] Tim LaHaye, fundamentalist Christian coauthor of the bestselling *Left Behind* series, and with the late Jerry Falwell an initial cofounder of the Moral Majority, wrote, "the god they believe in is definitely NOT the God of the Bible, either in the Old or New Testaments."[25]

These empty claims all play into the more extreme interpretations of Islam where the mullahs are only happy to point out that those Muslims who try to reach out and speak of inclusivism are not achieving rapprochement with dignity and honor. In the anguish of the hostile response of most Americans to Muslims after 9/11, when Muslims were generally portrayed as the enemy, many followers of Islam turned to the mosques, Islamic centers, Muslim Students' Associations on campuses, and Islamic schools to "ease the pain of increased bigotry, stereotyping, and hate crimes."[26] The mosque is no longer simply a place of worship: it has become a bastion of identity, of solidarity, where activists can find receptive ears for their preaching of horrors committed by "the Jews" in Israel against Palestinians. Almost on a daily basis, stories are uncovered about alleged war crimes committed against Muslims in Iraq or Afghanistan.

---

21. Muhammad al-Ghazali. *Kayfa Nata'amal ma al-Qur'an* (Herndon, VA: International Institute for Islamic Thought, 1992) 80–84.

22. Abu'l Qasim al-Musawi al-Khu'i, *The Prolegomena to the Qur'an*, trans. Abdul Aziz Sachedina (New York: Oxford University Press,1998) 186–253.

23. Abu Yousuf al-Corentini, "The Concept of Abrogation in the Qur'an" *Journal of Religion and Culture* 10 (Winter/Spring 1996) 63–75.

24. Richard T. Cooper, "General Casts War in Religious Terms," *Los Angeles Times* October 16, 2003; online: http://articles.latimes.com/2003/oct/16/nation/na-general16/.

25. Tim LaHaye "The Prophetic Significance of Sept. 11, 2001," *Pre-Trib Perspectives* 6/7 (October 2001) 1–3.

26. Genevieve Abdo, *Mecca and Main Street: Muslim Life in America after 9/11* (Oxford: Oxford University Press, 2006) 6.

Capacity for Theological Self-Critique

Herein lies one of the greatest hurdles of contemporary Islam; for medieval, chauvinistic, and misogynist inanities have ossified themselves into a seemingly indestructible edifice of Islamic creed. In truth, I think it is easier to start a new religion than to seek to reform any of the cherished constructs of Islam. Later triumphalist, absolutist teachings have so supplanted the pristine Quranic worldview that they are now viewed as the pure Islam of the early generations (and purveyed as "salafism"). The retrogression of many later ideas to Muhammad means that the prophetic veneer now protects what under any unbiased examination should be clearly problematic. To even question, much less seek to bring about any change in, contemporary Islam is to court charges of heresy in some Islamic countries. The fields of legal interpretation, Quranic exegesis, or almost any aspect of Islamic thought are almost solely the domain of a group of thinkers that can collectively be described as overwhelmingly narrow minded, legalistic, antimodern, and in many cases obsessed with maintaining a distinctive apartness from the world community.

One only has to examine the cases of Nasr Abu Zayd, Muhammad al-Ashmawy, Abdel Karim Soroush, and Mahmoud Taha—to focus on some of the more well known examples. Nasr Abu Zayd (now deceased) was declared a disbeliever in his native Egypt simply for claiming that the Quran should be treated as any piece of literature. Muhammad al-Ashmawy, one of the finest brains in Egypt, is confined to his home because his views clash with that of the extremists. In Iran, Abdul Kareem Soroush was assaulted because he was seen as being in opposition to the orthodoxy of Shi'i thought. Mahmoud Taha was hanged in the Sudan because he dared opine against normative interpretation of the Quran. In the United States, especially after 9/11, the cases of Khalid Abou El-Fadl, Abdul Aziz Sachedina, and me are instances where the Muslim world makes the absurd seem so normal: many traditional scholars seek to use the pulpit to marginalize anyone who dares question the traditions of the past.

The events of 9/11 play a great part in spreading this malaise. It became painfully clear that the Westernized intellectuals of the Muslim world were ineffective at organizing the masses or providing any support against the terrible backlash that scourged the Muslims. Rather, it was the radical Islamist groups who organized themselves, and as they had been for decades, were relatively successful. They were the ones who offered effective financial aid and social support to the victims in the Muslim countries. Here in the United States, imams, instead of cringing and cowering, became more defiant in asserting their perspective of what Islam ought to be. In seeking to convince their congregations that Islam had always surmounted its challenges, they drew upon images of the past—that vaunted parahistory where Islam reigned supreme because the Muslims adhered to the Quran and the traditions of the prophet.

In response to largely Christian apocalyptic expectations, many Muslims have turned to their own eschatological traditions wherein Jesus comes back as a Muslim to defeat the forces of evil. Certainly it cannot be argued that this is a post-9/11 phenomenon, as the Muslim Jesus traditions date far back in Islamic history. But what 9/11 has done is to create the need for hope and succor from the present situation, and the redemptive reappearance of Jesus and the Mahdi to lead Muslims to final victory seem the ideal expectation. Now the Quran says nothing of this Second Advent, and the idea is actually imported from Syrian Christianity.[27] Since it, however, affords the believer some type of expected solace, any challenge of this idea is considered opposed to the core of the religion itself. No one asks why Jesus, who appears in the Quran as a messenger to the children of Israel, would be sent another time to descend among the Muslims, presumably speaking a language other than his own.

In 2003 at the Global Anti-Semitism Conference in Montreal, I gave an interview to Montreal's English-language newspaper, the *Montreal Gazette*. I stated that many mosques teach anti-Semitism and explained that the normative interpretation of the last verses of the first chapter of the Quran is that God is angry with the Jews, and that the Christians are misguided. The leaders of the Muslim community, instead of admitting I was right, came out in absolute denial and accusation. They accused me of outright lying, and of destroying the bridges of rapport that had been established between Islam and the other religions. Since the *Montreal Gazette* refused to print my rebuttal to the criticism, the local community was left to assume that I had none. The only forum I could find for publishing an answer was an academic journal, and I showed how the Muslim leaders were hiding the truth in order to prevent theological self-critique.[28] The problem is that my article was restricted to the academic community, and few Muslims or participants at the conference got to read my response.

---

27. Khaleel Mohammed, "The Jewish and Christian Influences on the Eschatological Imagery of Sahih Muslim," MA thesis (Concordia University, Montreal, 1997) 24–34.

28. Khaleel Mohammed, "Produce Your Proof: Muslim Exegesis, the Hadith and Jews," *Judaism* 53 (Winter/Spring 2004) 3–11.

Trialogue and Terror

The rise in popularity of interreligious dialogue brings to light an issue related to the lack of self-critique: that of religious leadership. The Jewish and Christian communities are well organized in the United States and Canada, and can afford to have ordained rabbis or priests represent them. The Muslim population is largely still an immigrant one, and in most cases individual communities are not well established enough to afford the services of a religious scholar. Many of the leaders and spokespersons of the Muslim community, therefore are chosen based, not upon their religious qualifications, but rather on their status or financial contributions, or simply their ability to communicate effectively. In many cases, such people are doctors and professionals—certainly outstanding in their fields of specialization but not necessarily in comprehending the finer points of their faith. The "Dr. Mohammed," therefore, who leads a mosque, and who so proudly uses the doctoral title, may be a physician. This in and of itself is not problematic, but it does become so when interfaith delegations assume that the title *Dr.* indicates graduate-level studies in his religion, and that the designated leader can truly expound the beliefs of Islam. Such a person is often afflicted with—to use Scott Appleby's term with an extended meaning—"religious illiteracy."[29] He does not have the capacity for any meaningful research into theology or even for moral reflection, and will often only repeat the age-old beliefs that have been passed on to him.

In some cases, where mosques can afford an imam, they often hire someone who comes from a foreign country and culture, and who has not had much—if any—experience in being a minority group or having to answer critical questions about religious constructs. Such persons, in many cases, come from the madrassahs in India, Pakistan, or other parts of the Arab world and do not generally question the material that they purvey. In some cases, where the governments of Arab countries pay the salaries of the leaders, it is unlikely that the leaders will raise any issues of self-critique, as doing so would probably get them fired. The academics who do attempt to criticize are often blamed for being too Western—*magrebzadehs* and as trying to Americanize or Canadianize themselves at the expense of their religion. That the writings of Yusuf al Qaradhawi, Abu'l Ala al-Maududi, and Sayyid Qutb—all purveyors of radical Islam—are still in high demand at many mosques is an indication of the crisis situation in which Muslims find themselves.

---

29. R. Scott Appleby, *The Ambivalence of the Sacred: Religion, Violence, and Reconciliation*, Carnegie Commission on Preventing Deadly Conflict Series (Lanham, MD: Rowman & Littlefield, 2000) 69

Before the French Reformation, the Christian Testament was in a language understood only by priests; the illiterate masses had no access to the sources. At least in the Christian world, this has largely changed—priests no longer have the monopoly on access to the Scripture. If it is argued that the masses may read but not truly understand the proper interpretation and context of what they are reading, the fact is that they nonetheless have access. In the Islamic world, much is made of the fact that there is no priesthood and that from the earliest times Muslims were taught to memorize and read the Quran. The truth is that today traditional Muslim scholars impress the community by citing tenth-century texts rather than by showing any new insights into legal, exegetical, or creedal matters. It matters not that these texts have nothing to do with modern society—and that their social world has been outdated centuries ago. Obviously these texts have none of the ideas of current globalization, much less the terminology of contemporary society. Yet, it is these texts that our vaunted *Ulama* (scholars) will peruse to find ideas about how to deal with modernity, globalization, human rights, feminism, pluralism, and artificial insemination among other topics.

Conclusion

Thus far this chapter insofar as any room for constructive interfaith trialogue goes, must seem overwhelmingly negative. My coreligionists may take issue with me for being so absolutely critical of the religion I am supposed to represent. But at the very beginning of my essay I wrote that my Scripture commands me to be honest, even if it means going against my own, and I could not depart from that imperative. Interestingly, the most distinguished scholars involved in interfaith discussion stipulate this type of honesty as a prerequisite for meaningful encounter. Leonard Swidler, distinguished professor and editor of the *Journal of Ecumenical Studies* states, "Each participant must come to the dialogue with complete honesty and sincerity. No false fronts have any place in dialogue."[30] Hans Küng, the famous Catholic theologian, noted that interfaith discussions must, *inter alia*, give priority to clearing up misunderstandings and healing traumatic memories.[31]

---

30. Leonard Swidler, "Ground Rules for Interreligious Dialogue," in *Interreligious Dialogue: Facing the Next Frontier*, ed. Richard W. Rousseau, Theological Themes (Montrose, PA: Ridge Row, 1981) 9–12.

31. Hans Küng, "Foreword," in *Rivers of Paradise: Moses, Buddha, Confucius, Jesus,*

Trialogue and Terror

I want to let participants in a trialogue have realistic expectations, and that we are up against tremendous hurdles. Yet, however, I strongly feel that there is room for hope. In the Muslim world, there is a rising swell of dissent against retrogression and malaise. If these voices were only those of Muslims living in the West, it would not be so significant, for it is easy to speak out against something when one is outside the locus of the problem. The voices are, surprisingly, in the heart of the Muslim world, and of the highest authorities. Dr. AbdulHamid AbuSulayman, while rector of the International Islamic University in Kuala Lumpur, Malaysia, published *Towards an Islamic Theory of International Relations*, harshly criticizing the traditional Islamic approach to international relations.[32] He followed this with another book, *Crisis in the Muslim Mind*, listing the various symptoms of problems in the Muslim world.[33] Dr. Taha al-Alwani, former professor of Islamic Law at Imam Muhammad bin Saud University (Riyadh) recently authored a book *Towards a Fiqh for Minorities* wherein he, for perhaps the first time among Muslim scholars, asserted that Muslims have to realize that there must be a new methodology for interpreting Islamic law, especially for Muslims who are a minority in the West.[34] Dr. Ahmed Al-Baghdadi, lecturer in political science at Kuwait University, wrote in the Arab media on April 12, 2006, that Muslims themselves are responsible for the detested image of Islam in the West.[35] Abd el-Hamid al-Ansari, former head of the Shariah College at the University of Qatar noted in the Arab press that the religious curricula squander the future of the sons of Islam, wherein imams issue fatwas of hate and aggression.[36] Shirin Ebadi, Nobel Peace Prize laureate from Iran, give an interview in which she noted that freedom in her country was still curtailed by the president and his council of conservative religious leaders.[37] Recently, I

---

and Mohammed as Religious Founders, ed. David Noel Freedman and Michael Clymond (Grand Rapids, Eerdmans, 2001) ix.

32. AbdulHamid AbuSulayman, *Towards an Islamic Theory of International Relations*, 2nd ed. (Herndon, VA: International Institute of Islamic Thought, 1993).

33. AbdulHamid AbuSulayman, *Crisis in the Muslim Mind* (Herndon, VA: International Institute of Islamic Thought, 1993).

34. Taha Alalwani, *Towards a Fiqh for Minorities* (Herndon, VA: International Institute for Islamic Thought, 2003) xi–xx, 9.

35. Reform in Arab and Muslim world, special report 1157, www.memri.org dated May 5, 2006.

36. Reform in Arab and Muslim world, special report 968, www.memri.org dated Aug 25, 2005.

37. Reform in Arab and Muslim world, special report 942, www.memri.org dated July 26 2005.

attended a conference in Washington sponsored by a special section of the Kuwaiti Ministry of Islamic affairs, promoting a more modern outlook for Islam. All the foregoing clearly shows that Muslims are beginning to realize that they must shock themselves out of the medievalist mentality.

The process, however, is not going to be a short one. This truism needs to be pointed out to Americans, who seem to think that every problem can and must be solved within a specific time frame. This is simply not going to happen in the case of the Abrahamic religions. There are still too many agendas floating around, and mistrust still pervades. Along with the problems within Islam, there is the problem from without. I am aware that many come with warped views of Islam, and often selectively quote the Quran or Hadith, misinterpreting texts to give the impression that Islam is inherently violent. Muslims, as a result, often boycott these conferences; many see them as simply occasions for vilifying Islam. There are those who try to derail conferences by their own political agendas—such as those Muslims who make the Palestinian issue the main agenda item, or those Jews who seek to do the same for Israel.

In this modern world, we need to focus on a simple fact: religions themselves don't preach hatred: people do. Judaism, Christianity, and Islam are, after all, abstract concepts. These concepts come to life through the actions of people who claim to follow those faiths. Too much focus is given to selective citation of traditions and Scripture, and too little to the human element in interpretation. The Abrahamic Scriptures are all set in a time long past, and their details are necessarily outdated in today's world. Their edicts, especially as they pertain to human interaction, are often not compatible with modern concepts of globalization. These Scriptures can only be meaningful if examined for their ultimate goal, which is to make the world a better place. This situation does not mean we have to forget our individualities, but simply to recognize that others have theirs as well, or to put it another way, acceptance of pluralism must not deny our diversity.

Jet Li's recent film *The Hero* brings out this point beautifully. There is a scene where he has, out of haste, planted rice seedlings too closely together. They have to be replanted because if each seedling does not get its own space to develop and grow, it will die. This is precisely the case with religions: if they seek to impose themselves on each other, they will all suffer. Each one needs to respect the other and accept certain differences for what they are. Leo Pinsker pragmatically summed it up best when in September 1882 he wrote: "We cannot of course, think of establishing perfect harmony. Such harmony has probably never existed, even among other nations. The millennium in which national differences will disappear, and the nations will merge into humanity, is still indivisible in the distance. Until it is realized, the desires and ideals of the nations must be limited to establishing a tolerable modus vivendi."[38]

38. Leo Pinsker, "Auto-Emancipation: An Appeal to His People by a Russian Jew," in *The Zionist Idea*, ed. Arthur Hertzberg (Philadelphia: Jewish Publication Society, 1997) 181–98.

twelve

The Semitic Solution

Renewing the Natural Alliance between Jews and Muslims[1]

ANOUAR MAJID

Nothing has excited me more in recent years than my discovery of the common bonds between Jews and Arabs, or, more generally, the tenuous cultural and religious kinship between Judaism and Islam. The realization that such religious communities were more often than not interchangeable in the Christian European imagination was promising, but I also knew that the furies of the Israeli–Palestinian conflict and the fog of 9/11 have made the process of reacquainting the Jew with the Arab a nearly impossible task. At the time I am writing this, Muslims and Arabs, whether used as synonyms for each other or not, are firmly ensconced in the Western imagination as members of a despotic East, a place unwilling, if not unable, to live up to the loftier cultural achievements of modernity.

Jews, meanwhile, whether living in the West or in Israel, are often depicted as full partners in the achievements of Western civilization. The gulf that had long divided Christianity from Judaism was bridged by the hyphenated legacy of the Judeo-Christian tradition. There is no question now (except, possibly, among deranged white supremacists) that the intellectual legacy of the twentieth century would have been unimaginable

---

1. A fuller treatment of this topic can be found in Majid, *We Are All Moors: Ending Centuries of Crusades against Muslims and Other Minorities* (Minneapolis: University of Minnesota Press, 2009).

without the towering influence of Jewish intellectuals, or that contemporary life would simply not be the same without the vital role of the small but dynamic Jewish communities around the world. From the long-term historical perspective, this is a remarkable turn of events in world history.

Without a doubt, Jews are now living through a new golden age, one that compares favorably with Jewish life under Muslim rule in ninth- and tenth-century Baghdad and in Muslim-ruled Spain, or Al-Andalus, in the medieval period. This new golden age, however, has meant the geographical displacement of the Jew. Just as Western Christianity bears little resemblance to Christian practices in poor African or Latin American nations, so is Judaism today seen as part and parcel of the Western heritage, not part of the decrepit cultures of the East. Nothing would be more far fetched nowadays than to imagine Jews as the natural allies of Muslims. Who would think that Jews could be members of sleeper cells intent on undermining the march of European civilization, or that they are the hit men of bearded and turbaned caliphs from the lands of Islam? No, if one thing could be claimed with any degree of certainty, it is that Jews bear little resemblance to Muslims. Their assimilation into the West is a *fait accompli*.

Yet the successful integration of Jews into the Western body is the misfortune of both Jews and Muslims. It blocks out the possibility for solidarity by preventing the two religious communities from wearing their long-discarded Semitic garb. The Semitic designation is, of course, culturally meaningless. One cannot count on an eighteenth-century European concept to capture the uneasy relationship and unintentional bonds between Jews and Muslims throughout more than a thousand years of history. But the expression crystallizes the long European refusal to see both religions as anything other than dangerous heresies and mortal threats. If Judaism and Islam were not completely alike—as they are not—then they were made to be alike. They were alike in their own alternative visions—the questionable knowledge of Judaism's fathering principle and Islam's intolerable plagiarism of the biblical script. The racially defective Semite was juxtaposed to the biologically superior Aryan partly because, as Gil Anidjar points out in his book *Semites*, race and religion operated on one and the same register. Religion, a nineteenth-century European concept, was simply a cover for race. This explains why the prominent French philologist Ernest Renan's declared war on *"la chose sémitique"* (the Semitic thing) targeted Jew and Arab indiscriminately because both religious communities represent "the Semitic spirit" in its purest form.

In this reading, ancient Israel is part of Arab culture—a defective one, to be sure, as the eighteenth-century German philosopher Immanuel Kant stated in his description of Jews as Palestinians. Thus, in Renan's quest for a higher social order, the "eternal war" on the Semite "will not cease until the last son of Ishmael has died of misery or has been relegated to the ends of the desert by way of terror."[2] But now that the Jew has been fully integrated into the West, only his *semblable*, the Muslim, is left out. Worse than this, a few Jews have joined hands with previously anti-Semitic European parties to fight the Islamic menace in Europe and the West generally. This is certainly not the best way to mend differences.

By reaching out, and back, to Muslims, Jews could do more to bring Muslim and Jew together than the typical interfaith meetings about the possibility of coexistence and the repeated attempts to highlight the common elements in both faiths. It's not that such matters are not significant—they are. But they also have the strange effect of papering over real theological differences, eschewing the conundrum of the exclusionary provisions in every monotheistic faith. Such interfaith assemblies leave out Islam's deliberate rupture with Judaism, which meant, among other things, redirecting prayers away from Jerusalem. The quest for a separate identity, a new voice, a different Scripture, and new rituals could only be accomplished through a sort of violent rejection of Judaism's master influences. Let us be clear, then: Islam will never develop a perfect opinion of Judaism or Christianity, just as the two other monotheistic religions cannot give Islam equal status, or see the youngest monotheistic religion as anything but a deformed offshoot of their faiths. Questions of authenticity and truth are notoriously impossible to sort out, so talking about living together, despite unbridgeable differences, is the best Jews and Muslims (and Christians) can do.

There is, in my opinion, another way to approach the problem, and that is by resurrecting the Semite from his untimely death. If the Semite did not have a happy career in the modern European imagination, we could change that and endow his profile with life-saving powers. We could, for instance, remind ourselves that Jews, like Arabs, often saw themselves as Oriental people, close cousins to Islam, even when Europe opened the doors for Jewish emancipation. Quite a few prominent nineteenth-century Jews saw no wall between their faith and Islam, and some proudly proclaimed themselves to be Muslim. They were not eager to identify with

---

2. See Gil Anidjar, *Semites: Race, Religion, Literature* (Stanford: Stanford University Press, 2008) 6, 31–32, 115–16, n. 37.

European civilization, believing that they were heirs to the greater Islamic tradition. Both Sephardim and Ashkenazim agreed that the "Moorish-style synagogue" was an inextricable expression of their sacred faith. It is on such grounds, for instance, that Florence's Accademia delle Arti del Disegno blocked a neo-Renaissance design in 1872, explaining that "as every nation has stamped its own history on [its] monuments, and most of all its religious monuments, so a building with the said function must manifest at first sight so effectively a marked character that it recalls the dates and the places that are of most interest for this religion, and a character such as cannot be confounded with the religious or secular monuments of other nations and religions."[3]

Ludwig Förster, who designed the Vienna-Leopoldstadt synagogue (1853–1858) put the case succinctly:

> It is known to be a difficult task indeed to build an Israelite Temple in a form required by the religion and suitable for its practice, and at the same time corresponding, at least in its essential features, to the hallowed ideal of all temples, the Temple of Solomon. It is doubly difficult insofar as [the building's] external architecture is concerned, for the existing records cannot nearly provide us with a reliable picture; and those Houses of God that belong to a later time either lack any distinct style or carry features that are in their inner being entirely alien to the Israelite religion.
>
> In my humble opinion, the right way, given the circumstances, is to choose, when building an Israelite Temple, those architectural forms that have been used by Oriental ethnic groups that are related to the Israelite people, and in particular the Arabs.[4]

If one thinks about it, this was a remarkable act of self-assertion, one that reflects the depth of cultural kinship between Jews and Muslims. Just when Jews were given the opportunity to become full members of European nations like Germany, they refused easy assimilation and held on tenaciously, and proudly, to their Semitic identity. The Orientalist Paul de Lagarde[5] was taken aback by this defiance in 1881: the Jews' "alien nature is stressed every day and in the most striking fashion by the Jews—who nevertheless

---

3. Quoted in Ivan Davidson Kalmar, "Moorish Style: Orientalism, the Jews and Synagogue Architecture," *Jewish Social Studies: History, Culture, and Society* 7/3 (2001) 86.

4. Quoted in ibid., 78–79.

5. Editor's note: Lagarde was notorious for his anti-Semitism.

wish to be made equal to Germans—through the style of their synagogue. What is the sense of raising claims to be called an honorary German and yet building the holiest site that one possesses in Moorish style, so as to never ever let anyone forget that one is a Semite, an Asiatic, a foreigner?"[6]

The Semitic factor could renew the long-frayed alliance of Jews and Muslims. As Islamophobia spreads throughout the world, Jews who are aware of the common destiny of Jew and Arab could enter the fray by expressing their unambiguous solidarity with Muslim immigrants or minorities. No religiously defined community is more aware of its persecutions at the hands of a Europe that claims to be superior to the cultural background of its minorities, so the Jews' silence in the face of the condemnation of generations of Muslims living in Western societies to various policies of exclusion and discrimination only adds to the bursting store of suspicions and mutual recriminations. It is true that a certain Judeophobia—the expression of Muslim fanatical literalists and the outcome of the simmering Israeli-Palestinian conflict—makes it difficult for Jews to overcome the more pressing commitment to Israel, a state they see as endangered by political manifestos denying is existence. That is unquestionably a serious issue, but it is by no means theoretically insurmountable. There is no reason why historical memory should evaporate in the heat of land disputes, suicide bombings, or bomb shelling. The Semite, in his or her various guises, is a millennial figure that survives the politics of the moment. He cannot be allowed to become mere collateral damage to a war over land. Or at least, we could suspend our moral and ideological commitments in the unfolding battle pitting Israelis and their supporters in the Diaspora, on one hand, against Palestinians, Arabs and Muslims, on the other, to make room for the far more valuable lessons of history. Without reviving the Semites' history of common suffering at the hands of Europeans, there would be little impetus to move beyond locked positions and worsening suspicions and hatreds. The Semites must come back to rescue what was once an alliance by default.

If the solution is one of recognition, the problem is one of avoidance. The encounter between Jew and Muslim has become too loaded to be natural. Too many prejudices need to be examined and overcome. Let's start with everyday language in the Arab and Muslim worlds. Muslims often see Jewish organizations monitoring anti-Semitism in the Muslim world as too politically motivated to be taken seriously. In their victim narrative, Muslims cannot be faulted for prejudice, for in the order of things, one is

---

6. Quoted in Kalmar, "Moorish Style," *Jewish Social Studies* 7/3 (2001) 89.

either oppressor or oppressed, colonizer or colonized, Crusader or *jihadist*, and Muslims are powerless to cause any hurt. But the truth is one can be both, often more, and so while such self-serving narratives relax the demands on our responsibility, they do not promote understanding, let alone the pursuit of a genuine culture of coexistence.

As a kid growing up in the cosmopolitan city of Tangier in Morocco, a place that is historically friendly to minorities and Jews, one that still boasts today an active synagogue with its distinctive prayers, I experienced first hand the plight of Jewish minorities in our midst. Because the *lihud* (Jews) symbolized treachery and greed, to call someone a Jew was an insult. Muslims do talk a lot about their respect for the "People of the Book," but these are merely ready-made excuses for not examining the fabric of our social patterns critically. *Dhimmitude*, the second-class status conferred on Christians and Jews in Islamic regimes, one that is often presented by Muslim apologists as a testament to the tolerance of minorities in Islam, does not meet the minimum human rights expectations in nation states. Under this theological legal code, Jews lived precariously among Muslims, relying, at best, on the ruler's protection against the ever-lurking violence of the mob. That an occasional courtesan would rise to positions of prominence and power in no way meant that the collective rights of the Jewish community were secure. Without royal protection, Jews and Christians in Muslim societies were but one sermon away from catastrophe. To be fair to Muslims, few other societies, certainly not Christendom, had a better human rights record, but to say (as many Muslim fundamentalists do) that a medieval formula for coexistence could still apply today is a gross abdication of *ijtihad*, the intellectual effort necessary to keep updating basic principles to the demands of new centuries and societies.

On the whole, part of the Muslim violence is born out of ignorance. But it is, in some ways, a willed ignorance—the persistent refusal to measure the Muslims' complicity in the systematic discrimination against those who don't share their faith. The ongoing conflict between Israel and Palestine should not erase the precarious status of the Jew in Muslim societies. Organizing colloquia over the Holocaust in order to downplay the horrors visited upon European Jews is both a futile and pernicious attempt to take away from centuries-old realities that cannot be challenged. Even if the goal were to shed light on the victimization of the Palestinians, the collateral damage of what George Bensoussan has termed Europe's "genocidal passion,"[7] this approach only makes sense within the callous logic of a monstrous calculus.

While historical Palestine, or modern-day Israel, may be a contested territory, such is not the case for the place of Muslim and Jew in the European imagination. As with the case of Israel, one can understand the shifting of alliances on the part of Jews, and one should not dismiss the real lure of European secular civilization, as problematic as it may have been—and still is—for a number of Jews, whose Semitism placed them squarely outside Western culture. But the automatic alliance erases the long Jewish struggle against the very Western project deployed now to belittle the heritage of Muslims. And it is the history of Jewish struggle against Europe's "genocidal passion" that needs to be foregrounded, so that Muslims may shatter two myths at once: that Jews are an inextricable part of Europe's crusade against minorities and Muslim nations, and that integration, with some degree of autonomy, is possible within the West. In other words, even as the Israelis and Palestinians and, by proxy, Jews and Muslims, are wrestling over a small but symbolically rich land, Jews—and I am singling out Jews here because they are, as a group, better integrated and more successful in the new world order—need to develop a narrative that both asserts Jewish resolve against their enemies and contributes solutions to Muslims struggling against discrimination or various forms of colonialism. This multilayered approach would have the effect of demonstrating to Muslims that Jews are not the natural enemies of Islam; only, but not always, the adversaries of Palestinians in the contest for land in the Middle East.

It may do us well, therefore, to recall the main lines of the common destiny of Jew and Arab in world history, particularly within the confines of Christian European civilization. Through trials, migrations, triumphs, defeats, and diasporas, early Jewish history was staged in what is today the larger Middle East. Though Jews survived the second loss of Jerusalem to the Romans in AD 70 through the adoption of a rabbinical system with its Scriptures (particularly the Babylonian Talmud), and after enduring Greek and Roman anti-Semitic persecutions, the rise of Islam may very well have given the Jews a new lease on life, as they were now, with minor exceptions,

---

7. George Bensoussan, *Europe. Une passion génocidaire: Essai d'histoire culturelle* (Paris: Mille et une nuits, 2006).

united, for the first time, by a common language across Muslim lands and protected by law from random persecution. "Aramaic-speaking Jews and Hellenized Jews" were brought together by the Islamic expanse and the lingua franca of Arabic. Thus, noted the eminent historian and Orientalist Bernard Lewis, Arabic "became the language of science and philosophy, of government and commerce, even the language of Jewish theology when such a discipline began to develop under Islamic influence."[8] While living in Cairo in 1190, the celebrated rabbi/philosopher Maimonides (1135–1204) wrote his famous treatise, *Guide to the Perplexed*, in Arabic, before it was translated into Hebrew. So intertwined were the two religions that one could talk about a "Judaeo-Islamic" culture or tradition, one that parallels "the Judaeo-Christian tradition of which we are accustomed to speak in the modern world." In fact, "the emergence of a Jewish theology took place entirely in Islamic lands," and Arabic had a significant impact on Hebrew philology.[9]

After their expulsion from Spain, the Sephardim (Jews of Spain) were welcomed with open arms by Ottoman sultans and experienced, for about a century and a half, yet another golden age under the auspices of Islam. A fifteenth-century French Jew was so impressed by the status of Jews in Turkey that he called on his coreligionists to leave Christian lands and join him there.[10] Again, the Jewish kinship with Islam is also not entirely surprising, given the two faiths' similar theological and cultural outlooks. Not only did the Semites originate in Arabia, but Moses is also by far the most cited biblical figure in the Quran. Islam may be the younger progeny of the Jewish monotheistic cosmogony, but if Arabic is the youngest of the Semitic languages, it is also the most archaic one, "probably the nearest to the ancestral Semitic language," the "most widely spoken and written of all the Semitic languages," with Hebrew, revived as a common language for Zionists, the second. (In fact, before the term *Semitic* was coined in 1781, the German Gottfried Wilhelm von Leibniz classified Hebrew as a member of the "Arabic" languages.)[11] It is therefore as fellow Semites (to use,

---

8. Bernard Lewis, *The Jews of Islam* (Princeton: Princeton University Press, 1984) 76–77; Joseph Pérez, *History of a Tragedy: The Expulsion of the Jews from Spain*, trans. Lysa Hochroth, Hispanisms (Urbana: University of Illinois Press, 2007) 11.

9. Lewis, *The Jews of Islam*, 76–77, 81

10. Quoted in Lewis, *The Jews of Islam*, 135–36.

11. Pierre Lory, "Le judaïsme et les juifs dans le Coran et la tradition musulmane," in *Juifs et musulmans: Une histoire partagée, un dialogue à construire*, ed. Esther Benbassa and Jean-Christophe Attias (Paris: La Découverte, 2006) 19; Lewis, *Semites and Anti-Semites: An Inquiry into Conflict and Prejudice*, 50, 55–57, 44.

once again, this European category profitably) that Jew and Moor stand on the stage of European history to face the long arm of persecution. Before the birth of Israel, such quarrels were minor enough to inspire prominent Jews to boast of their Muslim or Arab descent.

In their massive historical study, *The Jew as Ally of the Muslim*, and through an exhaustive comparatist approach, Allan Harris Cutler and Helen Elmquist Cutler even made the astounding argument that classical anti-Semitism, rooted in Christian medieval charges of deicide or in social rivalries, was given new life by anti-Muslimism, born out of the millennial clash between Christianity and Islam. Christian anti-Semitism, which had been "dormant" during the three centuries prior to 1000, emerged as a corollary of the Crusades, since the Jews came to be seen as the natural allies of the Muslims. At the end of their first campaign, Christian crusaders ruthlessly slaughtered Muslims and Jews alike in Jerusalem, seeing them both as "the shadow-self of Christendom," in the words of the noted interfaith historian Karen Armstrong.[12] Because of their perceived closeness to Muslims, Jews were persecuted and murdered. Indeed, the Cutlers go so far as to assert that "had there been no such outburst of Christian hatred against the Muslims, anti-Semitism might well have died out altogether in Western society."[13] The edicts of the Fourth Lateran Council of 1215, imposing distinctive clothing and a "badge of shame" on Jews (and Muslims), was part of a messianic policy whose final aims were the reconquest of Jerusalem and the degrading of its Muslim inhabitants. The fate of Jews in Spain, their persecution by the Inquisition after their sincere conversion in the late fourteenth and early fifteenth centuries, and the Jewish *conversos*' reaction by going back to their ancestral fate were all the result of the clash between Christians and Muslims. Moreover, "the Iberian Inquisition and its demonic attack upon thousands of innocent people in Europe and the New World circa 1480–1825 must ultimately be traced to the Islamic conquest of Spain in 711."

Major scholars who have studied the roots of modern anti-Semitism in the medieval period, such as Joshua Trachtenberg, author of *The Devil and the Jews* (1943), and Norman Cohn, author of, among other important works, *The Pursuit of the Millennium* (1957), "acknowledge the importance of the association of Jew with Muslim by medieval Christians as

12. Karen Armstrong, "We cannot afford to maintain these ancient prejudices against Islam," *Guardian*, September 18, 2006.

13. Allan Harris Cutler and Helen Elmquist Cutler, *The Jew as Ally of the Muslim: Medieval Roots of Anti-Semitism* (Notre Dame: University of Notre Dame Press, 1986) 6.

a factor in the history of anti-Semitism."[14] Pope John XXIII's conciliatory attitude toward Islam in the mid-twentieth century may have prepared the ground for the Church's new attitude toward the Jews in Vatican II. But the problem of anti-Semitism, despite changing Catholic theology, particularly after Vatican II, cannot be truly solved without addressing, and coming to terms with, anti-Muslimism. This is a particularly daunting challenge, for anti-Muslimism "as well as racial, ethnic, and political passions and enmities, remain very powerful forces." Written during the cold war, the Cutlers' argument may appear dated, now that anti-Semitism seems to appear mostly in its Islamic guise, triggered mostly, as we have seen, by political disputes and armed conflict over land in the Middle East. Still, "this approach to the history of anti-Semitism via anti-Muslim and ethnopolitical tensions makes a far greater contribution to modern efforts to fight and cure the chronic and pernicious social disease which is anti-Semitism than the approach via Christian theology and the deicide charge!"[15]

The Crusades, then, inaugurated a new era in the long saga of anti-Semitism. "Was it mere coincidence that neither blood nor desecration-of-the-host libels were known in Western Europe before the Crusades?" the Cutlers asked. "Was it sheer coincidence that the first known instance of the blood libel in Western Europe, at Norwich, England, 1144, occurred during the decade of the Second Crusade, while the first known instance of the desecration-of-the-host libel, at Belitz, near Berlin, 1243, occurred the year before the Christians lost Jerusalem to the Muslims[?]"The first "major international persecution of the Jews," following on the heels of scattered accusations in Spain, France, and Italy, "is clearly and unequivocally attributed by the Christian primary sources to the charge that the Jews were in league with the Muslims (specifically, in league with al-Hakim, the Fatimid Caliph of Egypt, who destroyed the Holy Sepulchre in Jerusalem circa 1010),"[16] thereby setting the tone for the persecutions of 1096 (First Crusade). The Jews seemed like the natural allies of the caliph, or of Muslims, because of their similar theological and ritual practices, and because the Jews of Western Europe had come, directly or indirectly, from Muslim lands, where many still maintained contact.

The stock motifs of classical anti-Semitism were engendered during this Christian clash with Islam. During the First Crusade, when Jerusalem

14. Ibid., 121.
15. Ibid., 7–8, 12, 121, 344 (n2), 13–14.
16. Ibid., 92.

was literally submerged in its dwellers' blood, crusader chroniclers, such as Raymond d'Aguilers, justified Christian massacres with the charge that Muslims "torture and mutilate crucifixes, icons, and the Eucharist, or even Christian children," accusations that would later justify "many a pogrom, from the thirteenth century to the twentieth."[17] In 1146, when Peter the Venerable of Cluny wrote to Louis VII supporting the Second Crusade, he thought it natural to conflate Muslims and Jews: "Why should we pursue the enemies of the Christian faith in far distant lands while vile blasphemers far worse than any Saracens, namely the Jews, who are not far away from us, but who live in our midst, blaspheme, abuse, and trample on Christ and the Christian sacraments so freely and insolently and with impunity!?"[18]

There were differences, to be sure. For Bernard de Clairvaux (1090–1153), the prominent Cistercian abbot who, according to the late Norman F. Cantor, the renowned medievalist, "seems to have dominated the western church" in the middle of the twelfth century, "the Muslim exemplifies the passion for violence, conquest, and slaughter, [whereas] the Jew that for money and material profit." But such differences were merely academic, since, in Clairvaux's view, "the crusade expedites triumph over both."[19] The Protestant Reformation inherited the same legacy. Johannes Brenz (1499–1570), a colleague of Martin Luther and author of *How Preachers and Laymen Should Conduct Themselves if the Turk were to Invade Germany* (1537), written after the first Ottoman siege of Vienna in 1529, joined Luther in linking Jew and Turk.[20]

Thus, the genocidal impulse that Bensoussan traces cannot be separated from Europe's crusading spirit against Islam because, according to Richard Southern in his *Western Views of Islam in the Middle Ages* (1962), "the existence of Islam was the most far-reaching problem in medieval

---

17. John V. Tolan, *Saracens: Islam in the Medieval European Imagination* (New York: Columbia University Press, 2002) 117.

18. Quoted in Jeremy Cohen, "The Muslim Connection, or On the Changing Role of the Jew in High Medieval Theology," in *From Witness to Witchcraft: Jews and Judaism in Medieval Christian Thought*, ed. Jeremy Cohen, Wolfenbütteler Mittelalter-Studien 11 (Wiesbaden: Harrassowitz, 1997) 155.

19. Ibid., 159; Norman F. Cantor, *The Civilization of the Middle Ages* (New York: HarperCollins, 1993) 339.

20. Benjamnin Braude, "'Jew' and Jesuit at the Origins of Arabism: William Gifford Palgrave," in *The Jewish Discovery of Islam: Studies in Honor of Bernard Lewis*, ed. Martin Kramer (Tel Aviv: The Moshe Dayan Center for Middle Eastern and African Studies, Tel Aviv University, 1999) 79.

Christendom."²¹ Although Muslims occasionally appeared as "new Jews," making anti-Muslimism an extension of anti-Judaism,²² it is simply impossible to disconnect the rise of medieval Christian anti-Semitism from the Christian crusades against Islam.

It is not for no reason, then, that the Nazis called the most helpless and degraded of their Jewish victims Muslims (*Muselmänner*, plural for *Muselmann*)²³ because that is how this category of doomed Jew was designated in the made-up Nazi idiom. In the Nazi artificial language, *Lingua Terii Imperii* (LTI), Muslims were the Jews who had given up all hope of struggle and survival, the "men and women reduced to staring," in the words of Inge Clendinnen, "listless creatures, no longer responding even to beatings, who for a few weeks existed barely—and who then collapsed and were sent out to the gas."²⁴ It designated, in the words of Elie Wiesel, "those resigned, extinguished souls who had suffered so much evil as to drift to a waking death," those "who were dead but didn't know it."²⁵ Primo Levi remembered the *Muselmänner* as the "backbone of the camp, an anonymous mass, continually renewed and always identical, of non-men, who march and labor in silence, the divine spark dead in them, already too empty to really suffer. One hesitates to call them living; one hesitates to call their death death, in the face of which they have no fear, as they are too tired to understand." The *Muselmänner* crowded Levi's "memory with their faceless presence" because they were the very embodiment of humanity's evil to humans. "If I could enclose all the evil of our time in one image," wrote Levi, "I would choose this image which is familiar to me: an emaciated man, with head dropped and shoulders curved, on whose face and in whose eyes not a trace of thought is to be seen."²⁶ So horrific was the case of the "Muslims" among the internees that Emil Fackenheim described them as "the most truly original contribution of the Third Reich to civilization."²⁷ "It is for [the *Muselmann*]," wrote the Hebrew novelist

---

21. Richard W. Southern, *Western Views of Islam in the Middle Ages* (Cambridge: Harvard University Press, 1962) 3; quoted in Cohen, "The Muslim Connection," 145.

22. Cohen, "The Muslim Connection," 147.

23. Gil Anidjar, "Postface: Réflexions sur la Question," in *Juifs et musulmans*, ed. Esther Benbassa and Jean-Christophe Attias, 130.

24. Inge Clendinnen, *Reading the Holocaust* (Cambridge: Cambridge University Press, 1999) 35.

25. Elie Wiesel, "Stay Together, Always," *Newsweek*, January 16, 1995, 58.

26. Primo Levi, *Survival in Auschwitz: The Nazi Assault on Humanity*, trans. Stuart Woolf (New York: Collier, 1993) 90.

27. Quoted in Gil Anidjar, *The Jew, the Arab: A History of the Enemy*, Cultural

Yehiel De-Nur, better known as Ka-Tzetnik 135633, in *Moni: A Novel of Auschwitz*, "that Auschwitz was created."²⁸

The term "Muslims" was chosen to designate Jews in their most helpless state because, Inge Clendinnen and Giorgio Agamben postulate, it makes the connections between the docility of the victims and the widespread view of Islam as a religion of fatalism. "The term," though, "like the condition, was current in many camps among prisoners and guards: a small linguistic indicator of the coherence of the *univers concentrationnaire*." In Buchenwald and Ravensbrück, for instance, the *Muselmänner* were known as "tired sheikhs" and "*Muselweiber* (female Muslims)."²⁹

It is this remarkable fate, this overlapping of Jewish and Muslim identities in the European imagination, that has been, in the opinion of Gil Anidjar, largely unexplored. For as Anidjar emphasized at the end of an encounter in France, for a frank dialogue between Jews and Arabs or Muslims, "the Jewish question has never been anything but the Arab question" because, in truth, one doesn't exist without the other. "From the Crusades to accusations of ritual murder, from Shylock and Othello to the perverse distinctions that the French colonial regime established between Jews and Arabs in Algeria and in France, the Jew, the Arab [a phrase that Anidjar borrows from Jacques Derrida] has been in turns the theological or political enemy, but also the military, religious and ethnic enemy against whom the West fails." Hence, "holy wars and expulsion, colonialism and genocide, mission civilisatrice and secularization [*laïcisation*], Islamophobia and Judeophobia have always been the two faces of the same and only question, the same strategy."³⁰

⸻

A vigorous Jewish contestation of Zionism as a Western project in the Middle East will also do much to bring Jews and Muslims together. Most Muslims see Zionism as an extension of European colonialism in Arab lands, but Zionism was, in many ways, the affirmation of Judaism's Middle Eastern roots. It was part of a strong nineteenth-century Jewish view that Jews were part of the Islamic world. Prominent Arab poets, like the Iraqi

Memory in the Present (Stanford: Stanford University Press, 2003) 141.

28. Ibid., 147–49.

29. Clendinnen, *Reading the Holocaust*, 35; Giorgio Agamben, *Remnants of Auschwitz: The Witness and the Archive*, trans. Daniel Heller-Roazen (New York: Zone, 1999) 44.

30. Anidjar, "Postface: Réflexions sur la Question," 115, 125, 127.

Ma'ruf al-Russafi, denied any animosity toward the project of Zionism per se: The Arab poet was proud to call Jews "our uncles" related to Arabs through common ancestry (in Ishmael) and language.[31]

In his book *Genesis 1948: The First Arab–Israeli War*, Dan Kurzman recounts the encounter between King Abdullah of Transjordan and Golda Meir in 1948, during which the king invited Meir to consider joining his kingdom, with fifty percent of the seats in parliament allocated to Jews, thereby creating a powerful Arab-Jewish Palestinian country. Meir refused, even as she reminded the king that "the Jews are the only friends you have." This led the king to make the following comment:

> I know that very well. I have no illusions. I know you and I believe in your good intentions. I believe with all my heart that divine providence has brought you back here [to Palestine and the Middle East], restoring you, a Semitic people who were exiled to Europe and shared in its progress, to the Semitic East which needs your knowledge and initiative. Only with your help and your guidance will the Semites be able to revive their ancient glory. We cannot expect genuine assistance from the Christian world, which looks down on Semitic people. We will progress only as the result of joint efforts. I know all this and I believe it sincerely, but conditions are difficult. One dare not take rash steps. Therefore, I beg you once more to be patient.[32]

King Abdullah here treats Jews as the Arabs' long-lost siblings, perhaps like a Semite or Oriental delegation bringing back European knowhow to the Orient, a fact that is central to the vision of many prominent Zionists and figures like Dr. von Weisl who, in the 1920s, thought it most natural to publish the periodical *The Nile and Palestine Gazette* in Egypt and try to covert Arabs to his Zionist cause. It may sound condescending to those who are attuned to Orientalist prejudices, but when the poet Uri Zvi Greenberg stated his hopes in lines like "Believe: our race's sister, the Arab, is here/. . . we will come to instruct him, great in wisdom and experience,"[33] it sounds as if he were simply stating the obvious fact

---

31. See ibid., 202.

32. Dan Kurzman, *Genesis 1948: The First Arab-Israeli War* (New York: New American Library, 1972) 209; quoted in Cutler and Cutler, *The Jew As Ally of the Muslim*, 84–85.

33. U. Z. Greenberg, "The World of the Son of Blood" [Hebrew], in *Shield Area and the Word of the Son of Blood* (Tel Aviv, 1930); quoted in Ranen Omer-Sherman, "Introduction: The Cultural and Historical Stabilities and Instabilities of Jewish Orientalism," *Shofar* 24/2 (2006) 4. Omer-Sherman describes Greenberg's statement as

The Semitic Solution

that Diasporic Jews had benefited from European knowledge and were bringing it back to their ancient lands.

Looking back at the strong Jewish-Muslim bonds through the ages, there is no reason to believe that Zionism could not coexist with full Palestinian rights. In 2004, during an encounter between Arabs and Jews in France, Patrick Klugman, member of the board of directors at the Conseil representatif des institutions juives de France (CRIF), did not hesitate to sum up his convictions with this statement: "I am a pro-Palestinian Zionist."[34] Even when all Muslims have become suspect in the Western imagination after the terrorist attacks of 9/11, and Jewish-Muslim relations have deteriorated even further in the wake of the West-Islam conflict, Jewish leaders are still defending Muslim rights. When Muslims gathered in Rosemont, Illinois, in early September 2007 to talk about their collective plight after 9/11, the president of the Union for Reform Judaism, Rabbi Eric H. Yoffie, denounced such maltreatment in language reminiscent of that from nineteenth-century Jews who defended Islamic causes: "The time has come," the rabbi told the opening session, "to stand up to the opportunists, the media figures, the religious leaders and politicians who demonize Muslims and bash Islam, exploiting the fears of their fellow citizens for their own purposes."[35]

What the Arab historian Ibn Khaldun said to explain the negative view of Jews in the Middle Ages could be reciprocated today by Jews willing to put the deteriorating image of Muslims and Arabs in its proper social context. Many Jews in Arab lands have not yet given up on Muslims. The dwindling but steadfast community of Jews in Morocco continues to believe in the project of a shared destiny. In fact, Morocco's sense of kinship with its ancient Semitic heritage used to be displayed on the emblem of the nation, for the Moroccan flag, before the French colonialists brought their own prejudices, once featured the Seal of Solomon (Star of David), not the five-pointed star (pentagram) we see today. When Muslim terrorists attacked a synagogue (among other targets) in Casablanca on May 16, 2003, one million Moroccans, including Muslims and Jews, refused to be intimidated or divided, joined hands, and walked out in protest—a remarkable event described by the American Israel Public Affairs Committee (AIPAC) as "an amazing, and unprecedented, sight." Almost four years

---

"unfortunate" for its condescending views, but I don't see it as such. Such views anticipate King Abdullah's statement quoted above.

34. See Anidjar, "Postface: Réflexions sur la Question," 101.

35. Neil MacFarquhar, "Abandon Stereotypes, Muslims in America Say," *New York Times*, September 4, 2007.

later, Serge Berdugo, the president of the Moroccan Jewish community's Council, wrote: "As the flames of anti-Semitism continue to be fanned across much of the Islamic world, there is a risk that today's youth will grow up believing that Arabs and Jews were simply not meant to coexist, let alone thrive together. That idea conflicts with history—and is a falsehood today."[36] As if to illustrate his point, a Berber (Morocco's native non-Arab population)-Jewish association was established in 2007 to (among other things) help reconnect Moroccan Jews in Israel with their ancestral homeland (thereby causing some consternation among Arab nationalists). That same year, a Jewish woman and author of books on Jewish life in Morocco, the fifty-four-year-old Maguy Kakon, a member of the newly created Parti du centre social (Party of the Social Center), who traces her family origins back to the fourteenth century, ran for a parliamentary seat in the elections of September and was helped and warmly received by her head-covered Muslim fellow-citizens in some of the poorest districts in Casablanca. (She was one of five Jewish candidates.)[37] This tenacious will not to succumb to the false dichotomies of our time is probably the surest path to a Semitic renaissance, one that brings "Mosaic Arabs" (Jews) and "Mohammedan Arabs" (Muslims), in the description of Benjamin Disraeli, in a fulfilling and lasting union.

---

36. See "Rising Tide," Online: www.aipac.org/documents/risinger060903.html; David Sharrock and Adam LeBor, "Jews Welcome the Support of Muslims," *London Times*, May 19, 2003; François Musseau, "'Nous, les juifs marocains, n'allons pas capituler," *Libération* (France), May 21, 2003; Serge Berdugo, "Morocco: A Model of Muslim-Jewish Ties," *Christian Science Monitor*, January 9, 2007.

37. "Maguy Kakon, femme, citoyenne et juive," *Le Matin* (Morocco), August 31, 2007. For a good sketch of the shrinking but still dynamic and proud Moroccan Jewish community, see Marc Perelman, "From Royal Advisers to Far-Left Militants, Moroccan Jews Embody Coexistence," Forward.com/, October 10, 2007.

thirteen

Islam and Peacebuilding

A. RASHIED OMAR

The dramatic turn of world events at the dawn of the twenty-first century—including the collapse of the Oslo Peace process in September of 2000 in the face of a renewed and ongoing cycle of violence in the Middle East; the terrorist attacks on the United States of America a year later in September 2001, and the Bush administration's subsequent "war on terror" in Afghanistan and Iraq—have all served to reinforce the widespread perception that Islam is in some special way linked to terrorist violence. Even conventional academic perspectives regard Islam as having a predilection for violence.[1] Never before in recent history has the Muslim commitment to a more peaceful and human world being challenged as it is at this time.

Against this backdrop, an examination of the role of Islam and peace takes on momentous proportions. It is a task that I and an increasing number of other Muslim scholars and activists have undertaken and continue

---

1. The stereotype of a bellicose and inherently violent Islam, so pervasive in the media, has wide currency among Western policymakers. For two of the most popular academic accounts that depict Islam as inherently violent see, Bernard Lewis, *What Went Wrong?: The Clash between Islam and Modernity in the Middle East* (New York: Harper Perennial, 2002); and Samuel P. Huntington, *The Clash of Civilizations and the Remaking of World Order* (New York: Simon & Schuster, 1996). There has also been an alarming amount of anti-Islamic propaganda published in the wake of the attacks of September 11, 2001. Two particularly sinister works that attempt to demonize all politically active Muslim individuals or organizations are: Steven Emerson, *American Jihad: The Terrorists Living among Us* (New York: Free Press, 2002); and Daniel Pipes, *Militant Islam Reaches America* (New York: Norton, 2002). Both of these works brand all American Muslims who are critical of Israeli policies as potential terrorist threats, and they incite suspicion against American Muslims by claiming that many of those Muslims are taking part in a secret conspiracy to promote terrorism in America.

201

to undertake with great passion and commitment, since it counterbalances the current preoccupation with Islam and violence.[2] A number of key questions undergird my research on the role of Islam in peacebuilding:

1) How consonant or disparate is the Islamic definition of peace from that of the leading perspectives?
2) Why is peace so elusive in many Muslim majority societies?
3) How should the core Islamic values of Compassion and Justice be configured in an Islamic theology of peace?
4) What concrete strategies and practices could Muslim peace activists adopt in pursuit of a more just and humane world?

This essay addresses the above four questions and concludes with four modest proposals that may create the conditions for the recovery of the Islamic principles of peace and making them part of the fabric of contemporary Muslim culture. I argue that the complex justice struggles in which many Muslim social movements have been engaged during the past century have led to the erosion of the core Islamic value of compassion, and consequently, the loss of peace. It might be expedient to begin with a definition of *peace*.

Locating an Islamic Definition of *Peace*

As is the case with almost all key terms, defining them is a perennial problem. Our definitions of key terms provide us with lenses through which we see the world, and are therefore inherently contested. A number of contending interpretations of *peace* exists in the literature.[3] The disparate definitions of *peace* can be plotted on a horizontal graph, with one axis called *negative peace* and the other *positive peace*. Negative peace has also

---

2. In August 2000, I temporarily left my post as a full-time Imam of a local mosque in Cape Town, South Africa, and joined the Joan B. Kroc Institute for International Peace Studies, at the University of Notre Dame to deepen my own understanding of the causes of religiously motivated violence, and, more important, to identify resources for peacebuilding within Islam and Muslim societies.

3. For a useful introduction to the contending definitions of peace in the literature see David Barash, *Introduction to Peace Studies* (Belmont, CA: Wadsworth, 1991) 5–30. For a deeper reflection on the meaning and sources of peace, see Kenneth Boulding, *Stable Peace* (Austin: University of Texas Press, 1978).

been described as a minimalist definition of peace, and positive peace as a maximalist definition.[4] Negative peace is simply the absence of war.[5]

The alternative to this conventional understanding is positive peace. It stresses the importance of recognizing the existence of a more indirect and insidious form of violence called structural violence. This form of violence is less dramatic and often works slowly, eroding human values and eventually human lives. Its progenitor and most ardent advocate is the Norwegian peace scholar and activist Johan Galtung. According to Galtung, violence can be built into the very structure of the sociopolitical, economic, and cultural institutions of a society.[6] Structural violence has the effect of denying people important rights such as economic opportunity, social and political equality, and human dignity. When children die of starvation or malnutrition, a kind of violence is taking place. Similarly when human beings suffer from diseases that are preventable; when they are denied a decent education, housing, and opportunity to raise a family; or to participate in their own governance, a kind of violence is taking place.[7]

An examination of the Islamic concept of peace reveals that it is closer to that of positive peace and traverses between two core values in Islam, namely, that of compassion and justice. This is underscored by the strong emphasis the most primary source of Islamic guidance, the Quran, places on these two principles of compassion and justice. Both these core ethical precepts are employed numerous times in the Glorious Quran. The word *rahma* ("compassion," "mercy," and "tenderness") and its various derivatives occur more than 326 times. According to Imam Raghib al-Isfahani in his famous lexicography, *Mufradat al-Quran*, the term *rahma*

---

4. I am indebted to a former Peace Studies teacher of mine, Professor Siobhan McEvoy-Levy for first introducing me to the contending definitions of peace in the literature.

5. According to R. Scott Appleby, negative peace is a condition in which no direct, physical or instrumental violence is perpetrated either by the state or by paramilitaries or resistance/rebel movements. See Appleby, *The Ambivalence of the Sacred: Religion, Violence and Reconciliation*, Carnegie Commission on Preventing Deadline Conflict (Lanham, MD: Rowman & Littlefield, 2000) 296.

6. Johan Galtung "Violence, Peace and Peace Research," *Journal of Peace Research* 6/3 (1969) 167–91.

7. For a related idea due to the Galtung distinction between direct violence (children are murdered), structural violence (children die through poverty), and cultural violence (whatever blinds us to this or seeks to justify it), see in Hugh Miall et al., "Introduction to Conflict Resolution" in their *Contemporary Conflict Resolution*. (Cambridge: Polity, 1999) 15 [5–22].

means "softening of the heart towards one who deserves our mercy and induces us to do good to him/her." It is interesting to note that the womb of a mother is also called *rahm*. A mother is always very soft and gentle towards her children (*raqiq*); she showers love and affection on them.[8]

The Quran uses two terms to refer to justice: *qist* and *ʿadl*. These two terms are used interchangeably and basically mean "to give someone his or her full portion."[9] In fact the Quran regards "actions for justice as being the closest thing to piety." (5:6)[10] The Quranic verses pertaining to justice are often specific about those areas of social affairs wherein lapses are most likely to occur, such as the trusts and legacies of orphans and adopted children (4:3; 33:5), matrimonial relations (4:3; 49:9), contractual and business dealings (2:282), judicial matters (5:42; 4:56), interreligious relations (60:8), economic relations (11:65), and dealing with one's adversaries (5:8). This strong emphasis on justice has led some Muslim jurists, like the renowned Ibn Qayyim al-Jawziyyah (d.1350 CE), to argue that justice is the *raison d'être* of the establishment of religion: "God has sent His Messengers and revealed His Books so that people may establish justice [*qist*], upon which the heavens and the earth stand. And when the signs of justice appear in any manner, then that is a reflection of the *shariah* and the religion of God."[11] In short, therefore, the Islamic concept of peace is integrally related to the struggle for justice. It resonates well with the following exhortation from Pope Paul VI, "If you want peace, work for justice."[12]

In order to balance the picture of the Islamic concept of peace I have sketched thus far, it is necessary to bear in mind that, as important as justice may be in the comprehensive matrix of Islamic values, I argue that it is certainly not *the* preeminent one. This is underscored by the fact that *al-Rahman*, or the Compassionate One, is undoubtedly *the* most important attribute of God in Islam. It is the equivalent of the Christian preeminent understanding of God as Love. One of the best-known Quranic verses with which Muslims commence every action is, "*bismillahir rahmanir*

---

8. For a useful discussion of the concept of compassion in Islam see Ashgar Ali Engineer, "On the Concept of Compassion in Islam"; online: http://newark.rutgers.edu/~rtavakol/engineer/compassion.htm/.

9. See E. W. Lane, *Lane's Arabic-English Lexicon* (Beirut: Librairie du Liban, 1980, q-s-t).

10. All translations of the Quran are my own.

11. Ibn Qayyim al-Jawziyya, *Al-Turuq al-Hakimiyyah fi al-Siyat al-Shar'iyyah* (Cairo: n.p., 1953) 14–16.

12. Quoted in R. Scott Appleby, *The Ambivalence of the Sacred*, xi.

rahim," translated as, "In the name of God, the Most Compassionate, the Dispenser of Grace." Compassion is so central to God's existence that it embraces all that exists in the universe (40:7). The Quran describes the *raison d'être* of the prophet Muhammad's mission as *rahmatan lil ʿalamin*, a source of compassion and mercy to the world (21:107). It is this understanding of Islam that has allowed Muslim mystics, *sufis*, to develop the doctrine of what is called *sulh-i-kul*, that is, peace with all, which means no violence and no aggressiveness.

I have thus far argued for an Islamic concept of peace that navigates between two core values in Islam, namely, justice and compassion. I have also argued that whenever these two core values of Islam come into tension with each other, compassion trumps. In my view, therefore, a struggle for justice *(jihad)* that claims Islamic legitimacy has to locate itself within an ethos of compassion. Without compassion, struggles for justice invariably end up mimicking the oppressive orders against which they revolt. Ironically, it is precisely here that the crisis of contemporary Muslims is located, and consequently where the challenge of a credible Islamic peace resides. How does one balance between the two critical concepts of justice and compassion in constructing a viable project of Muslim peacebuilding?

It is my considered view that the numerous struggles for social justice, starting with the anticolonial wars of the first half of the twentieth century, the watershed Afghan war against the Soviet invasion in the 1980s, and the continuing struggles against secular elites in the postcolonial period that have engaged many parts of the world with Muslim-majority populations have inevitably led justice to be the hermeneutical key through which Muslims view Islam. This obsession with justice has in turn led to an erosion of another central Islamic concept of compassion. The kind of wanton violence into which many Muslim struggles for justice have degenerated can in large measure be attributed to this phenomenon: justice struggles without compassion. How can the central Islamic concept of compassion be recovered and reinvigorated such that it once again becomes part of the fabric of contemporary Muslim culture. This is indeed the critical challenge facing contemporary Muslims.

Concrete Proposals for Muslim Peacemaking

I suggest four modest proposals that may create the conditions out of which a credible Muslim role in peacebuilding could be spawned. My suggestions emerge primarily from my own assessment of the current geopolitical realities and the corresponding Muslim crisis of extremism.

First, Muslims must not become weary of stating again and again, loudly and unequivocally, that acts of wanton violence and barbarism are contrary to the teachings of Islam. And the news media must do more to make sure their voices are heard. In Islamic ethics, the end does not justify the means. Religious extremism has no virtue in Islam and has been unequivocally condemned by the prophet Muhammad. He is reported in an authentic prophetic tradition (*hadith*) to have declared thrice, "The extremists shall perish."[13] For contemporary Muslims, this means to acknowledge, no matter how painful it is, that they do have extremists (*mutatarrifun*) in their ranks. This is, of course not unique to Islam. What is peculiar to Islam is that extremists appear to have a disproportionate voice within their ranks, not least because of the proclivity of the media for sensationalism. Muslim leaders have an especially onerous challenge of condemning violent overreactions and not allowing to go unpunished misguided individuals who act in a thoroughly reprehensible and depraved way in responses to perceived provocations against Islam.

Second, there is dire need for more rigorous academic studies of the potentially fertile sources of nonviolence and peacebuilding in Islam and Muslim societies. At the time of this writing, a keyword search on the Library of Congress subject catalogue for resources on *Islam*, *nonviolence*, and *peace* produced fewer than a half a dozen items. A similar search for items on *Islam* and *violence*, by contrast, produced a plethora of materials. It is palpable that Islam and Muslim societies are rather neglected areas of peace studies and peace research. Reflecting on this bias in the current peace research agenda, Mohamed Abu-Nimer, in the most pioneering book to be published recently in the field, *Nonviolence and Peace Building Islam* (2003), argues that shifting the emphasis from war and violence to peace and conflict transformation in the study of Islam and Muslim societies can contribute significantly to buttressing and reinvigorating courageous peace initiatives that are already in progress in many different Muslim settings.

Two useful examples of such Muslim peacebuilding initiatives are the British Muslim Peace and Reconciliation Initiative in Darfur, led by the Muslim humanitarian agency, Muslim Hands, and the Philippines Center for Islam and Democracy, which runs peace education programs

---

13. This prophetic tradition is found in the famous compilation of *Sahih Muslim*, translated into English by Abdul Hamid Siddiqui (New Delhi: Kitab Bhavan, 2000).

from an Islamic perspective in order to transform conflict and to engender a culture of peace in Mindanao. Abu-Nimer's groundbreaking book establishes a theoretical framework for peacebuildng and nonviolence in Islam and deals comprehensively with almost all the major academic contributions to this field.[14]

Not surprisingly, despite the paucity of publications directly on this topic, the field is rich and includes leading Muslim scholars from diverse countries and cultures, such as Abdul Aziz Sachedina (USA), Jawdat Sa'id (Syria), Mawlana Wahiduddin Khan (Pakistan), Ashgar Ali Engineer (India), Chandra Muzaffar (Malaysia), Chiawat Satha-Anand (Thailand), and Rabia Terri Harris (USA).[15] Notwithstanding the sterling efforts of these courageous scholars, the field of Islamic peace studies and conflict transformation remains inchoate and urgently needs much more attention.

Third, there is an urgent need for the nurturing and training of a new critically minded class of *ulama* (Muslim religious scholars). The established Muslim religious leadership in many Muslim-majority countries, such as Saudi Arabia, Egypt, and Pakistan, have abandoned their role as the moral conscience of their societies by speaking out more coherently on the human rights violations and injustices that permeate their societies. Many of them, while speaking out against certain forms of injustices against Muslims, are providing religious legitimacy to despotic and oppressive regimes. Moreover, nonviolent civil resistance campaigns are not tolerated in most Muslim countries, and progressive religious leaders are either incarcerated or exiled. Drawing on the theoretical insights gleaned from the recent deluge of studies on the causes and prevention of religious conflict, the conclusion is unmistakable: Religion does not spawn violence independently of predisposing social, economic, and political conditions as well as the subjective roles of belligerent leaders.[16] The studies of two historians of religion, Bruce Lincoln and Scott Appleby, have offered similar but independent arguments in support of this theoretical assertion. Appleby has, for example, proposed that because of the ambivalent

14. Mohamed Abu-Nimer, *Nonviolence and Peace Building in Islam: Theory and Practice* (Gainesville: University Press of Florida, 2003).

15. For a useful list of publications on Islam and Peacebuilding, see Mohammed Abu-Nimer's bibliography in *Nonviolence and Peace Building in Islam*, 213–28. An outdated but comprehensive bibliography on Islam-Peace-Nonviolence was also compiled by Karim Douglas Crow and can be found online: http://www.members.tripod.com/nviusa/islam.htm/.

16. Carnegie Commission on Preventing Deadly Conflict, *Preventing Deadly Conflict: Final Report with Executive Summary* (New York: Carnegie Corporation of New York, December 1997).

nature of the sacred (it can be interpreted in the service of peace as well as violence), the role of religious leaders is decisive.[17] He contends, "corrupt, craven or merely indecisive religious leadership invites interlopers, claimants who would associate the energies and purposes of religion with their own."[18]

In light of this finding, as well as the existing crisis in Muslim religious leadership, it seems to me critical that we contribute urgently toward the emergence of a new generation of religious scholars who are well versed in *both* the traditional Islamic sciences and the modern social sciences. Peace education and conflict transformation skills grounded within the key Islamic principles of compassion and justice must form an integral and essential part of this formation and training for future imams. A useful starting point might be to offer training programs and scholarships to enhance the knowledge horizons of existing imams, especially the younger ones. Fortunately, a few such programs have begun, although their numbers and ranks need great expansion. Another idea is to foster exchange programs between existing students from Muslim, Christian, and Jewish seminaries. Fortunately a few people are already beginning to work on exactly such an initiative.[19]

Last but not least, peace scholars need to consistently highlight the fact that the current iniquitous global conditions do not lend themselves well to credible Muslim peacebuilding. A number of scholars have already pointed this out. For example, the renowned scholar of Islam John Esposito has ominously warned in his most recent book, *Unholy War: Terror in the Name of Islam* (2002) that "if foreign policy issues are not addressed effectively, they will continue to be breeding ground for hatred and radicalism, the rise of extremist movements, and recruits for the bin Ladens of the world."[20]

---

17. R. Scott Appleby, *The Ambivalence of the Sacred*, 54–56.

18. Ibid.

19. It was a privilege for me to represent the Kroc Institute at the Global Dialogue Institute's 25th International Scholars Annual Trialogue in Skopje, Macedonia, from May 10 to 14, 2002. The trilateral dialogue was cosponsored by a wide range of international organizations, including the Macedonian Center for International Cooperation, the World Conference on Religion and Peace; the event was partially funded by the United States Institute of Peace. One of the most exciting dimensions of the trialogue was the sessions held at the Orthodox and Islamic theological seminaries. A bold proposal was made for exploring creative ways of interreligious collaboration in the theological formation and education of the students at these two seminaries.

20. John L. Esposito, *Unholy War: Terror in the Name of Islam* (New York: Oxford University Press, 2002) 157.

In line with this analysis, peace advocates need to support the call for a public debate concerning the most effective means to counteract Muslim and other forms of extremism. Interreligious activists need to join the many voices all over the world who are questioning the wisdom of the current strategy pursued in the "war on terrorism." They also need to back the call for a serious reassessment concerning the controversial United States foreign policy which abets authoritarian Muslim regimes in the Middle East, and elsewhere, as well as its uncritical and too often unilateral support for the present policies of the state of Israel.[21] The belligerent environment that is currently being engendered is not helpful in ameliorating the root causes that provide a fertile ground on which extremism thrives. On the contrary, it is generating conditions that favor extremism, thus rendering the task of developing Muslim peacemaking initiatives extremely difficult. More importantly, such an unequivocal call for justice in the Middle East and elsewhere coming from Jewish and Christian institutions and leaders, will help rebuild trust and confidence in the beleaguered initiatives of Muslim peacebuilders and their support bases.

Conclusion

Returning to one of the initial questions: why is peace so elusive in many Muslim societies? In our response we should remember that the contemporary global order is not by any stretch of the imagination a just one. Furthermore, Islam places a strong emphasis on social justice as an integral part of its concept of peace. Muslim legitimization of violence does not occur in a sociohistorical vacuum but rather within concrete human settings in which power dynamics are paramount. Against this backdrop, the Muslim preoccupation with justice has led to an erosion of the core Islamic value of compassion. Extremists have a disproportionate influence within the ranks of Muslims and the global communications media have inadvertently became their ally. Our primary strategy towards combatting Muslim and all other forms of violence and terrorism should be that of ameliorating the root causes that provide fertile ground on which extremism can thrive.

This chapter has offered four concrete proposals that can make a modest contribution toward creating the conditions necessary for a more positive peace role for Islam to counterbalance the disproportionate yet

21. Support for this view is presented in Graham E. Fuller, "The Future of Political Islam," *Foreign Affairs* (March/April 2002) 60.

awesome power of Muslim extremists. There exists a dire need for the followers of Judaism, Christianity, and Islam, as well as of all other traditions, to retrieve our common humanity and to end the horrific dehumanization currently taking place on such a wide scale. The challenge of peace for Muslims in particular is to develop a theology of healing and embrace (*ta'aruf*) so eloquently described in the following verse of the Quran: "O Humankind! We have created you into a male and female and fashioned you into nations and tribes, so that you may come to know each other (not despise one another). The most honoured of you in the sight of God, is those who display the best conduct. And God is All-Knowing, All-Aware" (49:13).

fourteen

Transformation through Dialogue

A Muslim Scholar's Search for Identity

MUHAMMAD SHAFIQ

This is the story of transformation: of my own, primarily, but also that of the two cultures by which my life has been shaped—the culture of Pakistan, the land of my birth, and the culture of my adopted country, the United States. The religion of Islam has played a key role in these transformations. So have the events of September 11. But the real story is about interfaith dialogue. At first presenting itself to me as a way to deal with an intense personal dislike of controversy, interfaith dialogue has become *my* way of life. It has also become my mission, required of me by my Muslim faith and greatly needed by a fear-imprisoned world.

Growing Up in the Khyber PakhtunKhwa (North West Frontier Province) of Pakistan

I was born in a poor, remote farming village in the district of Karak, in the Khyber Pakhtunkhwa Province of Pakistan. My parents, members of the Pashtun tribal culture, had no education in religion or in anything else. Our village had no drinking water. I recall that my mother would wake me at dawn to accompany her as she brought water home on our donkey from a source miles away. There was no electricity, no roads, and no clinic. Very few children in our village went to school in those days. Of my two brothers, one did not go to school at all, and the other went secretly to a nearby city where he received religious education in a madrassah. Madrassah education in Pakistan was and still is free.

My First Experience of Religious Controversy

Once in the late 1960s controversy erupted in a village near ours over the congregational prayer led by a member of Jamat-i-Islami, a religiopolitical party that followed the teaching of its founder, Mawlana Abul A' la Mawdudi. The *imam* (religious leader) of the village asked the congregants to redo the *Salat* (worship), since the person who had led the *Salat* that day was *Mudil* ("led astray"), according to him. Confusion and controversy followed. I was in high school and could not understand what was going on. This was my first exposure to rancorous intrareligious rivalry in Pakistan. My reaction to such rivalry as a child remains with me today: I was saddened and grieved by it.

My second exposure occurred during the summer a few years later when two top leaders of Jamʿiyyat al ʿUluma al Islam (another religiopolitical party), Mawlana Hazarvi and Mawlana Mufti Mahmood,[1] came to our village. My elder brother was a graduate of the madrassah and had associated with them. In his lecture to the villagers, Mawlana Hazarvi used very harsh, even abusive, language against the members of Jamaʿat-i-Islami, labeling them *Dal* and *Mudil* (those who not only go astray themselves but who lead others astray as well). These two religiopolitical parties both derive from the Deoband school of thought in India[2] but differ in

---

1. Mufti Mahmood was different from Hazarvi in attitude and dealings. He was respectful, humble and a wise leader. After his split from Hazarvi, he became a highly respected national figure. He also became the Chief Minister of the North West Frontier Province of Pakistan in 1970s and later led a successful opposition movement against Zulfiqar Ali Bhutto and his People Party accusing them of rigging the national polls in Pakistan. I met with Mufti Mahmood a few times in the 1970s and was impressed by his character. He, in contrast to Hazarvi, taught me that a respectful and humble character with wisdom can take one to a higher place in society.

2. The Deoband school called in Arabic: Darul ʿUlum Deoband in the town of Deoband, Uttar Pradesh, India represents the Hanafi Sunni brand of Islam. Darul ʿUlum was established to preserve and train the youth in Islamic knowledge. The pedagogical philosophy of Deoband focused on teaching revealed Islamic sciences to Indian Muslims primarily in the Hanafi tradition. Initially the School adopted a non-political policy. But soon its leaders formed Jamʿiyyat al Uluma al Hind and supported the Indian national Congress to win India's freedom from the British. Deoband scholars believed in a democratic government in which Hindus, Muslims, Sikhs, Christians, and Parsis could live together in peace. The Darul ʿUlum Deoband opposed the establishment of Pakistan.

their interpretations of Islamic tradition. Shocked by the violence of Mawlana Hazarvi's denunciations, I asked my brother why he could not have expressed his criticisms calmly and gently.

College Years: Discovering my Identity as a Religious Leader

In September 1968, during my first year in Government College Kohat, I was asked to lead *Salat* in the dorm for students. Taking me for a clergyman, people would come with their problems and ask for my special prayers. I had learned some of these prayers from my brother and my teachers in the madrassah. One day a cook in our dormitory came to me soon after I had finished leading the afternoon worship. In tears he told me that his buffalo was refusing to give milk to her new calf. He added that this buffalo's milk, along with the small salary he was receiving as a cook, was the basis of his family's sustenance. Grieving for him, I asked him to go home and bring me bread and some wheat flour. He promptly did as I had asked. I recited some Quranic verses in blessing over the bread and flour. Then I told him to mix the flour in water and to let the buffalo drink it and to feed her the bread as well. Once he'd done so, the buffalo began to give milk. News spread that the young imam was a spiritual healer. People from nearby towns would invite me just to pray for them!

More Controversies

The religious controversies I had known as a child now manifested themselves at the College. A severe controversy exploded one day over how to pronounce the words of the *fatiha* (the opening chapter of the Quran) correctly, especially a word containing the Arabic consonant *dad*. I recall people even refusing to pray in company with those who (in their minds) pronounced *dad* incorrectly. There was strife as well over whether to say *ameen* ("amen") out loud or silently after the imam finished proclaiming the *fatiha*. I also recall heated debates over the *ameen* issue between the Ahl al Hadith (people who claim that *ahadith*—the tradition of the

---

The Deoband school became highly influential in a very short period. Students came from all over and its graduates established madrassahs in their regions across South Asia, Afghanistan, South Africa, and the United Kingdom. Some madrassahs established in America and Canada today are influenced by the Deoband method of teaching Islam.

prophet Muhammad—are the ultimate criteria to be followed in determining the practice of worship) and between the ʿUlama (scholars) of the Hanafi school of thought (people who claim that legal schools shall be followed). Some of these disputes resulted in bloodshed. The violence disturbed me and left a deep mark on my early life.

The religious controversies were even worse between the Sunni and the Shiʿa in Pakistan. During my college studies, some of our teachers would not hesitate to call the Shiʿa *Kafirs* (disbelievers), and some Shiʿa leaders also adopted a hard tone against the Sunnis. People normally rejoice in celebrating the New Year, but in Pakistan, the Muslim New Year celebrations began to turn into riots and violence between the Sunni and the Shiʿa communities. Police were put on high alert to prevent violence and bloodshed over ʿAshura (the tenth day of Muharram, the day on which Imam Hussein was martyred in 626 CE) between the Sunni and the Shiʿa communities.

Taliban

My beliefs and lifestyle in Government College and later at the University of Peshawar resembled those of the Taliban: I was rigid, traditional, and backward looking. Yet the Taliban in those days were very different from the contemporary Taliban. They were humble, cooperative, and forgiving. They avoided violence. Yes, they had a history of severity and patriarchalism. They would not allow music of any kind, and they discouraged girls from going to school. They insisted that women wear the *burqa* (the complete covering). But later they became a bit tolerant. When we were in school, our Islamic studies teacher, a member of the Taliban, was very intolerant in the beginning. Then he was transferred to the city. When he returned to our school two years later, he was a different person: gentle and tolerant. When once we students asked him about the change, he only smiled. I followed a similar trajectory during my high school and college years, moving from conservative rigidity to openness.

The modern sense of the word *Taliban* is political, and refers to people shaped by their fighting in the Afghan-Russian war. There are very few madrassah graduates actively supporting these political Taliban.

America's Influence on Me

My journey to America in 1976 for higher education at Temple University opened a new chapter in my life. I was amazed to observe, first of all, how students dialogued in the classroom with the teachers and among themselves. Even when class discussion was heated, no one lost patience or showed disrespect. Many Muslim students would usually stay silent at such times. Once a professor asked me why some Muslim students remained silent and why, whenever any one of them would raise a question, he would become red faced as if he were fighting or bearing up under a heavy load. This professor did not know that many of us come from institutions where dialogue is considered disrespectful. Even in situations where our teacher was clearly wrong, we students didn't dare to correct, for fear of retribution. Our Temple professor did not know that Muslim students were trained in *Samiʿna wa Ataʿna* (we hear and obey).

I was especially amazed while attending a student demonstration against a state budget cut for the university. Thousands of students stood shouting from the open ground in front of the university's main library building. Two of us standing there were Muslims. We both thought that the angry crowd would burn the library to the ground that very day. So we were astonished to find that after hours of shouting, the leadership resolved to write letters to State Assembly members and to send a delegation to the State capital at Harrisburg to meet personally with legislators. When we saw the peaceful, constructive way the demonstration developed, we lamented the situation in our own homelands. Student protests there usually ended in the destruction of property and the loss of lives. We vowed that we would work to change these conditions once we returned home.

Something else that astonished me was the behavior I observed at a Christian ecumenical conference in New York City in 1978. I was surprised to observe how peacefully various Christian denominations dialogued with one another there. Many of these denominations had in the past called one another apostates or heretics. Their relations continued to be scornful and divisive for centuries after the periods of the Renaissance and Reformation. But then their leadership, realizing their mistake, initiated ecumenical dialogue. (*Ecumenical* comes from a Greek word meaning "household.") Although the denominations differed sharply over issues of theology and ritual, they nevertheless emphasized respect for each other's dignity, especially in their writings and discussions. Their behavior inspired me to try my best to initiate such respectful ecumenical dialogue among our various disputing religious groups in Pakistan.

Trialogue and Terror

I was able to deepen my understanding of Christian ecumenical dialogue thanks to my work in the ecumenical library of the Religion Department at Temple University under the supervision of Professor Leonard Swidler. In my research position I went through many articles and essays on dialogue. The next two-years of my stay at Temple gave me direct experience of such dialogue and bolstered my intention of transporting its lessons to intra-Muslim dialogue.

Returning to Pakistan

I returned to Pakistan soon after receiving my PhD in 1982. One day in 1983, I spotted two flyers attached to the side of the door of Islamabad's Red Mosque[3] as I exited after Maghrib (Sunset) prayer. One flyer was from Sipahi-i-Sahaba (the soldiers of the Companions of the Prophet, a movement founded by a Sunni group called Ahl al Hadith[4] to protect the dignity of the companions of the Prophet), and another one from Sipah Muhammad (the Soldiers of Prophet Muhammad, a movement that was founded by a Shi'a group to protect the honor of the Prophet). This was a frightening discovery. These two movements were violently opposed, and are banned today, but while they existed they enormously damaged Sunni-Shi'a relations.

Worse was to come. The Iraq-Iran war of the 1970s had greatly inflamed religious differences between Pakistan's Sunni and Shi'a communities. For example, the enmity between the Sipahi-i-Sahaba and Sipah Muhammad groups resulted in religious riots, killings, and bombings. Hate literature was translated into and printed in all Pakistani languages. The pro–Ahl al Hadith literature openly referred to the Shi'a as *Kafirs* (non-Muslims); the Shi'a group responded in kind. Their behavior poisoned the state of intra-Muslim relations.

I did what I could to change the situation by participating in the Shi'a-Sunni *Ittihad* (unity) movement on the Peshawar University campus. I established relations with religious scholars and academics from both sides to bridge the gap, but the gap was widening. I also built connections with

---

3. The Red Mosque in Islamabad, known as Lall Masjid, gradually became the center of Taliban activities. President Musharraf took military action against the leaders of the mosque in 2006.

4. Ihsan Ilahi Zaheer was the leader of Ahl al Hadith in Lahore, Pakistan. He published many books denouncing Shi'as, calling them *Kafirs* (disbelievers). He fomented controversy and was eventually assassinated. Many believed that he was killed by the Shi'a.

people of other faiths. I took my comparative religions graduate students to churches at Peshawar; to the Buddhist site at Taxila, Pakistan; and to a Gurdwara of Sikhism in the same city, in an effort to foster interfaith understanding.

But I and others like me were up against strong divisive forces. For example, the madrassah systems representing the different religious schools of thought in Pakistan were just as hostile to each other as they had been in my childhood. However, I now understood the intellectual basis of their hostility: their absolute adhesion to a single point of view. For example, *Tafsir* (Quran exegesis) in the Deobandi madrassahs was under the exclusive control of the Deoband ideology. Similarly the *Tafsir* taught in the Barelvi madrassahs[5] did not deviate from the teachings of Raza Khan, their founder. Madrassahs run by Jamat-i-Islami espoused a certain orthodoxy (*Tafhim al Qurʿan*, by Maududi), and the same was true about the madrassahs run by the Shiʿas and others too. Most students of these different madrassahs graduated with a rigid ideological focus that encouraged disrespect for each other's school of thought.[6] Trying to steer clear of all ideologies, I sought to build relations with all of them in the hope of eventually developing better understanding among them and convincing them to adopt inclusive curriculum for their respective madrassahs.

The Skies Darken

Soon after the assassination of President Zia ul-Haq in 1988, I found the situation in Pakistan rapidly deteriorating. The deterioration was most noticeable among the Pashtun tribal peoples.

Though the Pashtun followed Deobandi teachings by tradition, they were barely educated. The Pashtun tribes of both Afghanistan and Pakistan followed the strict discipline of Pashtunwali, which emphasizes family honor, a tribal code of ethics, and respect for tribal leaders. The Pashtun were brave fighters with their own gun factories (Landi Kotal and Khayber Bazar, known as Darra between Peshawar and Kohat) where

---

5. The Barelvi Madrassahs represent Hanafi Sunni Islam with Sufi influence. The Barelvi School came into existence soon after the Deoband School. Though both are Sunni from the Hanafi School, they differ on many legal issues.

6. I myself studied in a madrassah run by the Deoband ideology and remember when the teacher would apply the words *Daal* ("gone astray") and *Mudil* ("make others to go astray") to rival schools of thought. The teacher did not hesitate to accuse the rival schools of heresy.

they manufactured all sorts of small weapons. Because of their war-like nature, the men of the tribes were encouraged to become freedom fighters in Kashmir both before and after the partition of the subcontinent to support the Muslims of India. The tribal leaders were accustomed to receive bribes from government authorities when their services were needed. But they in turn were often exploited to satisfy political agendas potentially harmful to them.

Such exploitation rose to a new level with the Afghan jihad against the Soviet invasion. The Pashtuns suddenly found themselves exposed to ideologies of a more complex sort than they had ever encountered before.[7] The Afghan jihad itself took the form of a jihad against the Russians. The West, including America and some Middle Eastern countries, joined their resources to fight this war. Their slogan was "to save Asia from the red and keep it for the green." (The color red stood for communism while green represented people of faith.) But later the ideology expanded to include, after the liberation of Afghanistan,[8] the liberation of Palestine and then of Saudi Arabia from foreign occupation At this point the Pashtuns were first exposed to Wahhabism[9] and then to the cause of destroying Israel. The Pashtuns, who believed they were the descendents of the lost tribes of Israel, now found themselves directed to hate all Jews, and America as

---

7. The Pashtuns were first exposed to such ideologies through the movement of Syed Ahmad Shaheed of Rai Bareilly, India, and Shah Isma'il Shaheed of Delhi, India, in 1825. Syed Ahmad went on pilgrimage and perhaps became influenced by the Wahhabiyya Movement in Saudi Arabia. He was against the British occupation of India, and believed in the courage and strength of the Pashtun tribes to support him. He toured India gathering some followers and then came to Peshawar to mobilize the Pashtun tribes. Instead of fighting the British to liberate India, Ahmad started his movement to liberate Punjab from Sikh domination. He defeated the Sikh army in a number of places initially and was moving toward the mainland of Punjab when he declared his brand of Shari'ah (Islamic Law). This disillusioned many Pashtun tribes who ceased supporting him. He and many of his followers were killed at the fierce 1831 battle in Balakot (Pakistan). There are many writings available on the subject.

8. Abdullah 'Azzam was the key leader of this movement, receiving Bin Laden's support. Bin Laden became well known only after 'Azzam's assassination.

9. How much the Pashtun were against the Wahhabi ideology before the Afghan war can be seen in this story: There was a Hindu shopkeeper in Afghanistan. As was customary, he used to send fresh vegetables to the Imam's house every morning when he would open his store. His business went down and he stopped sending it to the Imam's house. In reaction the Imam told his congregation that our Hindu shopkeeper has become a Wahhabi. First how could a Hindu be Wahhabi? But his congregants without understanding the real issue boycotted the shopkeeper. The shopkeeper restarted the vegetables to save his business. The Imam told his congregants that the shopkeeper had repented. This story shows the intensity of hatred towards the Wahhabi ideology among many Pashtuns.

well, because of its support for Israel. It was not unusual to hear Pashtun processions chanting, "Israel and America Murdabad" (death to Israel and America).

Returning to the United States and Coming to Rochester, New York

In October 1991, I returned once again to America, accompanied by my family, to serve the Islamic Center of Rochester, New York, as its imam and executive director. Soon I was encountering challenges much like those I had left behind in Pakistan: challenges caused by people's inability or unwillingness to tolerate difference. I was experienced enough to know that leading a Muslim community like the one in Rochester, composed of different ethnic groups and with different religious backgrounds, would not be easy. Sure enough, soon after I came to the Center, I had to deal one day with a dispute between two brothers from different ethnicities who were blaming each other for the widening gap between them as they stood in line during *Maghrib Salat* (sunset prayers). They quarreled and were on the verge of fighting till others intervened. Which was more sinful—a gap in prayer, or fighting? The challenge was how to lead such a community peacefully.

Misunderstandings and misconceptions abounded. On one occasion, while addressing someone's question as to whether angels can enter homes where photos are hanging, I tried to differentiate between photos and statues. Without giving me an opportunity to explain further, two men stood up and started shouting, accusing me of disrespect for the *Sunnah* (Prophetic tradition). I heard some people debating that taking US citizenship is an act of *Kufr* (disbelief), that voting in a non-Muslim country is *Haram* (forbidden), and that democracy is the work of *Shaytan* (the devil). Some Muslims would not hesitate to call another Muslim *Fasiq* (a mischief maker) if the offending party had spoken against his accuser's point of view. Some considered interfaith dialogue *Haram* (forbidden), and those who participated were labeled acting as *Kafirs* (disbelievers).

After much effort trying to keep the community united despite such disputes, I came to the conclusion that the differences of opinion would not just disappear; but if I succeeded in creating an atmosphere of listening, where people could express their differences gently and respectfully, then unity would follow. I devoted almost all my *Khutbas* (Friday sermons) and lectures to moderation of behavior as the true sign of Muslim character. I extolled manners, etiquette, and the art of dialogue.

I had ample opportunity to promote dialogue with non-Muslims as well. Upon my arrival in Rochester, I joined the city's interfaith forum. One of our first acts was to create in 1993 the Commission on Christian-Muslim Relations, the first ever of its kind in America. The Commission called for bridge building between members of the two faiths by creating educational programs, by calling public attention to media bias against Islam and Muslims, and by arranging visits to each other's houses of worship.

The most difficult area for interfaith dialogue was not between Muslims and Christians, however, but between Muslims and Jews, since both communities were, and remain, caught up in gridlock over the Israel-Palestine conflict. Yet the Muslim community of Rochester supported my efforts to reach out to the Jewish community leadership for better relations. The late Rabbi Judea Miller of Rochester's Temple B'rith Kodesh, an active member of our interfaith forum, was very interested in building bridges and better relations between the Jewish and Muslim communities. Soon the Reform Jewish Community of Temple B'rith Kodesh and the Islamic Center joined hands in promoting many activities, especially during the Bosnia crisis. One of those activities stands out. It was a jointly sponsored fundraising dinner for Bosnian victims of war held at the temple in 1993. There was a large audience, which included state and federal government representatives. It was there at the temple that the *Adhan* (call for worship) was given for the first time in a Rochester synagogue, and Muslims prayed in the worship space. This was indeed a historic occasion.

Rabbi Miller, a recognized leader of the Reform Jewish community, took great initiatives in building good relations. He was also a humble and spontaneous man. If he had a new idea to share, he would come to the Islamic Center to talk to me, sometimes without calling ahead. On one occasion, Rabbi Miller called me early in the morning at home from the airport to express sadness over the incident in which a Jewish man fired on Muslims during congregational worship in the Hebron mosque in Israel-Palestine. He asked me to call a joint press conference for the next morning to condemn the incident. The Center was packed with media personnel as well as community leaders on both sides of the Israeli-Palestinian conflict. During the press conference, Rabbi Miller called the attacker "an impostor, a betrayer of the Jewish faith." He asked the Jewish government of Israel and the Jewish people to make amends for the betrayal.

Transformation through Dialogue

When I first arrived in Rochester, I was told that some local officials had publicly stated that they would never let Muslims gain a foothold in "their" town. The Muslim leadership of the Islamic Center wanted me to counter that bias. I did so not only by participating in interfaith programs but also by being present at all those meetings that dealt with a Rochester community issue. Encouraged by Rabbi Miller's example, I appeared on TV and on radio networks, wrote articles explaining Islam in Rochester's daily newspaper, *The Democrat and Chronicle*, and raised my voice in favor of tolerance and dialogue wherever and whenever I could. The Rochester Muslim community was small in number, but its voice was being heard with increasing respect.

September 11, 2001

September 11, 2001, catastrophic for all Americans, was catastrophic in a special way for American Muslims. No American Muslim could believe at first that the disaster involved Muslims, or that any Muslim group was even capable of perpetrating it. I was on my way to St. John Fisher College for my morning class when I heard on the car radio the first news of the attack. At that point little was clear about the perpetrators. I stayed in the car listening to the radio once I'd reached the college in order not to miss new information. Soon I began to hear reports of Muslim involvement. I immediately restarted the car and rushed back to the Islamic Center, where I found myself greeted by the police. Nothing serious had happened, they reassured me; they said they had come just to ensure the center's safety. Entering the building, I called the Muslim leadership and the imams of the other Rochester mosques, urging them to attend an emergency meeting at noon in the Center. I also called the interfaith leadership. Almost everyone I'd called arrived at the center on time if not early. While the local media waited at the main entrance, we passed two resolutions: one from the interfaith community and another from the imams of the local mosques. We then emerged to read them to the media and to hold a press briefing. Both resolutions unanimously condemned the attacks. We declared our solidarity with the American people and asked for patience and prayers at this difficult moment.

The next day, Rochester's PBS affiliate, WXXI, arranged a town-hall meeting at Nazareth College, with WXXI's talk-show host Bob Smith as moderator. Roman Catholic bishop Matthew Clark, Rabbi Larry Kotok, and I were on the stage. The three of us condemned the attacks and made brief remarks. I said in my remarks that while 9/11 was a tragedy for all Americans, it was a triple tragedy for Muslim Americans—first, as Americans themselves, Muslim Americans shared the same pain from the attack as everyone else; second, we as Muslim Americans would be suspected of disloyalty; and third, this suspicion would make life with our non-Muslim neighbors difficult for the foreseeable future. Most of the audience questions were directed at me, and some were harsh and hard. Yet thanks to our previous efforts to build interfaith understanding, the bishop and the rabbi were there to come to my defense.

My words alone weren't enough to quell the growing suspicion, of course. Extraordinary steps had to be taken. The Islamic Center was opened to the public so that non-Muslims could have a close look at us. The Commission on Christian-Muslim Relations offered seminars on understanding Islam. The interfaith community arranged for suppers at the Islamic Center to give opportunities to people to eat together and to see the way Muslims worship. Registration for these suppers was amazing; we kept the waiting list for a long time so that we could continue to keep inviting people to these and similar events.

Because of a widely based community effort, including from the Rochester police, no serious incident against the center or against Muslims occurred in the area. In gratitude, the leadership of Upstate New York Imams, meeting at the center some time after September 11, unanimously acknowledged that those mosques that engaged in interfaith dialogue were richly repaid by the interfaith community through its solidarity with the mosques after the September 11 tragedy.

The Effects of September 11

September 11 was a tragedy undoubtedly, but it was a blessing too. No tragedy is without blessing in religion. It has had a great impact on American Muslims.

First, 9/11 forced many American Muslims, including me, to put our divided loyalties behind us and to accept America as our true country. Many of us still looked back to our countries of birth as our real homes. All first-generation immigrants, Muslim or not, react similarly. For example, I was taking a taxi one day to the airport with a Haitian from Harvard Divinity School. My companion was telling me stories about his home country. Finally he told me that he was moving back to Haiti and taking his family with him.

I said, "But why? Haiti is very poor and you have a good life here."

"Yes," he replied, "but a good life does not mean dollars alone, it means where you feel at home." He said that he would live in Haiti among his relatives, and his children would grow in the culture. I knew exactly what my Haitian companion was talking about. I was typical in dreaming always of moving back to Pakistan someday, even if only to spend my old age there, or at least to be buried there. Typical too was my plan to send our children back "home" to learn the language and the culture. Many other Muslim Americans had kept a house in their birth country so that they would have a place for their return. Ironically, if predictably, our children never agreed with our plans to go "home." Their concerns were with finding a place among their American peer group. My youngest two children had grown up here. America was their country. But for us of the first generation, was America our country or not? September 11 challenged my cohort to declare our identity: are you an American, or are you not? My response, like that of many others, was, yes, I am. Along with that affirmation went a commitment to put our hearts and minds into America and to make the most of our new destiny.

A second impact was a parallel transformation in the attitudes of our religious communities. Our mosques and community organizations became more identified with American interests and values. We refused to allow or condone any activity that could be seen as anti-American. Before September 11, many of us would not care if someone in our mosques and community organizations spoke against America, but after September 11 we would not allow such activities. The Islamic Center of Rochester frowned on such activities even before September 11. For example, sometime in the late 1990s the imam who was leading the morning *Salat* suddenly raised his hands and prayed in Arabic for the destruction of the enemies of Islam. After the worship had ended, I raised an objection to what the imam had done, first explaining to the non-Arabic speakers among us what the imam had said. I took a lot of effort during the following two mornings to persuade the congregation that such prayers were not from Islam but had been adopted during the downfall of Muslims in the Abbasid period. After September 11, the Islamic Center's policy towards such language and behavior as the imam's became more restrictive.

A third impact was the integration of Muslim communities into mainstream American political discourse. Before September 11, many Muslims did not take an interest in American political, social, and economic discourse. As noted earlier, some avoided taking US citizenship.

Many others were sitting on the edge, thinking about leaving. After 9/11 many Muslims went to the polling both and became members of the Democratic and Republican Parties. Many voted for the first time in the 2008 presidential election. Similarly, many Muslim Americans started to invest in America instead of sending money back home, and took an interest in issues confronting the American economy and social life.

Fourth, the American Muslim community before 9/11 was divided mostly on ethnic grounds. People differentiated themselves based on categories they had brought with them from their places of origin. Their differences were not primarily ideological. For example, while ethnic divisions among the three major Muslim American religious organizations—the Islamic Society of North America (ISNA), the Islamic Circle of North America (ICNA), and the Muslim American Society (MAS)—existed before September 11, those divisions were not labeled conservative, liberal, or orthodox. The same was true of mosques and Islamic centers. Today, along with ethnic divisions, mosques are distinguished by their ideological labels (liberal, conservative, moderate, and the like). Some mosques use the Arabic word *Salafi* (which means, following the Sunnah of the Prophet more faithfully than others) to distinguish themselves from other mosques. Imams are also ideologically labeled. Once, when I was part of an interfaith dialogue at the Rochester Institute of Technology, a rabbi told the audience that he himself was labeled a Reform rabbi. The rabbi then asked the Muslims present how they would label Imam Muhammad Shafiq. I was amazed to hear them using the words *modern* and *liberal*. A few added *moderate* but none said *conservative*. Other causes of ideological labeling derive from the role of woman in mosques and from the degree of the community's participation in interfaith dialogue. Recently I heard a Muslim who had left the Islamic Center of Rochester for another mosque saying that he had left the Center for two reasons—one, because the Center participated in interfaith dialogue; and second, because women were very "free" and mixed with men after worship.

A fifth impact of September 11 was a resurgence of Muslim emphasis on socioeconomic justice. Such emphasis is actually at the heart of what Islam teaches. The Quran calls upon Muslims to take care of the poor, the weak, the old, and the less fortunate. The Quran actually institutes charity in the form of *Zakat* (taking care of the poor), the third pillar of Islam, as an obligatory act upon all Muslims who hope to have God's blessing. The Quran also encourages *Sadaqah* (charity), and promises great reward for those who spend the path of God in the service of humanity. Prior to September 11, however, Muslim charities interpreted this obligation to mean supporting welfare activities in foreign lands. Little attention was given to the poor and needy in America. African American Muslims often claimed, with justice, that Muslim charities paid only lip service to the needs of the American poor. The charities' indifference caused disenchantment between the immigrant and indigenous communities. Now, after September 11, since many of the old Muslim charities like Kind Hearts and the Holy Land Foundation were banned from operating overseas by the United States Office of Homeland Security,[10] new Muslim charities like the Relief Foundation of the Islamic Circle of North America are concentrating more on America's needs. They are opening halfway houses, shelter homes, soup kitchens, and free clinics.

A sixth and final impact of 9/11 on Muslims is greater commitment on the part of the entire Muslim American community to interfaith dialogue. The need for dialogue antedates September 11, of course. Islam has been and still is to a certain extent the most misunderstood religion in America. The Western media, both print as well as electronic and film, have all contributed over the years to this misunderstanding of Islam and Muslims. Islam is still looked upon as the religion of the sword, while Judaism and Christianity are considered religions of peace. Hollywood movies continue to picture Arabs as backward-looking barbarians, or else as monsters of deceit and violence.

September 11 intensified these misunderstandings by instilling fear both in non-Muslims and in Muslims themselves. Soon after September 11 some Muslims changed their names, especially those working in public positions. They feared discrimination or revenge or ostracism. The fear cut both ways. Muslim doctors told me that some of their co-workers would avoid them. Some Muslim doctors lost their patients once the patients realized their doctor was a Muslim.

The only answer to such a situation was and is interfaith dialogue, as the essential first step towards better understanding. This is a step that many American Muslims were unwilling to take prior to September 11, however. They felt comfortable within their ethnic enclaves. Many of the mosques that did participate in dialogue prior to September 11 made no public announcement of the fact for fear of repercussions from other Muslims. Those fears evaporated after September 11, allowing mosques to engage in interfaith dialogue openly and wholeheartedly.

---

10. The charity was shut down because of allegations by the United States Homeland Security Office that they funded Islamicist terror groups.

Rochester's Uniqueness

Rochester, New York, is unique in interfaith dialogue. This is the city where the Rochester Roman Catholic diocese and the Rochester Jewish community signed a historic accord in 1995. Eight years later, in 2003, the dioceses signed another historic accord with Rochester's *Masajid* (mosques). The Muslim–Catholic Alliance was formed as the implementing committee of that accord. Here also in Rochester the Commission on Christian–Muslim Relations was formed in 1993, and the Commission on Jewish-Muslim Understanding ten years later in 2003. Above all, there is the Rochester Interfaith Forum in which more than thirty-five different faiths dialogue together. Rochester's interfaith dialogue became so well established that interfaith leaders decided to take the next step by establishing an academic center to promote interfaith dialogue through teaching and training. Preliminary discussions about starting such a center began prior to September 11; September 11 gave the discussions urgency. The Center for Interfaith Studies and Dialogue (CISD) was formally inaugurated at Nazareth College of Rochester, New York, in 2003. Since its inception, CISD has promoted interfaith training programs, workshops, and certificate programs and seminars for nurses, schoolteachers, clergy, and hospice care providers. It has also offered credit courses for college students and professionals.

Believing as strongly as I do in interfaith dialogue, I have been pained to see certain Muslims still objecting to it. In order to persuade such Muslims to see the advantages of interfaith dialogue, I coauthored with Mohammed Abu Nimer, *Interfaith Dialogue: A Guide for Muslims*, published by IIIT Publications in 2007. The book is designed to serve as a guide to support Muslims interested in or already involved in building relations with people of other faiths, and particularly with people of the Abrahamic traditions. Some Muslims raise concerns about interfaith dialogue, pointing, for example, to the danger of mixing their Islamic teaching with the teachings of other religions. They fear interfaith dialogue is an attempt to create one religion by amalgamating the key principles of all faiths. They think that interfaith dialogue is meant to create a civil religion with common worship, rituals, and prayers. They believe any such concoction would be against God's design. The book deals with this and other concerns of Muslims. It explains that interfaith dialogue stands for a common understanding between people of different faiths. The greatness and uniqueness of each faith community is manifested when people practice their faiths freely and purely without any compromise and are respectful of each other's faiths at the same time. The book ends by presenting some models of dialogue between the Abrahamic faiths.

Concluding Remarks

September 11 changed many lives. It changed America as well. According to many overseas opinion polls, America reacted to September 11 by turning away from its commitment to human rights and by becoming harsh and taking extreme measures in its treatment of other societies. Americans themselves have become more polarized in their religious and political beliefs. I have already described some of the ways in which American Muslims have changed. They now see themselves as Americans, but in doing so they have experienced many of the ideological differences that characterize other American religious groups.

I sometimes wonder, what would have happened if I had gone to Saudi Arabia for higher education in Islamic studies rather than to the United States? I would, I believe, have excelled in the field, but I would have had a different outlook on issues of religion and social life. I have no regrets. In fact I am glad that I chose to come to America to learn the processes of a free, civil society at the same time that I was expanding my knowledge not only of Islamic studies but also of world religions. Religion without an understanding of civil society cannot grow, but instead becomes divisive and self-destructive. America does not deprive people of their religion. It does demand that people practice their faith within the norms of civil society.

September 11 inspired American Muslims to do as early Muslim immigrants to other lands had done: to make their new land their home. Those early immigrants became partners with other members of the civil society they had entered, and contributed to that society generously. When Muslims landed in Indonesia and Malaysia, for example, they soon accommodated themselves to those societies' civic norms. Impressed by the Muslim immigrants' piety and civic contributions, Malaysians and Indonesians became Muslims themselves. The same occurred in India; those who became Muslims did so voluntarily, having been impressed by Islam's Sufi circles. The engagement of Muslim Americans in America's civic life would win them respect and also could pave the way for the spread of Islam on this continent.

I end with a true story that, though humble in its details, can stand, perhaps, as a symbol of the value of dialogue.

Trialogue and Terror

Once in the 1980s, when my family and I were out driving in the Pennsylvania countryside, one of my daughters told us she needed to use a bathroom. We looked for rest areas but could not find any. Finally we saw a family out in their yard. I stopped, got out of the car, and approached them, ready to ask them politely if my daughter could use their bathroom. But as soon as I used my name, Muhammad Shafiq, in introduction, the mother and father took a step back, their eyes wide, repeating the name "Muhammad" in frightened voices. I smiled gently, explaining in a quiet voice that I was a student at Temple University and that we were making a daytrip just to see the beautiful countryside. I introduced my wife and daughter, and explained what my daughter needed. I could see how the couple's fear began to evaporate under the influence of genuine human contact. They were soon at peace, and my daughter was graciously allowed to use their bathroom.

At its best, all true interfaith dialogue follows such a course. Differences remain, but they become a stimulus for mutual understanding and for the fulfillment of each other's needs. Would that all societies could learn this simple lesson!

fifteen

Lifting the Veil

AKBAR S. AHMED

Who cannot marvel at the capacity of the human spirit to expand and change? When I first met Aijaz, he seemed fully set in his opinions, one whose world consisted of simple, clear-cut categories that differentiated friends from foes and good religion from bad religion. Author of *Jihad and Terrorism*, he seemed obsessed with "American barbarism" and "Israeli barbarism." There were no shades of gray in his worldview. Although intensely religious in a formal and orthodox manner, he had yet to develop a spiritual expansiveness that would coincide with the Quranic vision of a common humanity. Now, before me, was his e-mail, which had arrived only a few days after the team returned from the fieldtrip in mid-April, expressing the glimmering of a new vision or, as he put it, "guidelines."

After our visit to Deoband, Aijaz accompanied us for the next week as we met with various Muslims in Delhi in gatherings large and small. He had arranged some of the meetings himself, such as a visit to the headquarters of the Jamat-i-Islami, the orthodox Islamic party of South Asia. Throughout the week, he listened carefully to my speeches about my American friends—both Christians and Jews—which stressed that Americans are not all alike.

At every forum, he would hear me emphasize the need for dialogue and understanding as a Quranic duty, especially in view of the globalizing forces impinging on the *ummah* today. At times, Aijaz showed growing territorial pride when introducing me at my lectures. Initially at Deoband a week before, he had introduced me as a somewhat remote and distant "great scholar." Now, with some defiance in his voice and more than a hint of South Asian hyperbole, he was calling me the best model for the Islamic faith—indeed, for all faiths.

I believe we were the first Americans Aijaz had met and certainly spent so much time with. He had long conversations with Hailey, Frankie, and, later, Hadia about serious issues that had been agitating him regarding world affairs. Although he was initially reserved about speaking directly with Hailey and Hadia, he later opened up to them after spending a few days in the field with us, at last able to put a human face to what he had earlier called "American barbarians." These Americans were actually listening to his opinions and willing to discuss them seriously, in contrast to the stereotypical media commentators who labeled people like him "Islamic extremists' without any engagement or acknowledgment of their common humanity.

Toward the end of our visit in India, Aijaz said that he would like to translate my book *Islam under Siege* into Urdu. The book explores the idea of common humanity, especially after 9/11, explaining that today all societies feel under siege and off balance. It is vital for them to learn to trust each other, which can only be accomplished through dialogue and understanding. Later, as he began the translation, he seemed grateful beyond words that at last someone was actually trying to "explain the Islamic Concept in [the] contemporary world. May Allah Bless you, I pray to Allah Almighty for your good health and good serving of Islam."[1]

How clear it seemed that the principle of dialogue and understanding could indeed have an effect. Through the translation of *Islam under Siege* over Deoband's vast network of madrassahs and mosques, Aijaz would spread these ideas to thousands of young readers, and hopefully my message of dialogue with other world civilizations would take root. Instead of interpreting jihad as violence, young men might now think of it as a peaceful movement aimed at creating better understanding; maybe now they would think of the place of Islam in the twenty-first century in a more balanced and compassionate manner, prepared to reach out to other civilizations, or at least attempt to understand them.

If Aijaz could change his hard-line position, so could others taking similar stances, including Americans and even Israelis. Like Aijaz, other individuals might finally abandon their "us"-versus-"them" dialectic for

---

1. The quotation is attributed to Aijaz Arshad Qasmi in conversation with Akbar Ahmed, in Ahmed, *Journey into Islam: The Crisis of Globalization* (Washington, DC: Brookings Institution Press, 2007) 246–47.

one that encompasses all of humanity. For me, Aijaz's conversion was as momentous as an oil tanker reversing course in mid-ocean.

Aijaz's new awareness promised hope in an otherwise bleak landscape. He had done what the Buddha had recommended—challenged the poisons in himself. With his anger at and ignorance of Americans now in check, he had begun a journey of immense importance not only to the ummah but also to the world at large, though he was probably little aware of it.

"In Me, Where It Mattered"

Aijaz's spiritual progress did not entirely surprise me; life consists of a journey for all human beings, and they have the capacity to change as they progress through it. Religions and sages provide them with guidance or markers to signal its different phases. The trajectory of my own life has been marked by such change, without my being aware of it.

As a young man, I admired Aurangzeb because he seemed to embody the ideal Islamic ruler. He appealed to my youthful loyalty and passion for my religion, and I saw him as a champion of the faith. He would not compromise on matters that exposed Muslims to threat. Having grown up in an environment of large-scale religious riots, the memories of which have haunted me throughout my life, I felt that no Muslim could fail to be moved by Aurangzeb, the champion of Islam and the personification of the Deoband model.

Later in life, I discovered another Muslim hero in Jinnah. All the issues that my colleagues and I debated as undergraduates had been tackled by Jinnah when he led the Pakistan movement. Unlike Aurangzeb, Jinnah was prepared to interact with and even absorb foreign ideas about democracy and voting rights for women and minorities. Yet Jinnah would not compromise on the rights and security of his community either. I was thrilled to see him on the same level as Mahatma Gandhi and Jawaharlal Nehru, the Indian icons. As a Muslim, I took great pride in Jinnah's successful wresting of a Muslim Pakistan from the powerful grip of the British and the Indian National Congress. That he achieved this success within constitutional limits further enhanced his stature in my eyes.

As I grew older, I became more and more interested in the mystic and universalist Islam to which my father, who worked first in the government and later in the United Nations, had introduced me when I was a student at Lahore. He would ask me to accompany him to the shrine of

Dahta Sahib, the famous saint of Lahore—Lahore is also known as the Nagri or city of Dahta Sahib—which I would agree to do more to humor him than out of personal desire. He never insisted that I go with him or lectured me about his ideas of Islam. It was only toward the end of his life that he pressed me to spread the universalist message of *sulh-i-kul*, or "peace with all," as embodied by Dahta Sahib.[2] But something in those visits had touched a spiritual part of me I did not even know I possessed. Later, after completing my studies at Cambridge University, I returned to Lahore to attend the elite Civil Service Academy, the embodiment of the Aligarh model. I was still convinced of the merits of the Aligarh way of thinking and admired Jinnah and Aurangzeb as heroes of Islam, although I had begun to have doubts about the latter.

The young entrants to the Civil Service Academy in Lahore saw themselves as the personification of a modernist Islam—a true product of Aligarh—and were inclined to snigger at the ways of Ajmer and Deoband. To them, the mystics were too otherworldly, unrealistic, and confused, while the orthodox seemed fanatical, backward, and irrelevant. The former were sneeringly dismissed as "Sufis" and the latter as "damned mullahs." After all, the Aligarh model had successfully led the nation to independence from the British and would safeguard that independence into the future. Thus, my peers at the academy, who suspected I went to Dahta's shrine, were unsure of my motives. There was a conjecture and debate about why I really disappeared from time to time. They saw Ajmer and Aligarh as mutually exclusive. It was one or the other.

Looking back from the vantage point of four decades, I am mortified and amused in equal measure at that brash, cocky young man bursting with energy, ideas, and self-worth. One part of me said, "I have made it to the top. I am the best, the smartest, the greatest." The rest of me rejected that part, and the whole was easily able to contain it. My trips to the Dahta helped to check the intoxication of the academy. When I entered the shrine and began taking off my shoes and covering my head, the arrogance and self-importance induced by the academy evaporated.

When I accompanied my father to the shrine of the saint in Ajmer, who has a spiritual relationship with the saint in Lahore, I discovered the enduring beauty of the mystic message. Even in the midst of a swirling mass of humanity, a feeling of calmness would descend on me, erasing any traces of anger, arrogance, and ambition, and fill my soul with a sense

---

2. Akbar S. Ahmed, *Discovering Islam: Making Sense of Muslim History and Society*, rev. ed. (London: Routledge, 2002).

of divine spirit, making me feel that I was at one with everyone around me and that they too were experiencing the same connection to the divine through their acceptance of the other pilgrims, whether rich or poor, Muslim or non-Muslim. Although we all had arrived as strangers, we had become brothers and sisters in goodwill, recognizing our common humanity in this place of worship. There was no past or future, only the peaceful present. I could see clearly, as if a curtain had been removed from my eyes, how truly close humans are to each other and how ugly the barriers they have erected that prevent them from seeing the beauty in the world's diverse souls.

We can only see into each other's souls if we take the trouble—and sometimes the risk—to visit each other. Unfortunately, few Americans in the Muslim world venture out from behind the high security walls of their compounds to meet the ordinary merchant or cab driver on the street. Imagine the impact if a diplomat from the US embassy in Damascus visited the house of a well-known sheikh for a casual conversation. Imagine the cultural and psychological barriers that would be crossed.

Our team did just that. We traveled to Damascus, where we visited Sheikh Hussam Al-Din Farfour, the head of Fatah Institute, a well-known Islamic university. Looking stern in a white turban and well-trimmed white beard, with the black robe covering his large frame, the sheikh was waiting for us in his dimly lit office with over a dozen of his senior department and faculty heads, all seated on outdated furniture. They were talking nostalgically of their visit to universities in the United States and the United Kingdom. During the meeting, the sheikh's students came in with trays of juices for us to sip.

Although I began with some questions about Islam, the conversation eventually lapsed into another tedious and somewhat meandering description of the troubles with the United States. We had been treated to essentially the same lecture for the last few days, and I braced myself for a long and sterile afternoon. As the discussion wore on, my impression of the sheikh was that of a bureaucrat who had adapted Islam to the socialist rhetoric and system in which he operated. The official portrait of President Bashar al-Assad in the office and the sheikh's glowing acknowledgment of the president's services to the cause of the nation and Islam only confirmed this feeling. As we prepared to leave, the sheikh invited us for dinner at his home. I promised to let him know if I could come, leaving myself time to think of a good excuse because I was not sure I could take another session of this kind.

Trialogue and Terror

Despite my concern that we would be in for another wearying session, we turned up at the sheikh's home the next night. In characteristic Arab style, it was situated in a crowded alley with an obscure-looking entrance that led into a nondescript courtyard followed by a hallway and another courtyard, this one structured and elegant, which opened into a spacious and comfortable home with distinct quarters for men and women to preserve modesty, according to local tradition. We were ushered into the owner's grand study, filled with leather-bound books on Islam of the kind one would find in the home of any affluent and educated senior official in the Muslim world. Present were some of the same professors we had met at the university as well as some new faces, which included leading religious figures and disciples of the sheikh.

As the guests responded to us with obvious warmth and hospitality, the evening took on a new feeling. After a conversation that thankfully went beyond politics to the scholars of the past, the sheikh invited his guests into his dining room. The dinner, laid out on a wide table, consisted of a variety of delicious Arab dishes that must have taken days to prepare. We sat down with our plates, and the introduction of food made the guests more relaxed. In order to make Hailey feel more comfortable, the sheikh had invited his daughter-in-law, who was from Spain, to sit with her, as normally men and women are segregated. Hailey spoke Spanish, so the two began to chat about the daughter-in-law's conversion to Islam after her marriage.

The gathering began to reveal a complex interplay between the models identified in this book. What had seemed to be the Aligarh model, which calls for a synthesis with non-Muslim systems, in this case socialism, speared to dissolve into the Ajmer model, with its traditional mystic expressions of pace, compassion, and universal humanism. The change in rhetoric matched the body language of Sheikh Farfour, who had transformed from a formal, prickly, even slightly hostile-looking bureaucrat to a gentle, smiling, and welcoming Sufi master.

A Muslim may reflect Ajmer, Deoband, and Aligarh in different ways at different or even simultaneous moments in life. Progress from one model to another depends on personal growth, circumstances, and opportunities. In my case, the movement was part of the trajectory of my life; in Aijaz's case, it was a distinct shift in direction. Extrinsic factors and general societal attitudes influence the flow and popularity of these models within individuals. That makes it all the more important to understand what influences Muslims around the world and to reach out to the model of acceptance and love.

Using the Knowledge of the Sages in the Age of Globalization

As I moved through life traveling the world and developing spirituality, I gained some insight into the best path forward for those interested in peace. Along the way, I met more and more people who were not of my faith and culture but whom I grew to respect and admire. These relationships brought me to yet another new perspective: I found that my heroes, Aurangzeb and Jinnah, embodied forms of Islam that still acted as barriers to understanding. Aurangzeb was too much of an Islamic exclusivist; and Jinnah, while accepting the influence of Westminster on his politics, failed to appreciate the spiritual dimension and character of other cultures.

In my effort to encourage peace and dialogue between cultures, I thought the Ajmer model was so amorphous and its interpretation so personal that it was too idiosyncratic to stand up to the pressures of this age of rampant consumerism. I assumed that the only way forward lay in promoting the Aligarh model. At least it had the merit of being practical, and its frame of reference could be understood by both Muslims and the West. I believed that ultimately the Aligarh model, like that of Jinnah, could help to create a sense of modern nationalism. While Aligarh may promote the language of international commerce and politics, nationalism by definition creates boundaries that exclude neighbors and thereby prevents true understanding and lasting peace between cultures. Faced with globalization, the Aligarh model clearly has the potential to produce wisdom and justice, but it falls short of producing compassion, which is the only sure way to bring civilizations together in friendship. The young students of Aligarh our team met may well have spoken English and read Thomas Friedman, but few had gone deeper into the civilization they are at odds with to read the prose of Aquinas, the poetry of St. Francis, or even the plays of Shakespeare. They were unable to connect spiritually or culturally. As applied nowadays, the Aligarh model has been reduced to kowtowing to mainly superficial commercial transactions and consumer products of ephemeral value. In other words, the Aligarh model fails to make the all too necessary spiritual connection between cultures.

If the Aligarh model has its shortcomings, so does the Deoband, which is too easily inflamed into anger and emotion. It cannot function effectively in the age of globalization either, unless it begins to change. Muslims cannot remain an island of isolated believers in a sea of different cultures and faiths. As members of a world civilization, people are now too close to and dependent on each other to afford the luxury of ignoring and excluding others. Deoband must approach different beliefs with acceptance and compassion if it is to move forward. One of its most faithful sons, Aijaz, showed that this was possible.

Just as Aligarh creates political boundaries, Deoband creates religious ones. All those—Muslims or non-Muslims—who create boundaries around themselves on the basis of either nationalism or religion invariably exclude those on the other side. This exclusion easily degenerates into indifference to the pain of others and too often into violence against them. It is only Ajmer followers—whether Muslims or non-Muslims—who believe in a common humanity and thus are able to live comfortably with others and to adapt to them and learn from them. This is the great lesson that world history and the current impasse teaches. How else is civilization to live in peace and harmony in the future?

That brings one to the idea and practice of acceptance provided by the universalist Ajmer model. This is not to say that the looming problems of the planet will be readily solved by the dreamy and mystic side of the Ajmer model, which is sometimes dangerously tempted to withdraw from society altogether. Clearly, the accepting nature of the Ajmer model must be buttressed by the commitment and fervor that Deoband can provide, along with the skill and dexterity to negotiate with governments, organizations, and political parties, which is characteristic of Aligarh.

The strength of the Ajmer worldview is that it has the same spirit of acceptance inherent in other traditions. The Judaic texts, the Bible, the Quran, the Gita, and the Granth Sahib, the sayings of Confucius and Buddha—all have taught something more than how to intone prayer and observe external ritual. They have taught how to penetrate deep into their message and look for the one underlying and common theme in each: the importance of justice, compassion, and knowledge as the sure antidotes to the poisons that plague and pervert human society. It is but a matter of looking for and understanding the true spirit of faith.

The dire problems of poverty, population explosion, global warming, and religious and ethnic killings around the globe seem inexplicable at this point in history, when world civilization has inherited such a rich legacy of spiritual thought. One may well ask whether the three abstract philosophic precepts outlined in this book are able to help. The answer, I believe, is, not only can they help in a direct and personal way to uplift souls, but they can also elevate both national and international debate on precisely these global problems. But hard work will be required, in both the long term and the short term.

The solutions must take into consideration the interconnectedness of the world, the fact that everything happening in the United States is making an almost immediate impact in the Muslim world, and vice versa. Unless societies receive and are seen to receive justice, anger will continue spreading its poison throughout the world. The events of September 11 symbolized the anger of the Muslims, which provoked the anger of the Americans. So great was the outrage at the scale of the tragedy and loss of human life that it was unlikely and unreasonable to expect compassion and understanding from Americans at that time. It would have defied human nature itself. If cool thinking had prevailed, however, the first task at hand would have been to capture the perpetrators and then to consolidate the worldwide sympathy that had spontaneously expressed itself for America—even in anti-American countries like Iran—into a movement for a better common future for the planet. But this was not to be.

George W. Bush was to launch one of the most asymmetrical wars in history, using the most advanced technology known to humanity against two small, deeply divided, and impoverished Muslim nations, Afghanistan and Iraq. Torn by ethnic and political strife, their people—millions on the verge of starvation—looked to the United States for assistance and friendship. They were stunned when it launched an onslaught on them, which has resulted in many thousands of deaths. In addition, too many people have been tortured and sexually humiliated. The nightmare Bush had created for these Muslim societies very quickly involved large parts of the world, including his own society. Although Americans took time to realize it, they eventually saw that they were on a slippery slope that could lead to the suspension of civil liberties, universal surveillance, and mindless neurosis and hatred of others, with open discussions of interning Muslims in the United States. Torture was supported, with the vice president leading a campaign on its behalf, notably for waterboarding, but general criticism was muted.[3] The argument prevailed that terrorists must be defeated whatever the cost. The mood of anger that Bush had articulated fed directly and powerfully into the actions of the administration and the larger media, inciting fear and insecurity in people.

3. In a rare display of editorial candor, the *Washington Post* devoted its lead editorial of October 26, 2005, to Vice President Dick Cheney under the banner headline, "Vice President for Torture." The conclusion of the hard-hitting editorial was: "In other words, the vice president has become an open advocate of torture."

Trialogue and Terror

For several years after 9/11, opinion leaders in the United States, including television talk-show hosts, parading under the mantle of punditry, blindly echoed the administration's fear that another strike on US soil was imminent. Americans grew increasingly fearful that they were in immediate danger, and angry because their lives had changed so much. It was left to the comedians to introduce some perspective and point out notably after the invasion of Iraq what was incorrect, unjust, and absurd in the developments taking place around them. Their voices grew in volume after the disastrous news from Iraq became unstoppable, and soon people were tuning in to Jon Stewart and Stephen Colbert on Comedy Central for the news. I was personally grateful to know that Americans still retained their famed ironic humor, sharp intelligence, and feeling for the underdog.

None of us can predict how we would react to personal tragedy—the unexpected death of a spouse or a child or even a relative. When such a tragedy involves an entire community, it tends to be magnified, and if it is caused by traditional antagonists, then the overriding reaction is as much anger as it is hatred. Human beings are capable, however, of responding to the worst kind of attack with compassion and nobility of spirit. For writers such expressions of human graciousness are "saintly acts," and for poets they are "divine sparks." The events that took place on September 11 produced many such examples of these sparks. Our Voices Together, headed by the indefatigable Marianne Scott, was organized by those who lost relatives on that day.[4] One of the group's projects was to build educational centers in Afghanistan. Aware that al-Qaeda and bin Laden had lived among the people of Afghanistan, Our Voices Together wished to convert strangers into friends. Judea Pearl too made a similar gesture when he reached out in dialogue and then friendship to me with my Pakistani background. While his beloved son had been murdered in Pakistan, he overcame a natural revulsion for those who had committed this crime to reach out to those from the very nation that had produced the killers. The dialogues he and I have conducted from 2003 onward have helped to promote Jewish-Muslim understanding and to create bridges between communities.

Politicians too have shown that they can rise above common human emotions and attain an almost superhuman moral plane by insisting on compassion and justice in the face of massive death and destruction. Gandhi, Nehru, and Jinnah are three such statesmen. In the summer of 1947, Hindus, Muslims, and Sikhs slaughtered each other in South Asia; up to

---

4. See online: www.ourvoicestogether.org/.

two million people may have been killed and up to 15 million displaced from their homes to find a new one in a new land.[5] Yet each one of these three leaders stood firm against communal violence even if it meant challenging their own community. On several occasions, Gandhi began a fast unto death until Hindus stopped rioting against Muslims in India; Nehru declared that his nation had gone mad, and ordered his entire administration to check the violence as its top priority; and Jinnah, on the other side of the border in Pakistan, seeing an angry Muslim mob surrounding a group of Hindus in Karachi, threw himself into the crowd to stop the violence and declared, "I am going to constitute myself the Protector-General of the Hindu minority in Pakistan."[6] As a consequence, these leaders were threatened by their own communities. Gandhi eventually lost his life to an assassin who had complained of Gandhi's support for Muslims.

Jews, Christians, Muslims, Hindus, young and old, men and women, Americans, Pakistanis and Indians—countless examples from among them illustrate the capacity of human beings to attain moral heights in the most difficult circumstances. Thus, ordinary individuals become extraordinary ones, and those already recognized as extraordinary pass into the realm of folklore and legend.

The United States, especially, because it is relatively young and powerful, must construct a new philosophy toward other civilizations. Because it is dealing with Muslim nations of diverse social and political character, it needs to quickly appreciate the nuances of these societies Muslims widely complain of the lack of justice, widespread corruption, and collapse of law and order. Too frequently the United States backs strong military intervention, unaware of how this support encourages turmoil or how negatively this support is seen within a country.

American policymakers and diplomats can work with Deoband model regimes to promote US standards of justice, equality, and human rights, but it can only happen through dialogue. Visits to mosques and madrassahs and serious attempts at dialogue by American scholars and diplomats can make an impact. Dialogue does not preclude US action against those guilty of violence, but a finer distinction must be made between those who are actually guilty and those who happen to be part of their community. There needs to be much more research and truth

---

5. Akbar S. Ahmed, *Jinnah, Pakistan and Islamic Identity: The Search for Saladin* (London: Routledge, 1997); Stanley Wolpert, *Shameful Flight: The Last Years of the British Empire in India* (Oxford: Oxford University Press, 2006).

6. Rajmohan Gandi, *Eight Lives: A Study of the Hindu-Muslim Encounter* (Albany: SUNY Press, 1986) 178.

seeking before issuing accusations of the doings of "terrorist regimes" or announcements of "terror plots" which are later proven hollow. Even in the case of individual "enemy combatants" it is essential to respect the due process of law, which must operate swiftly and visibly so that the world knows that American justice is above reproach.

In dealing with the Muslim world, the West's commentators and policy planners need to understand the influence of the three models on Muslim politics. As noted throughout this book, leadership of many Muslim societies has been captured by the Deoband model, gaining the upper hand because the modern Muslim state has been unable to provide security to its people; or so much security, it terrorizes them; or to provide ordinary services such as proper health care and education. In times of national crisis, some states have failed even to ensure the integrity of national borders. Equally important, some Muslim states have not instilled a sense of national pride and identity that energized Muslims when achieving independence from Western colonial powers half a century ago. When a people feel their government no longer relates to their aspirations, they are alienated from it, and sense it has become an illegitimate and artificial reflection of the West's will.

The Deoband leadership has stepped neatly into the vacuum created by the failure of the state. It has not only provided health and education facilities, for example, but in many cases has also become the only champion of the nation itself against foreign forces—as Hezbollah has done in repelling the Israeli onslaught in Lebanon in 2006, and the Iraqis and Afghan Taliban have done in slowing the American war machine. These accomplishments against the most powerful army in the Middle East and the most powerful army in the world have only added to the luster and credibility of the Deoband model. In contrast, Aligarh-inclined governments have appeared weak and uncertain, almost to the point of being irrelevant.

Americans have made the fatal mistake of fighting the war against terror by resurrecting a strategy used in the cold war against the Soviet Union. This approach, however, fails to consider the complexity of Muslim society. All Muslims, whichever model they may follow, are committed to their faith, and all will defend it, and by extension their own homeland, in different ways against what they see as attacks from the outside. By contrast, Soviet citizens, terrorized and disillusioned by the entire state system and structure, lost their belief in the ideology of the state, whose collapse not only seemed inevitable but brought relief. Those hoping for a similar outcome from military campaigns in the Muslim world after 9/11 failed to recognize that Muslim society, buoyed by Islam, would rise to meet the challenge of what seems a global campaign against it. That is to say, Islam is a holistic and integrated system, and its different parts come into play at different times in history to preserve the larger whole.

For the West, condemning those inclined toward Deoband as terrorist, and refusing to talk to them, has led to an unrealistic and inevitably failed policy. Because so many Muslims are influenced by Deoband, the West needs to vigorously encourage and support the genuine forms of Aligarh—unfettered democracy and not a form that comes under the guise of military dictators posing as benefactors. The West must also look for and strengthen the Ajmer model, as it provides an authentic and permanent platform for global understanding.

For their part, Muslims need to review the three models with a view to adapting them for the present times, living as we are in the age of globalization. Islam encourages every individual to struggle to attain a higher spiritual plane. That endeavor, as mentioned earlier, is called *jihad*, which literally means, "striving." Muslims therefore need to rediscover the struggle, to improve life in a spiritual sense, which is the "greatest jihad"; Muslims also must actively discourage the interpretation that equates "lesser jihad"—the defense of one's family and community—with violent acts (even with those committed in self-defense).[7] "Muslims needs to recognize that the most effective "weapons" for addressing their grievances are knowledge and reason, rather than brute force. They must revive the ideals of *ijtihad*, which allows for innovative thinking to accommodate new conditions and needs of modern societies, such as the rights of women, minorities, and the less privileged. The deep loyalties to tribalism must be pushed aside in order to cooperate in a more integrated world. Educational centers of excellence need to be opened and supported by governments to revive the ideals of Islam.

Equally important, there should be no excuse for setting Quranic ideals of justice, compassion, and wisdom aside. Muslim leaders must strive to live up to their own vision of the ideal society. Too many Arab rulers use the crutch of Israel directly or indirectly to avoid working toward a democracy until that "problem" is resolved. For Pakistan's politicians and army generals, the crutch is Kashmir and the "threat" from India, which they use to delay introducing genuine democracy, human rights, and civil liberties. Too often Muslim leaders evoke an "enemy" to

---

7. See Ahmed, *Journey into Islam*, 3.

justify the suspension of civil law and to impose draconian regulations and brutal police methods. Even leaders in the United States and the United Kingdom have begun relying on crutches such as threats of terrorism and threats to security. Unless all societies live up to their own high standards and do not look for excuses to abandon them, they will ultimately descend into a world of legitimized terror.

What if the Muslim world had responded in the Ajmer way—or even the Aligarh one—after the American invasion of Afghanistan and Iraq? The Muslim restraint would have impressed people in the West and created sympathy for Muslim causes. As it happened, the beheadings, the suicide bombings, and the hyperbolic rhetoric of violence—all veering away from the Ajmer and Aligarh models—confirmed already existing stereotypes of Muslims. Very soon, people in the West began to equate violence and terrorism with Islam itself. Worse yet, they began to see all Muslims as inherently bloodthirsty creatures, a view that fed into the growing Islamophobia around the world, escalating its pejorative overtones. Even President Bush took to using the word *Islamofascism*, perhaps not realizing its implications and how much offense it has caused many Muslims, including his own allies.

Though the age-old poisons of greed, anger, and ignorance continue to afflict humankind, a far greater legacy is the wisdom of the sages. Their advocacy for compassion can today be the most effective tool for squelching the greed that drives powerful multinational corporations and even governments that ruthlessly exploit the natural resources of poorer countries and disregard the genuine needs of millions. This epidemic coming in the wake of globalization has led to the gap between a few individuals who live isolated lives of extravagance and millions who struggle for their daily food—what social scientists have called "global pillaging."[8] As the Ajmer model urges, nations must learn to live on less as a philosophy of life. They must use less power, less water, and less food if any of them, let alone the planet, is to survive. Each one of us must accept the invitation and challenge issued by Sir Jonathan Sacks, one of the truly outstanding religious sages of our age, to heal our fractured world.[9]

So too we must apply the sages' urge for knowledge. Without this, each human being is reduced to a world consisting of his or her own cell. Each of us needs to be much more sensitive to what is sacred or highly

---

8. Anthony Giddens, *Runaway World: How Globalization Is Reshaping Our Lives* (New York: Routledge, 2000) 34.

9. Jonathan Sacks, *To Heal a Fractured World: The Ethics of Responsibility* (London: Continuum, 2005).

Lifting the Veil

symbolic of a culture in other civilizations. Just as Muslims are—and will always be—sensitive to abuse of their Prophet and holy book, so Americans are sensitive to any desecration of their flag, which they see as the very embodiment of their nationhood and identity. Ignorance of other cultures leads to serious policy mistakes, whether conducting warfare or peace negotiations. With knowledge of other peoples and cultures, societies are less likely to see those others as disconnected from themselves. Once they recognize how closely dependent on each other they actually are, they will stop responding to provocation with more provocation.

To this equation must be added justice, which will prevent anger from consistently begetting crude force. Together, compassion and justice will stamp out the causes of violence, and I would encourage all nations to include this philosophy in their policymaking. The ongoing violent confrontations of our times can be resolved if worked out within such a framework. One of the most tragic and bloody of these conflicts has been taking place in the Middle East for half a century with little hope of resolution because of the perception on both sides that compassion and justice are missing. The milestones that create further hatred and violence are as fresh as the morning news in the minds of the combatants: the Muslim anger early in 2007 at the excavation alongside the Noble Sanctuary in Jerusalem (which reflects the Muslim feeling discussed in the last chapter that there is a sinister plot to demolish the mosque); the Israeli invasion of Lebanon in the summer of 2006, when Israel retaliated with overwhelming force against Hezbollah for the kidnapping of Israeli soldiers; the deaths and destruction caused by Israeli bombardment in Gaza and the West Bank; and the stirring of the Arabs to find more recruits for their crude and murderous suicide missions, killing passengers on buses and clients at pizzerias. The list is long. It is time for the two sides to come together as equals, working within each other's cultural and religious frameworks, and—with full consideration and compassion for each other's grievances—forge a lasting peace. Without compassion and justice, the cycle of death will only accelerate and involve more and more people in its path.

However, friendship and love must be present on both sides before the cycle can be broken. The Quran repeatedly asserts that when an individual has reached a certain stage of spiritual enlightenment, a veil or curtain is lifted from the eyes, and the individual is able to see the world and its truths clearly, free from attachment to worldly pleasures, pains, or selfish needs. If the poisons of globalization are overcome, then truth and reality may emerge, and the benefits of globalization safely reaped without toxic effect.

If asked to distill what I learned during my journey into Islam into a few words, it would be this: Be true to your own ideals. For the United States, this would mean staying focused on the practice of democracy and the promotion of education and justice, and using "diplomatic strings" to achieve those ends. For instance, US foreign policy could dictate that its support for Pakistan would be guaranteed only if a freely elected government were established within a specific time frame. At the time of this writing, the United States has given Pakistan about $5 billion since 9/11 alone (and it is estimated about the same outside the budget for security and terror-related activities) and could have demanded that this support be spent on building schools, training teachers, and translating books for Pakistanis, and in turn, for making Pakistani literature available to Americans—not on defense purchases. Pakistanis would benefit from the wisdom and elegance of the prose of Franklin and Jefferson, and Americans would appreciate the democratic character of Jinnah and the poetic vision of Iqbal. This simple change in policy and direction would ensure what the present course has failed to accomplish: it would create a genuine appreciation of American involvement in Pakistan among ordinary people and thereby lessen the security threat to Americans.

My recommendation to the Muslim leaders would be the same. Stay as close to your ideals as possible. Emphasize *ilm*, knowledge; *ihsan*, balance and compassion; and *adl*, or justice in your societies. At this time, your people groan under your rule because they see little of these attributes. Neither you nor the surrounding world can afford to keep the Muslim *ummah* from playing its full role on the world stage. That role will be positive and beneficial to everyone when it is defined by these great Islamic ideals. You need to keep in mind—just as Western leaders must—that according to current demographic estimates 25 percent of the world population of about 11 billion will be living in the fifty-seven Muslim-majority nations by 2050.[10]

It was in the spirit of dialogue and compassion that I traveled the world to discover the answers to the problems of our age. I spoke with presidents and prime ministers, and questioned scholars and students. I searched in synagogues, churches, mosques, and temples. I had set out to seek wisdom in the sayings and doings of the sages, and I glimpsed the

---

10. United Nations Population Division *World Population "Prospects": The 2004 Revision* (http://esa.un.org/unpp.index.asp ([January 22, 2007]).

glory of the divine in the hearts of the innocent and the pure. I saw love in the prayers of the pilgrims at the shrine, the kindness of a stranger, and the welcome of our hosts. I was not distracted by the strutting and bellowing of men who, like boys in a school play, convince no one but themselves. I have seen ignorant souls shout down those who spoke of peace and compassion. I heard voices loud and hoarse shouting, "Not now," and "Not here." But I also heard the sweet sounds of other voices through the noisy din, which said, "If not now, then when? . . . It is time; it is time." I heard the echo in the houses of worship, in the cities and villages, in the valleys and mountains: it *is* time.

Conclusion

While it is tempting to characterize the responses to 9/11 in this volume with labels such as "disappointment" [Jewish]; "hope" [Christian]; and "rage" [Muslim], the real situation is far more complex and nuanced then mere labeling implies. This complexity can be seen by summarizing the main points raised by the contributors. The Jewish thinkers, while emphasizing different dimensions of the trialogue, share several basic positions concerning the relationship between the three Abrahamic traditions. In the first place, they emphasize the importance of trialogue even while stressing the fact that bilateral discussion needs to continue and they underscore that the relationship between Judaism and Christianity is different than that between Judaism and Islam on the one hand, and Islam and Christianity on the other hand. Rabbi Riccardo DiSegni attests that in order to avoid illusions and to help achieve realistic results, three common denominators need stressing.

In the first place, there is the fact of "God's discovery of Abraham to whom each one of the three is connected." Next, the "history of the past" dramatizes the "possibility of self- and of other destruction based on religious principles and differences" and the "relatively rare but important positive developments that the exchange of experience produced." The third point concerns the urgency of the moment, and the craziness of these years. There now appears to be a "strong consciousness that something can be done by the religions in order to counteract violence." "Politically," he concludes, "it is important for the three traditions to meet in order to counter the diffidence and jealousy that may arise when the third party is excluded in a meeting between the other two."

The second point of agreement among the Jewish thinkers concerns both the post 9/11 rupture in Jewish-Muslim relations and the consequent need to find reliable dialogue partners. In Rabbi A. James Rudin's words: "owing to the "horrific anti-Zionist, anti-Israel, and ultimately anti-Jewish poison being spread by Muslim leaders in the world, a post-'Golden Age' dialogue based upon reasonable expectations with reliable and authentic partners is no longer a luxury, but a necessity." Rudin contends that the modern interreligious *Golden Age*, ushered in with the Vatican's promulgation of the theologically groundbreaking document *Nostra Aetate*, was ended by three major events: "the 9/11 terror attacks on America; Pope John Paul's II's death on April 23, 2005; and the July 1, 2004 vote by the General Assembly of the Presbyterian Church (USA) to support a selective divestment of holdings in multinational corporations doing business in Israel."

The third area of commonality among the Jewish contributors is the urgency of overcoming ignorance about the religious Other. Dr. Deborah Weissman speaks of the necessity "of developing a dialectical model for religious education." Her model strengthens particular identity and inculcates "a respect for the Other and the Other's faith . . . , an awareness that we are all human beings, of equal worth." Rabbi Gilbert S. Rosenthal reminds his readers that bloodshed between faith groups illustrates the point: "when people do not speak to one another, they do unspeakable things to one another." Authentic interreligious dialogue "*means consultation not confrontation, conversation not conversion.*"

Echoing Rabbi Rosenthal's call for engagement Professor David Patterson attests that unless a religion can include the Other in the world to come, then the Other will surely be excluded from this world as well. "Learning from their parent religion," he writes, "Christianity and Islam may—must—learn to include in their thinking about [the world to come] a place for the 'non-believer.'" Furthermore, he attests, authentic trialogue needs to include God as the fourth partner.

The fourth and final point on which the Jewish scholars agree is the necessity of never losing hope when involved in interreligious interchange. Rabbi Rudin speaks for all of his Jewish colleagues when in concluding his essay he cites the Hebrew prophet Zechariah who urged us to be "prisoners of hope" (9:12).

⸺

The Christian thinkers approach the question of trialogue and terror by focusing on three main points: a) The potential the terror attacks embody for being a bridge between the Abrahamic religions while acknowledging the distinctiveness of the Jewish-Christian dialogue; b) the immense impact of globalization on religion's quest for social justice; and c) the holiness of interfaith dialogue. Professor Theresa Sanders synthesizes the above by providing a post 9/11 reading of the Book of Job.

Professor Sanders begins with a query: "how (does) the private soul makes sense of the knowledge that someone wills to destroy it?" She responds to her own question by articulating four lessons from Job. The first lesson muddy's any effort to discern a correspondence "between righteousness and reward; the second lesson concerns the requirement "for humans to contest with God;" the third piece of instruction deals with the fact that because humans are "merely 'dust and ashes' is not an excuse for us to abdicate moral responsibility;" and finally " . . . the world is a frightening place . . . we are at the mercy of forces over which we have no control." However, "reconciling ourselves" to the dissonance between the ways of the world and what our sense of right and wrong is, "allows space for us to love" and this is the wonder.

The aftermath of 9/11 was profound and seemingly paradoxical. Doctor Eugene Fisher notes, "a deepening of Jewish-Christian dialogue and understanding, . . ." Christian and Jewish dialogue partners reached out to American Muslims differentiating between the religion as such and "the terrorism of the few." In addition, this outreach became a teachable moment for mutual respect and understanding. But lack of a peaceful response to modernity has resulted in an "imbalance between Jewish and Christian traditions, and the Islamic tradition." Consequently, the three "are not on the same page, or even in the same chapter, in their respective histories of development." However, American Muslims live in a pluralistic society which is based on "the separation of church/synagogue/mosque and state." This is the functional equivalent of "how faith traditions can and must recast themselves in the light of scientific and dialogic reasoning."

Dr. John Pawlikowski suggests that the emerging "dialogical model in Christian/Jewish dialogue, as a replacement for the traditional confrontational model," can impact positively on the "developing relationship between Christianity and Islam." There are of course major differences. Judaism was viewed as "having authentic revelation even though Christianity was seen to have absorbed that authentic revelation after Christ." The theological bonding between Christianity and Judaism is deep and profound. But Christianity "has never acknowledged authentic revelation within Islam." Finally, although Christianity will not accept "any notion of Islamic 'fulfillment' of Judaism and Christianity, it will need to become far more open to possible new authentic understandings of biblical revelation through the lens of Islam."

Professor Mary Boys views interreligious dialogue as "holy work" and calls for refinement in the task. She seeks "interreligious learning" which is "a form of interreligious dialogue emphasizing study in the presence of the religious Other and encounter with the tradition the Other embodies." This method has worked well in many Jewish-Christian settings. Its acid test will come in the context of Jewish-Muslim and Christian-Muslim dialogue. But it is imperative that dialogue which "doesn't preclude argument," should be thought of "as a *conversation*." Dialogue, like many creative efforts is "counter-cultural." The "increasing lack of civility and polarization in the public square suggests that sensibilities for dialogue need to be taught."

Professor Donald Dietrich notes that globalization "requires . . . [rethinking] . . . universal ethical principles." He offers the post-Vatican II Catholic model stressing the unity of humanity and encourage[ing] dialogue among religious traditions to assist in discerning the culturally pluralistic meaning of revelation." Moreover, as with the other contributors, Dietrich stresses the need for "a deep respect for those who hold differing beliefs." This is no easy task as is seen in the example of human rights. Judaism views these rights in terms of "national determination and . . . possession of Israel by the Jewish people. Western Christianity ". . . gives greater emphasis to the rights of individual persons, whereas many in Islam argue that these rights can only be achieved through submission to Allah in an Islamic state. Attaining the common good will not be a simple task in a complex world made more dangerous by terrorists committed to murdering those they think unfit to live

Muslim contributors have their own angle of vision on the contemporary Abrahamic trialogue. Four themes emerge from their essays. First of all, they attest, is the necessity of overcoming prejudice against Islam as a religion. In the second place, Islam needs to accommodate to globalization. The third theme consists of a critique of American policies and Western culture. The Final area of agreement is a commitment to dialogue.

The wish to resurrect common bonds between Jews and Arabs animates Professor Anouar Majid's essay. Looking behind and beyond 9/11, Majid seeks to renew what he views as the "natural alliance" between Jews and Muslims." Acknowledging the major impediments to this goal— "the furies of the Israeli-Palestinian conflict and the fog of 9/11"—Majid nonetheless contends that historically Muslims and Jews occupied a similar, negative, place in the European imagination which "saw both religions as "... dangerous heresies and mortal threats." He contends that "part of the Muslim violence" stems from a "persistent refusal to measure the Muslim's complicity in the systematic discrimination against those who don't share their faith."

The difficulties of post 9/11 dialogue are formidable, although there are certain hopeful signs. Professor Khaleel Mohammed addresses both polarities in his essay. "Othering," he writes, "is almost always negative." He observes that "almost every book of [Islamic] exegesis from the tenth century onwards seeks to explain away earlier [koranic] verses of inclusivism." This, coupled with the "rapid Islamic conquests" led to the view that the "world could be divided into two spheres: *Dar al Islam* [the territory of Islam] and the *Dar al Harb* [the territory of War]." Mutual animosity was engendered by the "inevitable clash with similar expansionist views of Christendom, and later European colonialism."

Four major factors work against Muslim participation in interfaith. Interchange. First of all, 9/11 was not a "single-occurrence" but rather "one of the most horrendous" acts of violence. Moreover, the "hateful post-event rhetoric represented centuries of ill feeling." The situation intensified as Muslim intellectuals were ineffective" in either "organizing the masses" or providing "any support against the terrible backlash" visited upon Islam. Unhappily it was the "radical Islamist groups" who were successful in these areas. In the third place, there is a leadership issue. Many who represent the Muslim community "are chosen, not for their "religious qualifications, but rather on their status or financial contribution, or simply their ability to communicate effectively." Finally, some mosques hire foreign born imams who have "not had much—if any—experience in being a minority group, or having to answer critical questions about religious constructs."

Yet, Mohammed sees reason for hope in what he terms "a rising swell of dissent against retrogression and malaise." Further these voices are coming from "the heart of the Muslim world and from the highest authorities." If Islam is to take its place among the Abrahamic traditions working for peace, the tradition must follow the example of those who "... realize that they must shock themselves out of the medievalist mentality." Globalization challenges contemporary adherents of the Abrahamic traditions to make the world better.

In the wake of 9/11 and the subsequent "war on terror," Professor A. Rashied Omar notes that compassion and justice are the two Qu'ranic principles necessary for peace. He suggests four proposals that "may create the conditions" for a credible Muslim role in peacebuilding." First of all Muslims must ceaselessly, loudly, and unequivocally state that "wanton violence and barbarism are contrary to the teachings of Islam" thereby countering extremist voices. Secondly, "rigorous academic studies" are needed to explore "sources of nonviolence and peacebuildng in Islam and Muslim societies." He cites two examples of Muslim peacebuilding: the British Muslim Peace and Reconciliation Initiative in Darfur... [and] "the Phillipines Center for Islam and Democracy... in Mindanao." Next, there is a crucial "need for... training... a new critically minded class of 'ulama (Muslim religious scholars). Finally, "peace scholars" must emphasize that "current iniquitous global conditions" are inimical to "credible Muslim peacebuilding."

Omar calls for the involvement of peace advocates and interreligious activists. The former should support public debate about how effectively to "counteract Muslim and other forms of extremism." Interreligious leaders need to "question the wisdom of the current strategy... in the 'war on terrorism.'" Furthermore, he contends that interreligious leaders "should also back the call for a serious reassessment concerning" [both America's] controversial foreign policy which abets authoritarian Muslim regimes ... [and] its uncritical and... unilateral support for the present policies of the State of Israel." Concerning the absence of peace in many Muslim societies, Omar attests that "Muslim preoccupation with justice has led to an erosion of the core Islamic value of compassion." The contemporary challenge for adherents of the Abrahamic, and other, traditions is to "re-trieve our common humanity and to end the horrific [and widespread] dehumanization." It is especially incumbent on Muslims seeking peace "to develop a theology of healing..."

Committing oneself to dialogue can be both transforming and challenging. Professor Muhammad Shafiq's essay illustrates both of these contentions. He discovered that interfaith interchange helped him deal "with [his] intense personal dislike of controversy." The Pakistan-born Shafiq writes of the need to create an atmosphere of listening" which encourages people to express their differences in a gentle and respectful way. Yet he correctly notes that "the most difficult area for interfaith" is the bi-lateral relations between Muslims and Jews as both communities are "caught up" in the Israeli-Palestinian conflict.

Shafiq attests that 9/11 was "catastrophic in a special way for American Muslims," resulting in a self-reflective impetus which changed many adherents of Islam in this country in several important ways. Chief among them were: "accept[ing] America as [their] true country;" the integration of Muslim communities "into mainstream American political discourse;" and, "a greater commitment on the part of the entire Muslim American community to interfaith dialogue."

Post 9/11 dialogue occurs in a global environment. Ambassador Akbar S. Ahmed reminds his readers that "people are now too close to and dependent on each other to afford the luxury of ignoring and excluding others." Ahmed points to the poison spread by anger as the root cause of 9/11 which "symbolized the anger of the Muslims, which provoked the anger of the Americans." In place of anger he argues for "compassion and nobility of spirit." Even after 9/11 there were acts which symbolized these "divine sparks" on both the organizational and individual levels. "Our Voices Together," organized by surviving relatives of those murdered in the 9/11 attacks built "educational centers in Afghanistan." Judea Pearl, whose son Daniel was beheaded by Muslim terrorists in Pakistan, joined in dialogue in various settings with Professor Ahmed. The goal of these dialogues was to "promote Jewish-Muslim understanding and to create bridges between communities." Appealing to the best in humanity, Ahmed writes "Jews, Christians, Muslims, Hindus . . . illustrate the capacity of human beings to attain moral heights in the most difficult circumstances."

Ahmed criticizes both the United States and Islam. America, he contends, fails to appreciate that it is dealing with "Muslim nations of diverse social and political character." Failure to recognize societal nuance leads to Muslim anger about the absence of justice and the presence of corruption. Muslims, for their part, "need to rediscover the struggle to improve life in a spiritual sense, . . ." Tribalism needs to be supplanted by cooperation "in a more integrated world." Furthermore, Arab rulers who use the "crutch of Israel" to avoid seeking democracy are complicit in perverting Quranic ideals of justice, compassion, and wisdom. A pathway to peace opens when "each of us [becomes] much more sensitive to what is sacred or highly symbolic of a culture in other civilizations."

⁓

The essays in this volume reveal two important facets of the post 9/11 trialogue. First and foremost is the fact that religion is not going away. It is true, as recent surveys indicate, that commitment to organized institutional religion appears to be waning.[1] However, if religion is diminished in the public square, it is squarely in place in the private sphere. In its various guises, whether as spiritualism, mysticism, or a search for transcendence, religion is an ineluctable part of the human search for meaning. The initial decade in the twenty-first century ushered in upheavals—both man-made and natural that threaten to continue to plague the world. In their wake, people seek certainty and reassurance. Moreover, there is a growing awareness of the common human vulnerability in an age of terror and the need to work cooperatively to seek understanding. Interfaith trialogue, although a relatively new phenomenon, is increasingly recognized as an important path to achieve this goal. In the second place, while not shying away from articulating real obstacles, the contributors to this book reveal the hopeful dimensions of the post 9/11 conversation among the Abrahamic traditions. It is clear that the trialogue conducted in this volume a decade after the catastrophic 9/11 terror attacks is imbued with a seriousness and maturity that will be needed to face and transcend the great and continuing challenges that lie ahead.

It is vital, as the contributors note, to keep open the lines of communication, notwithstanding the inherent difficulties. *At the very least, the essays in this book suggest a framework for ways of thinking about contentious issues* such as the scourge of Islamic, and other, terrorism; the Israeli-Palestinian situation; the "clash of civilizations"; and theological barriers to authentic dialogue/trialogue, as well as how to build trust. On the one hand, there are similarities and areas of agreement among the Abrahamic traditions, especially in the realms of concern for social justice; the giving of charity; the need to continue to speak and to listen to the Other. Furthermore, there have been some recent positive developments such as the journey to Dachau and Auschwitz (August, 2010) of eight influential American Imams and community leaders, including one woman Ms. Laila Muhammad, daughter of the late Imam W. D. Muhammad. Subsequently, the group issued a statement condemning antisemitism and Holocaust denial. More recently, Dr. Sayid M. Sayeed, National Director of the Islamic Society of North America's Office for Interfaith and Community Alliances—and one of the above noted eight—wrote an opinion piece "Anti-Semitism Has No Place in Islam" which appeared in the April 1, 2011 issue of the *Forward*.

---

1. The 2008 U.S. Religious Landscape Survey (Pew Forum on Religion & Public Life) finds that more than twice as many people are unaffiliated with any particular faith today than the number who say they were unaffiliated as children.

Conclusion

Reverberations of the Holocaust continue to echo over the post-Shoah interreligious landscape. The use of religious imagery and language to justify murder stands as a warning. However, this caution is not being heard equally. Fanatics claim to act on behalf of God or to be doing God's will. While the dialogue between Jews and Christians has deepened over the past six decades, the relationship between Judaism and Islam is just beginning, as is the dialogue between Islam and Christianity. Moreover, the evolving impact of globalization on religions is at the moment uncertain. However, at the very least it is most likely that this impact will be clearest in the area of perceptions of the religious Other. Whether this leads to a more liberal or more reactionary stance awaits further evidence. The challenge can be seen in the following question: Will any supercessionary theology attest that it bears only a part of the truth? But one thing is clear; Muslims living outside of Muslim majority lands will have to adjust to living as a minority if authentic dialogue is to occur.[2] This is especially the case within the American context of religious pluralism.

Readers of this volume should strive to ponder and, where possible, implement the suggestions of the authors. The task will not be easy, but it is necessary. The post-9/11 Abrahamic Trialogue faces a host of difficulties and obstacles which are significant and seemingly intractable. They include the millennial poison of anti-Semitism; continuing calls for violent Islamic jihad; the obscenity of Holocaust denial; the pledge to destroy the state of Israel; ugly rhetoric about the religious Other; and the goal of destroying all *infidels*. People everywhere are threatened. The challenge confronting humanity is nothing less than helping shape a future which recognizes the preciousness of the individual and the uniqueness of the whole. Precisely because the hour is late and the times unsettled the need for authentic trialogue has never been greater.

---

2. Europe where Christianity is in steep decline, and the number of Jews demographically inconsequential, represents a different dimension of the issue. Many countries including France, Germany, the Netherlands, Sweden, Denmark, and England have substantial numbers of Muslims, many of whom are immigrants who practice a fundamentalist form of Islam and are willing to become—or to support—jihadist terrorists. There is an unequal contest between, on the one hand, the substantial number of Muslim terrorists—some of whom are "home grown"—and, on the other hand, more moderate Islamic voices to see which will emerge as the European voice of Islam. One thing is certain: change in Islam, as in the other Abrahamic traditions, must come from within. How this struggle between violent and moderate Islam is resolved will bear directly on the possibility of a meaningful interfaith trialogue not only on the European continent, but in America as well.

Index

Abdullah (king of Transjordan), 198
Abraham, xiii–xiv, 12, 42, 85,
    162–63
Abrahamic traditions, essential
    differences among, xiii–xiv
abrogation, 176–77
Abu-Nimer, Mohamed, 206–7
AbuSulayman, AbdulHamid, 182
Accademia delle Arti del Disegno,
    188
acceptance, 236
Afghanistan, 169, 218, 237
afterlife
    Bible's rejection of, 25
    different schools of rabbinic
        thought on, 26–27
    as eternal damnation, 43
    excluding others from, 38
    Judaism's approach to, 43–46
    metaphors for, 37
    Pharisaic notions of, 26
    understanding of, 37–38
Agamben, Giorgio, 197
Ahl al Hadith, 213, 216
Ahmadinejad, Mahmoud, 10, 82
Ahmadiyya sect, 167
Ahmed, Akbar S., 172, 253
Ajami, Fouad, 33–34
Ajmer model, 232, 234–36, 241, 242
Akiva, 58
al-Alwani, Taha, 182
al-Ansari, Abd el-Hamid, 182
al-Arian, Sami, 9
al-Ashmawy, Muhammad, 178
Al-Azhar University, 82
Al-Baghdadi, Ahmed, 182

Ali, Ayan Hirsi, 35
Ali, Muhammad, 11
Aligarh model, 232, 234–36, 240,
    241, 242
al-Isfahani, Raghib, 203–4
al-Jawziyyah, Ibn Qayyim, 204
All about Eve (Mankiewicz, dir.), 22
Allam, Abdel Fattah, 82
al-Maududi, Abu'l Ala, 180
Al-Qaeda, 167
al-Russafi, Ma'ruf, 198
Ambrose, 49
AMC (American Muslim Council),
    10
American Israel Public Affairs
    Committee (AIPAC),
    199–200
American Jewish Committee, 8, 105
Angels of the Holocaust, 91
Anidjar, Gil, 186, 197
anthropology, 54
Anti-Defamation League, 105
anti-Islamic rhetoric, 201
anti-Judaism, 78, 79
anti-Muslimism, 193, 194, 196
anti-Semitism, 83, 193
    Benedict XVI rejecting, 107–8
    in Christianity, 78
    condemned by Catholics, 7–8,
        15
    distinguished from anti-
        Judaism, 78
    in Europe, 14–15. *See also*
        Holocaust
    from Muslims, 12–14
    medieval roots of, 193–94

anti-Semitism (*continued*)
   Muslims condemning, 254
   Protestants denouncing, 20
   Sacred Society of Pius X (SSPX), 19
Antoninus, 28
Appleby, Scott, 180, 207–8
Aquinas, Thomas. *See* Thomas Aquinas
Arabic, 192
Arab–Israeli conflict, 10–11. *See also* Israeli–Palestinian conflict
argument, 132
Armstrong, Karen, 193
Augustine, 142
Aurangzeb, 231, 232, 235
Auschwitz, 15, 16

Banki, Judith, 90, 91
Banki, Paul, 90
baptism, posthumous, 31–32
Barnes, Michael, 127–29
Baum, Gregory, 102–3
Begin, Menachem, 99
behavior, group norms for, 66
Ben Azzai, 58
Benedict XVI, 18–19, 80, 105, 118, 172, 173
   position in Catholic–Jewish relations, 106–8
   remarks on the Holocaust, 108–9
   theological perspective on Christian–Jewish relations, 109–14
Bensoussan, George, 190–91, 195
Berber–Jewish association, 200
Berdugo, Serge, 200
Berger, David, 84
Berger, Peter, 2
Berkovits, Eliezer, 67
Berlin, Isaiah, 32
Bernardin, Joseph, 115–16
Bet Din, 34
Bishops' Committee for Ecumenical and Interreligious Affairs (BCEIA), 92, 95, 96

Bodies of God and the World of Ancient Israel, The (Sommer), 118
Borelli, John, 87
Boyarin, Daniel, 117
Boykin, William G. (Jerry), 177
Boys, Mary, 250
Brenz, Johannes, 195
British Muslim Peace and Reconciliation Initiative, 206
Brown, Raymond E., 118
Buber, Martin, 41, 74, 97, 128
Buchmann, Margret, 132
Burbules, Nicholas, 126
Bush, George W., 173–74, 237

CAIR (Council on American–Islamic Relations), 10
Calvin, John, 142
Cantor, Norman F., 195
Cantwell Smith, Wilfred, 168, 175
Carter, Jimmy, 99
Cassidy, Edward Idris, 93–94, 95, 113
Catholic Church, 60, 66. *See also* Vatican
   Adult Catechism in, 19, 104, 105, 114
   Catholic social thought, 136, 143, 148
   defining itself over against Judaism, 102
   human rights, interpretation of, 147
   human rights, teachings in, 137–41
   relations with the state of Israel, 76–77
   rights talk in, 137
Catholicism
   centering on Christian–Jewish partnership, 119
   placed above all other religious traditions, 113
Catholic–Jewish Colloquium, 131
Catholic–Jewish relations, 7–8, 14–19

Index

Benedict XVI's position in, 106–8
dialogue since 9/11, 92–96
positive developments in, 114–15
in the U.S., 88
Catholic University of Leuven, 118
Center for Interfaith Studies and Dialogue (CISD), 226
Central Committee of German Catholics and Jews, 105
Chanukah, teaching about, 68
Chasidism, teachings on the stranger, 40
chauvinism, 55, 61
children, encouraging good behavior and developing understanding in, 65–66
children of Abraham, 12
Christ event, universal significance of, 92–93
Christian Identity and Religious Pluralism (Barnes), 128
Christianity
changing doctrinal aspects of, 84
creating a narrative of, grounded in Judaism, 123
divergence in, 4
growing respect in, for Jews, 79
historically committed to mission and evangelization, 119
Judaism viewing, as a true faith, 63
moral concerns of, 147
never acknowledging an authentic revelation within Islam, 120
parting ways with Judaism, 115–18
revitalizing the teachings of, 122
salvation in, 23
self-understanding of, over against Judaism, 122–23
spreading the faith, 31
understanding of human rights, 146
virtues of, 136

Christian–Jewish dialogue
concentrating on different aspects of, 84
deepened by 9/11, 90–92
developments in, 115
different from Muslim–Jewish and Muslim–Christian dialogues, 97–98
emerging model of, 120
history of, 4. See also *Nostra Aetate*
imperative for Christian theology, 121–22
mission as unresolved issue in, 105–6
new, 74
not an interfaith dialogue, 98
theological differences affecting, 83–84
Christian–Muslim clashes, 193
Christians
salvation for, rabbinical views of, 28–30
seeking self-identity through dialogue with Judaism, 74, 75
Christian saints, diatribes against Jews, 48–49
Christian Scholars Group on Christian–Jewish Relations, 122
Chrysostom, John, 49
Churchill, Winston, 32
Clairvaux, Bernard de, 195
Clark, Matthew, 221
clash of civilizations thesis, 4, 32, 33–34, 55, 134, 136
Clendinnen, Inge, 196, 197
co-evolution, 171
Cohen, Stephen P., 55
Cohn, Norman, 193
Colbert, Stephen, 238
Commission on Christian–Muslim Relations, 220, 222, 226
Commission on Jewish–Muslim Understanding, 226
Commission for Religious Relations with the Jews, 105

common good, 134–35, 139, 148–49
communitarian rights, 142
Companions of the Prophet, 216
compassion, as core Islamic value, 203–5, 208, 235, 243
Conference of Presidents of Major American Jewish Organizations, 32
Constantine, 117
conversation, 132–33
conversion, of the Jews, 18–19, 20, 73, 79–81, 83, 117, 193
Council of Jerusalem, 118
Covenant and Mission (USCCB and the National Council of Synagogues), 92, 93
creation story, 56–57
creative symbiosis, 171
Crisis in the Muslim Mind (AbuSulayman), 182
Crusades, 4, 99–100, 194–95
cultural pluralism (diversity), 53, 148
Curtis, John Briggs, 158–59, 161
Cutler, Allan Harris, 193, 194
Cutler, Helen Elmquist, 193, 194
Cyprian, 49

d'Aguilers, Raymond, 195
Dahta Sahib, 232–33
Damra, Fawaz, 9
Davis, Bette, 22
Dawkins, Richard, 1
death penalty, 48
deicide, 7–8, 103, 193
Dennett, Daniel, 1
De-Nur, Yehiel (Ka-Tzetnik 135633), 197
Deoband model, 212, 217, 229–32, 234–36, 239–41
Derrida, Jacques, 197
Devil and the Jews, The (Trachtenberg), 193
dhimmitude, 13, 190
dialogic pluralism, 143
dialogical universalism, 147
dialogue. *See also* interreligious dialogue; trialogue

communicative virtues of, 126
considered disrespectful in some Muslim education, 215
contemplative attitude regarding, 127
forms of, 133
humility and, 127
impossibility of, in context of exclusion, 46
interior, 127–28
meaning of, 97
requirements for, 38–39
respectful, 215
dietary laws, 57
Dietrich, Donald, 250
Dignitatis Humanae ("Declaration on Religious Freedom"; Vatican II), 138, 140
dignity, 66, 74, 138–40, 142, 144, 145, 161
Dignity of Difference, The (Sacks), 170
DiSegni, Riccardo, 247
Disraeli, Benjamin, 200
diversity, organization of, 64
Divino Afflante Spiritu (Pius XII), 100
Dominus Iesus (Congregation for the Doctrine of the Faith), 17, 113–14
Dulles, Avery, 103, 115, 119
Dupuis, Jacques, 109

Eastern religions, Judaism's view of, 63
Ebadi, Shirin, 182
ecumenism, 215–16
Egypt, 178, 207
El-Fadl, Khalid Abou, 178
Emden, Jacob, 30
Engineer, Ashgar Ali, 207
Enlightenment, religions' reactions to, 100–101
Episcopal Church, 21
Esposito, John, 208
eternal damnation, 45, 49
ethical principles, universalistic, 136
evangelical Christians

relations with Jews, 20–21
supporting Israel, 76
Evangelical Lutheran Church in
America, 123
evil, living with, 151–52
exclusivity, 236
exodus, 23–24
extra ecclesiam nulla salus, 35
extremism, 52. *See also* fanaticism
clashing with religious
humanism, 55
counteracting, 209
Islamic, 84
Islam's approach to, 206

Fackenheim, Emil, 196
faith
confusing religious certitude,
128
defending, 166
reason and, 144–45
"Faith and Doubt at Ground Zero"
(*Frontline*), 150–51
Falwell, Jerry, 155, 177
fanaticism. *See also* extremism
fanatics, 2–3, 32
Farfour, Hussam Al-Din, 233–34
Farrakhan, Louis, 11
fatiha, pronunciation of,
controversies over, 213
Federici, Tommaso, 94
Fischer, Shlomo, 61–62
Fisher, Eugene, 249
Fitzgerald, Michael, 113
forgiveness, 164
Förster, Ludwig, 188
Fourth Lateran Council, 193
Frankfurter, David, 117
Fredriksen, Paula, 117
Freire, Paulo, 127
Freud, Sigmund, 1–2
Friedman, Thomas, 55
Frontline, 150–51
full redemption, 80–81

Gabriol, Solomon Ibn, 13
Galtung, Johan, 203
Gandhi, Mahatma, 32, 231, 238, 239

Gaudium et spes (Vatican II), 139
Gehinnom, 45
Gemeaha, Mohamed, 9
*Genesis 1948: The First Arab–Israeli
War* (Kurzman), 198
genocidal passion, 190–91, 195
Gerer Rebbe, the, 57
German Episcopal Conference, 105
Gibson, Mel, 17
globalization, 135–36, 235–37,
242–44
global pillaging, 242
global reflexivity, 137
global rights, 142
Global Shemin Trialogues, xiii
God
affirmation of, 47
contending with, 157
omnipotence of, 35–36
as participant in trialogue, 48
Goitien, Shlomo, 171–72
Golden Age
interreligious, 7–8, 14, 20, 248
for Jews, 5, 12, 186, 192
Good, Edwin, 156
grace, 142
Graetz, Heinrich, 13
Greenberg, Moshe, 59–60
Greenberg, Uri Zvi, 198–99
Greenberg, Yizhak (Irving), 54n7,
125
Gregory of Nyssa, 49
group identities, 53–54, 56
group salvation, 23. *See also* national
salvation
Guide to the Perplexed
(Maimonides), 192

habituation, 65
Hadith, 48–49, 167
Halakha, 65, 98
Halevi, Yossi Klein, 5
Hamas, 170
HaMeiri, Menachem ben Solomon,
63
Hanafi school, 214
Hanahian, Joshua ben, 28
Harris, Rabia Terri, 207

Harris, Sam, 1
hatred, preached by people, 183
Hawking, Stephen, 1
Hazarvi, Mawlana, 212–13
Hebrew, 192
Hebrews, Letter to the, 103–4 115, 119
Henrix, Hans Hermann, 112
Hero, The (Li), 183
Herzog, Yitzchak Halevi, 69
Heschel, Abraham Joshua, 23, 36
Hezbollah, 240
Higgins, George, 99
Hillel school, 55, 58, 62, 71
Hitchens, Christopher, 1
Hollenbach, David, 147
Holocaust, the 3, 14–17, 19, 60, 66–67, 90–91, 255
   affecting Vatican–Jewish relations, 77–78
   Benedict XVI's remarks on, 109
   denial of, 82, 108, 109, 254
   Islam's impression of, 81
holy envy, 129
holy insecurity, 128
Holy Land Foundation, 225
honesty, as prerequisite for interfaith encounter, 181
hope, being prisoners of, 22, 248
Hotchkin, Jack, 87, 99
How Preachers and Laymen Should Conduct Themselves if the Turk were to Invade Germany (Brenz), 195
humanity, common, 56–59
human rights, 136
   finding a global ethic for, 147
   needing a dialogical or solidaristic approach, 145–46
   renewed priority of, for Catholics, 141
   respect for, 147
   understanding of, by the three religions, 146
   universality of, 141–42, 146
humility, 35, 127

Huntington, Samuel, 4, 32, 33–34, 35, 55, 134–35
Hyrcanus, Eliezer ben, 28

ideals, remaining close to, 244
identity
   attack on, 55
   politics of, 170
ideology, politics of, 170
idolatry, 47
Idols of the Tribe: Group Identity and Political Change (Isaacs), 53
ignorance
   leading to policy mistakes, 243
   overcoming, 248
I–It relationship, 97
ijtihad, 190, 241
imitatio dei, 59
Inquisition, 193
interdependence, 135, 148, 243
interfaith dialogue. *See also* interreligious dialogue
   foundations of, 3
   greater Muslim American commitment to, 225
   honesty a prerequisite for, 181
   Muslims fearing, 226
Interfaith Dialogue: A Guide for Muslims (Nimer and Shafiq), 226
interior dialogue, 127–28
International Catholic–Jewish Historical Committee, 87–88, 91
International Conference of Christians and Jews, 3n6, 122
International Council of Christians and Jews, 105
International Jewish Committee for Interreligious Consultations (IJCIC), 107, 114
interreligious dialogue, 36. *See also* dialogue; religious dialogue; trialogue
   achieving small gains through, 13–14
   as conversation, 132–33

Index

educational dimension of, 130
as holy work, 121
mission incompatible with, 119–20
as practice of faith, 127
priorities for, 70
ritualism in attempts at, 85
spirituality and, 125–29
virtues giving depth to, 129
interreligious encounter, 130–32
interreligious learning, 130–32
intrapersonal dialogue, 127
Iran, 169, 173, 178
Iraq, 237
Iraq–Iran War, 216
Isaac, Jules, 74
Isaacs, Harold R., 53
Islam
  absolutist teachings in, 178
  capacity of, for theological self-critique, 178–81
  contemporary, addressing, 167
  core values of compassion and justice in, 202, 203–5, 208
  critically minded scholars needed within, 207–8
  deteriorating image of, 34–35
  emphasizing socioeconomic justice, 224–25
  eschatological tradition of, 179
  evoking enemies, 241–42
  extremists dictating the behavior of, 5
  facing challenge of mosque-state separation, 5
  God of, considered inferior after 9/11, 177
  as holistic and integrated system, 241
  intrareligious rivalry in, 212–14
  issues in developing constructive relations with, 10–11
  Jesus traditions in, 179
  on Jewish and Christian holy scriptures, 98
  Judaism viewing, as a true faith, 63
  kinship with Judaism, 185
  lack of knowledge about, 3–4
  little new insight into, 180
  moderate U.S. voices for, lack of, 10
  mystic and universalist, 231–33
  negatively perceived in Europe, 186
  not yet reacting to the Enlightenment, 100–101
  at odds with the West, 4
  peacebuilding role of, 202, 205–10
  portrayed as inherently violent, 201, 242
  receiving most attention after 9/11, 1
  recovering its principles of peace, 202
  reforming, difficulty of, 178
  as religion of fatalism, 197
  resurgence of Islamic consciousness, 169
  rising dissent in, against retrogression and malaise, 182
  salvation in, 174–77
  self-image of, 81, 169
  spreading the faith, 31
  superseding all other religions, 175
  suspicion of, 34
  theology of the Other in, 168–74
  transforming into religion of conquest, 169
  as ultimate fulfillment of Judaism and Christianity, 11
  understanding of human rights, 146
  variety of thought in, 4–5
  violent disagreement within, 172
Islamic Center of Cleveland, 9
Islamic Center of Rochester (NY), 219–22, 223, 224
Islamic Circle of North America (ICNA), 224
Islamic rule, Christians and Jews living under, 12–13

Islamic Society of North America (ISNA), 224
Islamophobia, 170, 189, 242
Islam under Siege (Ahmed), 230
Israel, salvation of, 23–24, 27–28
Israel, state of, 10–11, 18, 189
    affecting Muslim–Jewish relations, 220
    as core center of Judaism, 76
    changing Jewish self-image, 193
    divestment from, 7, 21, 248
    leading to political–religious confusion, 82–83
    relations with the Vatican, 16
    U.S. Christians' attitude toward, 21
Israeli–Palestinian conflict, 53, 189
    affecting Muslim–Jewish relations, 220
    multilayered approach to, 191
Isserles, Loses, 29–30
I-Thou relationship, 74, 97
Ittihad (unity) movement, 216

Jabal Arabia, 172–73
Jamat-i-Islami, 212, 217, 229
Jam'iyyat al 'Uluma al Islam, 212
J.B. (MacLeish), 152, 163–65
Jerome, 49
Jesus
    relationship of, with Judaism, 116–17
    resituating, in Second Temple Judaism, 124
    as Torah, 112–13
Jesus of Nazareth: From the Baptism in the Jordan to the Transfiguration (Ratzinger), 112
Jew as Ally of the Muslim, The (Cutler and Cutler), 193
Jewish–Christian dialogue. *See* Christian–Jewish dialogue
Jewish covenant, validity of, 102–4
Jewish history, teaching of, 66
Jewish–Muslim dialogue. *See* Muslim–Jewish dialogue
Jewish People and Their Sacred Scriptures in the Christian Bible, The (Pontifical Biblical Commission), 110, 111–12, 114
Jewish Theological Seminary, 23
Jews. *See also* Judaism
    associated with the West, 185
    complex methods of identification, 83
    contributions of, recognized, 185–86
    deaths of, under Christianity and Islam, 73
    growing respect for, 79
    as minority without power, 75
    moving beyond identity as victims, 125
    positive associations with Muslims, 5, 188–89, 193, 194–95, 198, 199
    requesting that Christians stop teaching hatred, 75
    response to Christian request for dialogue, 74–76
jihad, 4, 169, 230, 241
Jihad and Terrorism, 229
Jinnah, Muhammad Ali, 231, 232, 235, 238, 239, 244
Job, book of, 152, 153–63
John XXIII, 91, 138–39, 194
John Paul II
    on the common good, 134
    death of, 7
    on human rights, 140–41
    Jewish groups' criticism of, 17
    improved Catholic–Jewish relations under, 14–17, 19, 77, 79, 92, 103–5, 107, 108, 123
Johnson, Luke Timothy, 119
Judaeo–Islamic culture, 192
judaicam superstitionem, 79
Judaism
    allowing room for the nonbeliever in the afterlife, 39, 41–42
    based on dialogue with God, 4

challenged to understand
    Christianity as partner, 125
changing doctrinal aspects of, 84
Christian teaching of contempt
    toward, 8
closed social structure of, 76
commandments of, distilled,
    58–59
development of, 124
educational model for, 69–70
embracing non-Jews not out to
    kill Jews, 49
Jesus's relationship with, 116–17
major festivals of, 67–69
Messianic era in, 64
negatively perceived in Europe,
    186
Paul's outlook on, 118–19
problematic texts in, for dealing
    with the other, 59–61
relations with Islam, 81–83, 185
salvation in, 23–24
on salvation for non-Jews, 28–31
setting Jewish people apart, 57
springing from divine
    revelation, 94
teachings of, regarding the
    stranger, 39–43
theology of other faiths, 30–31
understanding of human rights,
    146
understanding of the Jews as a
    people apart, 41
viewing Islam and Christianity
    as true faiths, 63
Judeophobia, 189
justice, 243
    as core Islamic value, 203–5,
    208, 235
    pursuit of, 47–48

Kabbalah, 31, 43–45
Kakon, Maguy, 200
Kant, Immanuel, 187
Kaplan, Edward, 129
Kaplan, Mordecai M., 23
Karo, Joseph, 29–30

Kasper, Walter, 92, 93, 94, 95, 106,
    110–11, 113
Keeler, William, 95, 113
Keller, Nuh HaMim, 176
Kennedy Institute Trialogue, 99–100
Khaldun, Ibn, 199
Khan, Mawlana Wahiduddin, 207
Khan, Raza, 217
Khatami, Muhammad, 173
Kind Hearts, 225
King Fahd Complex, 175
Klenicki, Leon, 89–90, 91
Klugman, Patrick, 199
knowledge, lack of, about other
    religions, 11
Kook, Abraham Isaac HaKohen, 64
Korczak, Janusz, 66
Koretzer Rabbi, the, 40
Kotok, Larry, 221
Küng, Hans, 2, 181
Kurzman, Dan, 198
Kuwaiti Ministry of Islamic Affairs,
    183

Lagarde, Paul de, 188–89
LaHaye, Tim, 177
Lampronti, Isaac, 29
Lee, Sara S., 130, 131
Lefebvre, Marcel, 19
legal distinctions, between three
    religions, demolished, 29
Leibniz, Wilhelm von, 192
Lennon, John, 53
Leo XIII, 137
Leuenberg Church Fellowship, 124
Levada, William, 105
Levi, Primo, 196
Levi, Yehudah Ha, 13
Lewis, Bernard, 192
Li, Jet, 183
life, understanding of, rooted
    to understanding of the
    afterlife, 37–38
Lilly Endowment, 131
Lincoln, Bruce, 207
Longitudes and Attitudes
    (Friedman), 55
L'Osservatore Romano, 18–19

Lustiger, Jean-Marie, 79
Luther, Martin, 49
Luzzatto, Simone Simhah, 29

MacLeish, Archibald, 152, 163–65
madrassas, 33, 180, 212, 213n, 217
Maglione, Luigi, 91
Mahdi, army of, 167
Maimonides, Moses, 5, 28, 59, 192
Majid, Anouar, 250–51
Many Religions, One Covenant: Israel, the Church, and the World, 110
Marcionism, 79
Markham, Edwin, 36
Martyr, Justin, 49
Marxist nations, human rights concepts of, 145
Mawdudi, Mawlana Abul A' la, 212
Meier, John, 116
Meir, Golda, 198
Meiri, Mehahem, 29
Mejia, Jorge, 88
Memory and Identity: Conversations between Millenniums (John Paul II), 17
Mendelssohn, Moses, 30
Messianic era, 64
Middle East, conflict in, 243
QY: midrash authors on 26–27?
Miles, Jack, 158, 159, 161
Miller, Judea, 220
Mishnat Rabbi Eliezer, 29n
Mishneh Torah (Maimonides), 28
mission, incompatible with dialogue, 119–20
missionaries, 31
Mitchell, Alan, 119
Modena, Yehudah Aryeh Leone, 29
modernity, assault on, 1, 3
Mohammed, Elijah, 11
Mohammed, Khaleel, 251
Mohammed, Warith Deen, 11
Moni: A Novel of Auschwitz (Ka-Tzetnik 135633), 197
Montreal Gazette, 179
moral diversity, 136
moral inquiry, 135

moral responsibility, 160
Mormon Church, 31–32
Morocco, 199–200
Moses, cited in the Quran, 192
mosque, becoming a bastion of solidarity and identity, 177
MPAC (Muslim Public Affairs Council), 10
Mufradat al-Quran (al-Isfahani), 203–4
Mufti Mahmood, Mawlana, 212
Muhammad, Laila, 254
murder
  divine prohibition against, 46–48
  in God's name, as desecration of the Name, 47
Muselmänner, 196–97
Muslim American Society (MAS), 224
Muslim Hands, 206
Muslim–Catholic Alliance, 226
Muslim–Jewish relations, 81–83, 84
  beginning with learning to live together, 187–88
  as creative symbiosis, 171
  improving, before 9/11, 8
  loaded nature of, 189–90
  after 9/11, 8–10
  paradoxes in, 13
  positive approaches to, 12–13
  potential closeness of dialogue, 97–98
  recalling main lines of common destiny, 191–
Muslims. *See also* Islam
  American, impact of 9/11 on, 221–25
  associated with the East, 185
  close contact and kinship with Jews, 5, 188–89, 193, 194–95
  inclusiveness among, 172–73
  leadership of, in North America, 180
  negative portrayals of, 172
  opening to spiritual progress, 230–31
  responding to 9/11, 166–67, 170

salvation for, rabbinical views of, 30
view of Zionism, 197–99
violence among, stemming from ignorance, 190
Muzaffar, Chandra, 207

Nader, Ralph, 135
Nanos, Mark, 112
National Council of Churches, 20
National Council of Synagogues, 92
national salvation, 23–24
Nation of Islam (NOI), 11
natural law, 31, 138, 139
Nazism, 77, 196–97. *See also* Holocaust, the
NCC. *See* National Council of Churches
negative peace, 202–3
Nehru, 231, 238, 239
Nemo, Philippe, 151–52, 155
Neusner, Jacob, 112–13
Nile and Palestine Gazette, The, 198
Nimer, Mohammed Abu, 226
9/11. *See* September 11, 2001
nonbelievers
    having a place for, 50
    place of, in the afterlife, 38–39, 41–42
non-Jews, salvation for, 28–29
Nonviolence and Peace Building Islam (Abu-Nimer), 206–7
Nostra Aetate (Vatican II), 3, 4, 7–8, 10, 75–76, 78, 93, 95, 102–6, 111, 122, 138, 139, 141, 142, 248
Notes on the Correct Way to Present the Jews and Judaism in Catholic Preaching and Teaching, 95–96
Nussbaum, Martha, 135

obedience, 65
Olam Haba, 50
Omar, A. Rashied, 251–52
Oral Torah
    discussion about, 62
    study of, 65

Origen, 49
Oslo Peace Process, 201
Other
    Islam's theology of, 168–74
    overcoming ignorance about, 248
othering, 52
Our Voices Together, 238

Pacem in terris (John XXIII), 138–39
Pahad Yitzhak (Lampronti), 29
Pakistan, 167, 180, 207, 211–14, 217, 241
Palestinian Liberation Organization, 170
Panikhar, K.N., 135
Panikkar, Raimundo, 127
particularism, 54–55, 57–58, 65
"parting of the ways" research, 115–20
Pascal, Blaise, 32
Pashtun peoples, 217–19
Passion of the Christ, The (Gibson, dir.), 17
Patterson, David, 248
Paul, outlook of, on Judaism, 118–19
Paul VI, 16, 77, 204
Pawlikowski, John, 249
peace
    Islam's definition of, 202–5
    multiplicity of, 64
    between religions, 36
peacebuilding, Islam's role in, 202, 205–10
peace studies, Islam neglected in, 206–7
Pearl, Judea, 238
people of the Book, 13
personalism, 139
Pesach, teaching about, 69
Peter the Venerable, 195
Pharisees, 25
Philippines Center for Islam and Democracy, 206–7
Pinsker, Leo, 183–84

Pius XI, 78, 137, 138
Pius XII, 78, 91, 100, 109
pluralism, 52, 136, 148
   dialogic, 143
   recognition of, 143
   religious, 2–3, 36, 140, 148
politics, changeability of, 84
Pontifical Biblical Commission, 98
Popular Front for the Liberation of Palestine, 170
positive peace, 202, 203
post-honor confrontation, 172
Praimnath, Stanley, 150–51
Presbyterian Church (USA), 7, 21, 248
"Pro Conversione Iudaeorum" (For the Conversion of the Jews), 18–19, 80
Pro Judaeis ("For the Jews"), 80
Protestant Reformation, 195
Protestant–Jewish relations, 7, 20–21
purification of the soul, 45
Purim, teaching about, 68–69
Pursuit of the Millennium, The (Cohn), 193

Qaradhawi, Yusuf al, 180
Quadragesimo Anno (Pius XI), 137
Quran, 167, 168
Qutb, Sayyid, 180

Rabin, Yitzhak, 32
Rainbow, the, 60
Ramadan, Obadiah, 173
Rashi, 57
Ratzinger, Joseph, 109–13. *See also* Benedict XVI
reason
   embedded in history, 143
   faith and, 144–45
redemption, 27, 125
Reflections on Covenant and Mission, 103, 104
Reform Jewish Community of Temple B'rith Kodesh (Rochester, NY), 220
relativism, 136, 144

Relief Foundation of the Islamic Circle of North America, 225
religion
   bad impression of, 51–52
   as cover for race, 186
   criticism of, 1–2
   double-edged sword of, 2
   exclusionary stance of, 38
   factoring into human existence, 2
   fanning flames of extremism, 51–52
   needing certain contexts to spawn violence, 207–8
   power of, 51, 170
   as reemerging model for identity, 72
   responsibility of, in political conflicts, 72
   resurgence of, 2
   violent forms of, 51–52
religious architecture, 188
religious consciousness, rise of, 170
religious dialogue. *See also* interreligious dialogue; trialogue
   Jews' reply to Christian request for, 74–76
   meaning of, 73–74
   as new form of communication, 74
religious education, dialectical approach to, 56
religious freedom, 139, 140
religious illiteracy, 180
religious pluralism, 2–3, 36, 140, 148
Renan, Ernest, 186–87
Rerum Novarum (Leo XIII), 137
respect, 66
resurrection of the body, 25–26
revelation, 142, 144
Righteous among the Nations, 42, 66–67
righteousness, 47–48, 155–56
Rivkes, Moshe, 30
Robertson, Pat, 155

Index

Rochester (NY), unique in interfaith dialogue, 226–27. *See also* Islamic Center of Rochester (NY)
Rochester Interfaith Forum, 226
Roman Catholic Church. *See* Catholic Church
Roncalli, Angelo, 91
Rosen, David, 108
Rosenthal, Gilbert S., 248
Rosenzweig, Franz, 30–31
Roth, Leon, 57
Rotta, Angelo, 90–91
Rudin, A. James, 247–48
Rushdie, Salman, 35

Sachedina, Abdul Aziz, 168–69, 174, 178, 207
Sacks, Jonathan, 170, 242
"Sacred Obligation, A" (Christian Scholars Group on Christian–Jewish Relations), 122
Sacred Society of Pius X (SSPX), 19, 108
Sadat, Anwar, 32, 99
Sa'id, Jawdat, 207
Salafist movement, 5, 178
Saldarini, Anthony, 116–17
salvation, 23, 92–93
　available to Jews, 94
　biblical view of, 24–25
　different schools of rabbinic thought on, 27
　individual, 23, 31
　Islamic concepts of, 174–77
　national, 23–24, 27–28
　for nations other than Israel, 28
Sanders, Theresa, 249
Santora, Christopher, 153
Santora, Maureen, 153
Satha-Anand, Chiawat, 207
Saudi Arabia, 207
Sauvage, Pierre, 66–67
Savage, Dan, 157
Sayeed, Sayid M., 254
Schweid, Eliezer, 54n7
Scott, Marianne, 238

Scroggs, Robin, 115–16
Second Vatican Council, 3, 4, 7–8, 17, 60, 66, 75–76, 92, 100, 103, 137. *See also Nostra Aetate*
　opening issues of religious freedom and pluralism, 140
　seeking to balance the rights of individuals and society, 139
　stressing dialogue and mutual inquiry, 144
Secretariat for Ecumenical and Interreligious Affairs, 104
Secretariat for Interreligious Relations, 99
Secretariats for Doctrine and Ecumenism and Interreligious Affairs, 95
self-esteem, 66
Semites
　origins of, 192
　resurrecting the identity of, 187–89
Semites (Anidjar), 186
Semitic, culturally meaningless designation of, 186
Sephardim, 192
September 11, 2001, 33
　altering the religious landscape, 1
　American response to, 237–38
　continuing emotions of children who lost parents, 161–62
　deepening Jewish–Christian dialogue and understanding, 90–92
　as end of Golden Age in modern interreligious relations, 7, 8–9
　historical meaning of, 72
　impact of, on American Muslims, 221–25
　local experience of, 87, 89
　reaction to, xiv
Shaaria law, 34
Shafi'i school, 176
Shafiq, Muhammad, 224, 252–53
Shammai, 62, 71

Shaprut, Hasdai Ibn, 13
shariah, 97–98
Shemin, Emanuel, xiii
Shemin, Rhoda, xiii
Shia, 4, 214
Shiite, 32
shiva, 43
Shoah. *See* Holocaust
Shriver, Sargent, 99
Shulhan Arukh (Karo), 29–30
Sipahi-i-Sahaba, 167, 216
Sipah Muhammad (the Soldiers of Prophet Muhammad), 216
Sklba, Richard, 106
Smith, Bob, 221
social density, 137
socialization, 54, 69–70
social vision, 135
solidarity, 14, 81, 85, 138, 141, 145
Solzhenitsyn, Aleksandr, 53
Sommer, Benjamin D., 118
Soroush, Abdel Karim, 178
soul
    immortality of, 25–26
    stages in the life of, 43–46
Southern, Richard, 195–96
Spain, Golden Age in, 12–13
spirituality, interreligious dialogue and, 125–29
spiritual regret, 129
SSPX. *See* Sacred Society of Pius X
Stein, Edith, 79
Steinsaltz, Adin, 45
Stendahl, Krister, 129
Stewart, Jon, 238
Stone, Suzanne Last, 61–62
stranger, Judaism's teachings on, 39–43
structural violence, 203
subsidiarity, 137–38
Sufism, 5, 205
Sulayman, Muqatil b., 175
sulh-i-kul, 232
Sunni, 4, 32, 82, 176, 214
Sunni-Shi'a relations, 167, 216
supersession, 79–80, 105, 113, 122, 124, 175, 255
Swidler, Leonard, 99, 181, 216

Swift, Jonathan, 1, 32
Synagogue Council of America, 103

Tafhim al Qur'an (Maududi), 217
Taha, Mahmoud, 178
Taliban, 33, 167, 214, 240
Talking Points (Evangelical Lutheran Church in America), 123–24
Talmud, 4, 48–49
tao, 65
Ten Utterances of Revelation, 46–47
territorial conflict, 10–11
Tertullian, 49
theism, commitment to, 134–35
theology, differences in, 11
Third World nations, human rights concepts of, 145
Thirty Years' War, 32
"This I Believe" (NPR), 121
Thomas Aquinas 49, 142
Tosafists, 63
Towards a Christian Theology of Religious Pluralism (Dupuis), 109–10
Towards a Fiqh for Minorities (al-Alwani), 182
Towards an Islamic Theory of International Relations (AbuSulayman), 182
Trachtenberg, Joshua, 193
Treaty of Westphalia, 32
trialogue, among Christianity, Islam, and Judaism
    barriers to, 50
    identifying common denominators for, 84–85
    importance of, 254
    necessity of, 85
    new oral tradition for, 49–50
    vs. trilateral dialogue, 97
tribalism, 52–53
tribal warfare, 53
triumphalism, 52
Trocmé, André, 67
truths, plural, 61–64
Turkey, 169–70
Tyson, Mike, 11

Index

ul-Haq, Zia, 217
Unholy War: Terror in the Name of Islam (Esposito), 208
United Methodist Church, 21
United States
    exclusionary religion in, 35
    intolerance in, among Muslims, 219
    Islamic community in, 11–12
    Jews partnering with Protestants and the NCC, 20–21
    Jews' relationship with evangelical Christians, 20–21
    Muslims in, coming to grips with pluralist society, 101
    needing a new philosophy toward other civilizations, 239–40
    Office of Homeland Security, 225
    people in, turning away from organized religion, 21
universalism, 56, 57–58, 61, 65
US Bishops' Advisory Committee on Catholic-Jewish Relations, 105
US Bishops' Committee on Doctrine, 104
United States Conference of Catholic Bishops (USCCB), 92, 95, 99, 103

Van Gogh, Theo, 34
Vanhoye, Albert, 104, 105, 119
Vatican, 87–88. *See also* Catholic Church
    relations with Israel, 16
    Waldheim's visit to, 16–17
    World War II records of, 17
Vatican Commission for Religious Relations with the Jews, 92–93, 95
victim narrative, 189–90
victims, solidarity with, 148

Wahhabism, 5, 33, 218
Waldheim, Kurt, 16–17
Wallenberg, Raoul, 91
Walzer, Michael, 54, 55
war on terrorism, 209
Wasserstrom, Steven, 171
Ways That Never Parted, The (Becker and Reed), 115
Weapons of the Spirit (Sauvage), 66–67
Weissman, Deborah, 248
"We Remember: A Reflection on the Shoah" (Vatican), 16, 77
Western civilization
    human rights concept of, 145
    opposition to, 72
Western Views of Islam in the Middle Ages (Southern), 195–96
Western world, relations of, with Muslim culture, 72
Wiesel, Elie, 160–61, 196
Williamson, Clark, 124
Williamson, Richard, 19, 108
Witte, John, 148
words, importance of, in Judaism, 41
workers' rights, 137
World's Parliament of Religions, 70
Woytyla, Karol Joseph. *See* John Paul II

xenophobia, in biblical and rabbinic texts, 59–60

Yad Vashem, 16
Yearley, Lee, 129
Yehudah Ha-Nasi, 28
Yoffie, Eric H., 199

Zayd, Nasr Abu, 178
Zionism, 197–99
Zohar, 41, 43
Zusia, 40